Land Rover Discovery Series 2 1999-2004 MY

Handbook

Publication Part Numbers
LRL 0459ENG-2nd edition
& LRL 0545ENG

© Land Rover 2001 and 2002

All rights reserved. No part of this publication may be reproduced, stored in a retrieval system or transmitted in any form, electronic, mechanical, recording or other means without prior written permission from Land Rover.

CW01657330

Owner's Handbook

This handbook covers all current versions of Land Rover Discovery petrol and diesel models and, together with the Service Portfolio book, provides information you will need to derive maximum pleasure from owning and driving your new vehicle.

For your convenience, the handbook is divided into sections, each dealing with a different aspect of the vehicle. These are listed on the title page and you will find it worthwhile to take a little time to read each one, and get to know your Discovery as soon as you possibly can. The more you understand before you drive, the greater the satisfaction once you are seated behind the steering wheel.

This handbook - LRL 0459ENG - 2nd edition have been updated to include information covering model years 2003 and 2004

Data covering these later models can be identified by the following symbol:

✱

© Copyright Land Rover Limited 2001 & 2002
and Brooklands Books Limited 2006

This book is published by Brooklands Books Limited and based upon text and illustrations protected by copyright and first published in 2001 & 2002 by Land Rover Limited and may not be reproduced transmitted or copied by any means without the prior written permission of Land Rover Limited and Brooklands Books Limited.

Whilst every effort is made to ensure the accuracy of the particulars contained in this book the Manufacturing Companies will not, in any circumstances, be held liable for any inaccuracies or the consequences thereof.

Brooklands Books Ltd., PO Box 146, Cobham,
Surrey KT11 1LG, England

ISBN: 9781855208438   Part No. LRL 0459BB   Ref: LRY99H 2244/12T3

IMPORTANT

The specification of each vehicle will vary according to territorial requirements and also from model to model within the vehicle range. Some of the information published in this handbook, therefore, may not apply to your particular vehicle.

Land Rover operates a policy of constant product improvement and therefore reserves the right to change specifications without notice at any time. Whilst every effort is made to ensure complete accuracy of the information in this handbook, no liabilities for inaccuracies or the consequences thereof can be accepted by the manufacturer or the dealer, except in respect of personal injury caused by the negligence of the manufacturer or the dealer.

Printed and bound in Great Britain by
Marston Book Services Ltd, Oxfordshire

Contents

BEFORE YOU DRIVE

WARNING

Your vehicle has a higher ground clearance and hence, a higher centre of gravity than ordinary passenger cars. This will result in different handling characteristics. Inexperienced drivers should take additional care, particularly in off-road driving situations and when performing abrupt manoeuvres on unstable surfaces.

SYMBOLS USED

The following symbols used within the handbook call your attention to specific types of information.

This recycling symbol identifies those items that must be disposed of safely in order to prevent unnecessary damage to the environment.

This symbol identifies those features that can be adjusted or disabled/enabled by a Land Rover dealer

*An asterisk appearing within the text, identifies features or items of equipment that are either optional, or are only fitted to some vehicles in the model range.

WARNINGS IN THIS HANDBOOK

WARNING

Safety warnings are included in this handbook. These indicate either a procedure which must be followed precisely, or information that should be considered with great care in order to avoid the possibility of personal injury or serious damage to the vehicle.

SECURITY CARD

The security card, supplied with the literature pack, contains important emergency information. It is ESSENTIAL that you keep the card safe from theft and ensure that it is passed to the new owner if you sell the vehicle.

- **Key number:** This is the number of the starter/door key - essential if you ever need to obtain a replacement.
- **Emergency key access code:** You will need this code in order to start the vehicle if the handset has been lost or damaged (see *'Emergency key access', page 18*).
- **Locking wheel nut number:** If your vehicle has locking wheel nuts, you will have been provided with a special wheel nut socket to remove them. You will need to quote this number to obtain a replacement socket.
- **VIN (vehicle identification number):** This identity number is unique to your vehicle and is essential proof of its specification. The number can also be found in various locations around the vehicle (see *'VEHICLE IDENTIFICATION NUMBER (VIN)', page 172*).
- **Radio security code number:** This unique code must be entered into the radio whenever the power supply has been disconnected. Without this code, the radio unit will not operate (see *'Security code'* in the *'In-Car Entertainment'* book).

WARNING

Never leave the security card inside the vehicle when it is unattended.

Memorise the emergency key access code, or keep the card on your person while driving, in case of emergencies.

SERVICE PORTFOLIO

The Service Portfolio book included in your literature pack contains important vehicle identification information, details of your entitlement under the terms of the Land Rover warranty, as well as useful consumer advice.

Most important of all, however, is the section on maintenance. This outlines the servicing requirements for your vehicle and also includes the First Service Voucher, and the service record slips, which the Dealer should sign and stamp to certify that the routine services have been carried out at the recommended intervals.

WARNING LABELS ATTACHED TO THE VEHICLE

Warning labels attached to your vehicle bearing this symbol mean: DO NOT touch or adjust components until you have read the relevant instructions in the handbook.

Warning labels showing this symbol indicate that the ignition system utilises very high voltages. DO NOT touch any ignition components while the starter switch is turned on!

GEARBOX SELECTOR LEVER LABELS

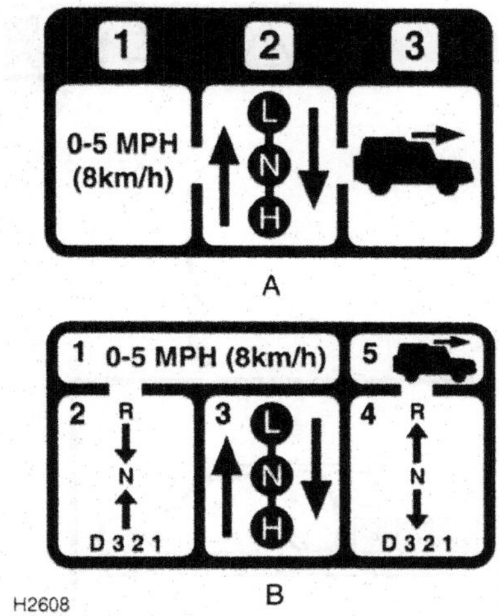

Information concerning operation of the transfer gearbox with either manual 'A' or automatic gearbox 'B' is printed on the centre console. This is important information and must be understood fully with reference to *'TRANSFER GEARBOX', page 113*, before using the transfer gearbox.

SUN VISOR LABELS

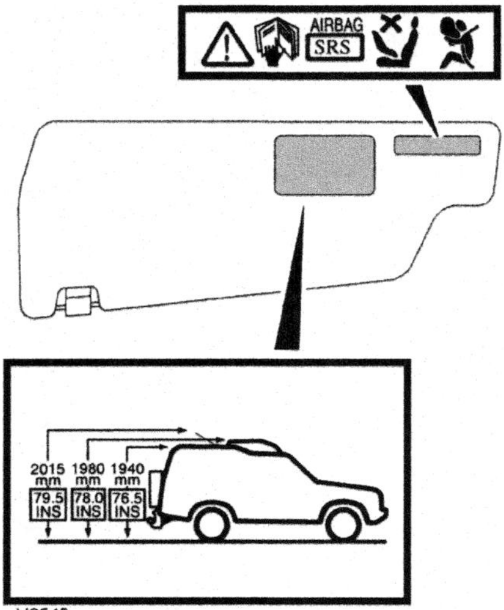

H2545

Always take careful note of warning information about the airbag SRS attached to the sun visor (illustrated above) or other parts of the vehicle.

Details of the vehicle's standard ride height, both with and without an open sunroof are printed on the drivers sun visor.

IN AN EMERGENCY

IMPORTANT INFORMATION

Remember the breakdown safety code

If a breakdown occurs while travelling:

- Wherever possible, consistent with road safety and traffic conditions, the vehicle should be moved off the main thoroughfare, preferably into a lay-by. If a breakdown occurs on a motorway, pull well over to the inside of the hard shoulder.
- Switch on hazard lights.
- If possible, position a warning triangle or a flashing amber light at an appropriate distance from the vehicle to warn other traffic of the breakdown, (note the legal requirements of some countries).
- Consider evacuating passengers through nearside doors onto the verge, as a precaution in case your vehicle is accidentally struck by other traffic.

Controls & Instruments

FASCIA

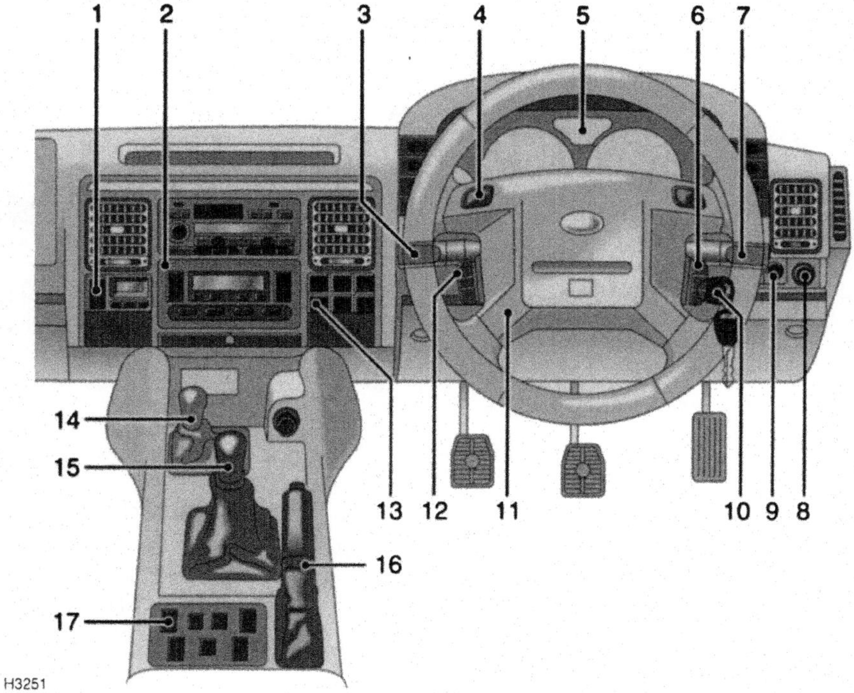

1. Door locking switch
2. Heater/air conditioning controls
3. Lighting and direction indicator controls
4. Horn switches
5. Instrument panel
6. Cruise control switches*
7. Windscreen wiper/washer controls
8. Electric mirror adjuster
9. Headlamp levelling control*
10. Starter switch
11. Steering column height adjuster
12. Remote radio controls*
13. Fascia panel switches
14. Transfer gear lever
15. Main gear lever
16. Handbrake
17. Electric window switches

NOTE: *The precise specification and location of the controls may vary according to territorial requirements and from model to model within the vehicle range.*

INSTRUMENT PANEL

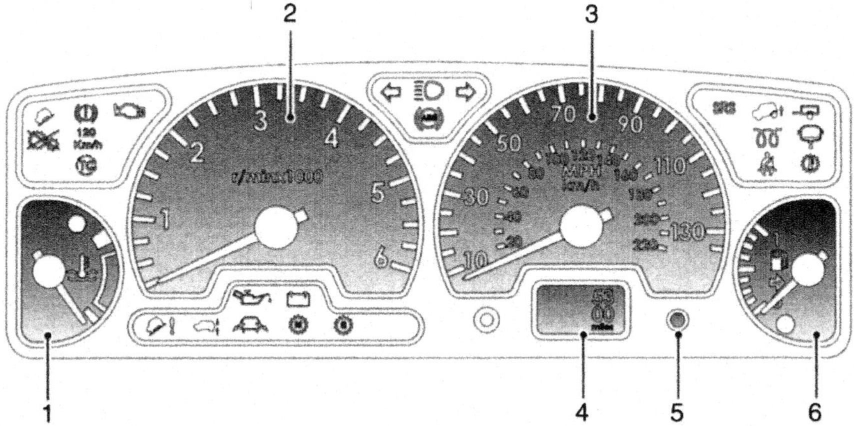

H2581b

1. Temperature gauge

   Under normal operating conditions the pointer will rise to a position within the white segment.

2. Tachometer

   Indicates engine speed in revolutions per minute (x 1000)

3. Speedometer

   Indicates road speed in miles per hour and/or kilometers per hour.

4. Total distance (odometer) and trip recorder

   NOTE: *On automatic gearbox vehicles the display also indicates the selector lever position*

5. Trip recorder reset button

6. Fuel gauge

   The pointer drops to zero when the starter switch is turned off, but quickly rises to show the level of fuel in the tank when the switch is turned to position 'II'.

NOTE: *This is a brief overview of the instrument panel, for a more detailed description of each instrument please refer to 'INSTRUMENT PANEL', page 45.*

*

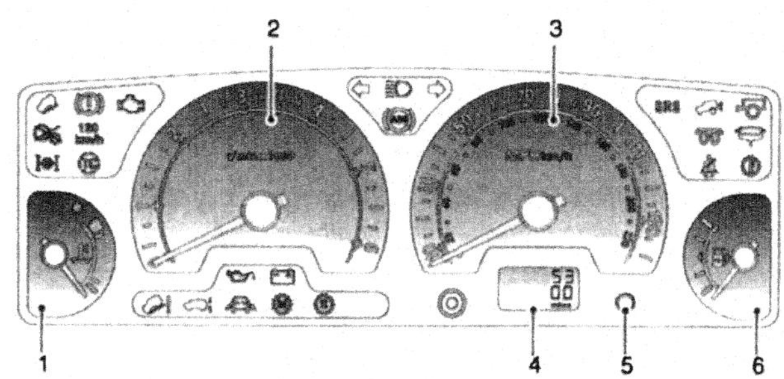

H4396

BINNACLE SWITCHES

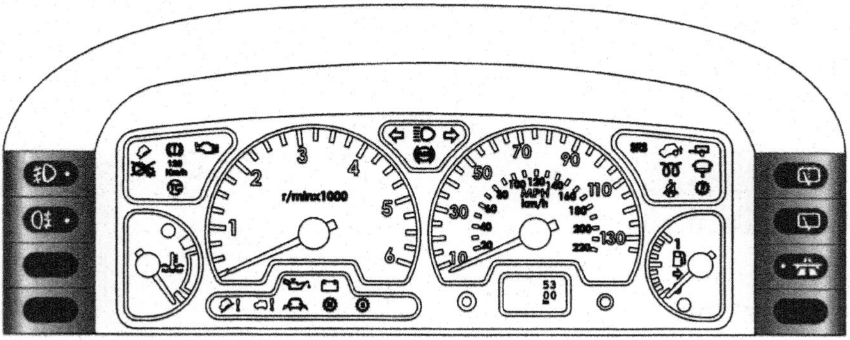

H2585b

Front fog lights*

Operation and function of the front fog lights are described under *'Front fog lights*', page 55.*

Rear fog guard lights

Operation and function of the rear fog guard lights are described under *'Rear fog guard lights', page 55.*

Rear window wash/wipe

The functions of the wash/wipe switch are described under *'Rear window wash/wipe', page 59.*

Rear window wiper

The functions of the rear window wiper switch are described under *'Rear window wiper', page 59.*

Cruise control

Operation and functions of the cruise control switch are described under *'CRUISE CONTROL*', page 115.*

*

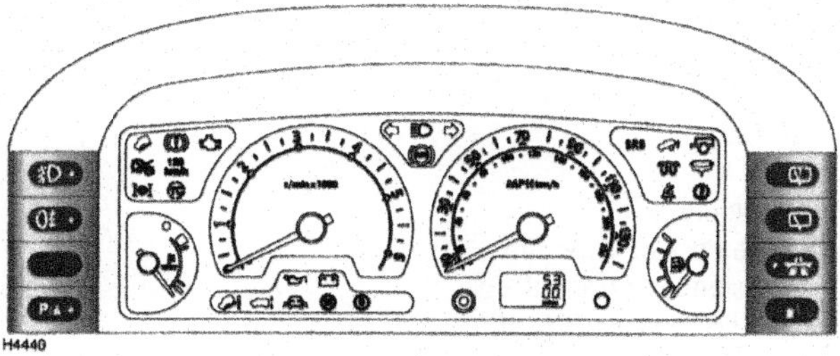

H4440

FASCIA SWITCHES

*

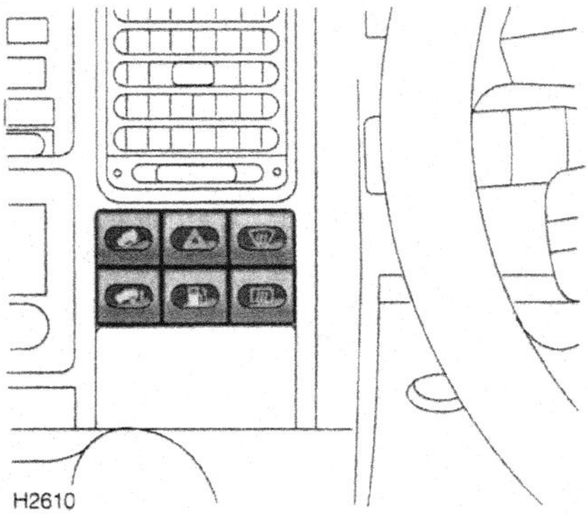

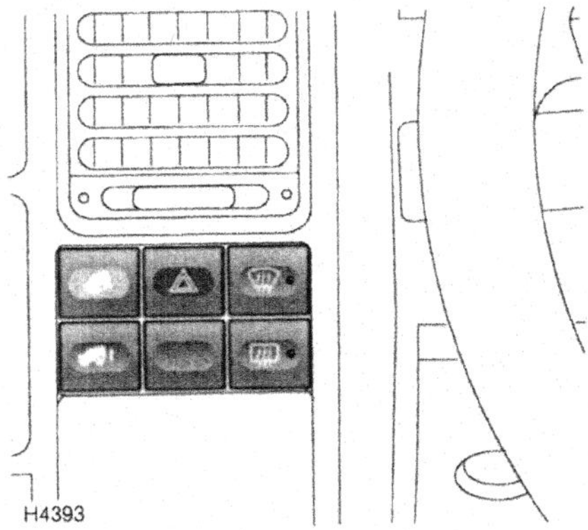

Hazard warning lights

Press to operate (see *'HAZARD WARNING LIGHTS', page 56*).

Heated front screen*

Press to operate (see *'Heated front screen*', page 74*).

Heated rear window

Press to operate (see *'Heated rear window', page 74*).

Fuel filler flap

With the starter switch turned to position '0' or '1', press to open the fuel filler flap.

Hill descent control (HDC)

Press to select hill descent control (see *'HILL DESCENT CONTROL', page 121*).

Off-road suspension mode*

Press to raise or lower the suspension to or from off-road height (see *'SELF-LEVELLING SUSPENSION*', page 125*).

KEYS AND HANDSETS

You have been supplied with two remote handsets with integral keys which operate all locks.

The key number is stamped on a tag attached to the key ring. Check that the key number has been entered in the space provided on your Security card.

If the remote handset is lost, contact a Land Rover dealer, who can supply replacement units.

WARNING

Keep the Security card and spare handset in a safe place - NOT IN THE VEHICLE!

ALARM SYSTEM

Your vehicle is fitted with a sophisticated electronic anti-theft alarm and engine immobilisation system. There are also a number of additional security features, some of which are selectable options and some are standard features of the vehicle. In order to ensure maximum security and operating convenience, you are strongly advised to gain a full understanding of the features and alternatives available, by thoroughly reading this section of the handbook.

IMPORTANT INFORMATION
FOR MAXIMUM SECURITY ALWAYS SUPERLOCK THE VEHICLE USING THE REMOTE HANDSET (except when passengers are to be left inside or if it is necessary to leave a window or sunroof open).

Using the remote handset

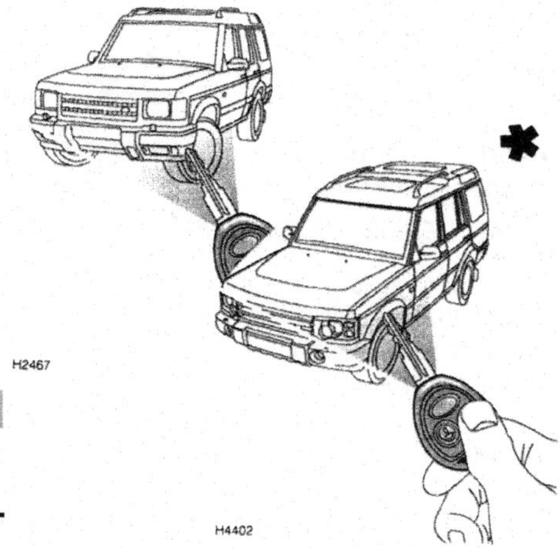

While it is not necessary to point the handset at the vehicle, the handset must be within range of the vehicle when a button is pressed. Note that the operating range may vary depending upon handset battery condition and may sometimes be limited by physical and geographical factors beyond your control. From a security point of view, it may not be wise to unlock unless you are within a few feet of the vehicle.

Locking

With the remote handset:

Press the lock (padlock symbol) button once:

- all doors are superlocked (see *'Superlocking', page 14*)
- engine immobilised
- perimetric alarm activated (protects the doors, bonnet and taildoor)
- interior space protection* activated

The direction indicator lights flash three times to confirm that the vehicle is secure and the anti-theft alarm indicator light (in the instrument panel) starts to flash.

With the key:
Insert the key and turn the door lock towards the rear of the vehicle:

- all doors locked (not superlocked)
- engine immobilised
- perimetric alarm activated (protects the doors, bonnet and taildoor)
- NO INTERIOR SPACE PROTECTION

The direction indicator lights flash once to confirm that the vehicle is secure and the anti-theft alarm indicator light (in the instrument panel) starts to flash.

Unlocking
With the remote handset:

- Press the unlock (Land Rover) button once to disarm the alarm and unlock the driver's door only (see *'Single point entry', page 16*).
- Press the unlock button twice to disarm the alarm and unlock ALL the doors.

In either case, the direction indicator lights flash once and the interior lights illuminate.

With the key:
While the doors can be unlocked using the key, this method is NOT RECOMMENDED - depending on the specification of the vehicle the alarm may not be disarmed.

NOTE: *If the handset does not operate after the vehicle has been parked for a long period, unlock the driver's door with the key and then try again. If the handset still fails to operate, enter the EKA code using the procedure shown later in this section.*

Superlocking
Provided all the doors are fully closed, the Superlocking feature is activated automatically whenever the vehicle is locked using the remote handset. Superlocking immobilises the interior door handles, thereby preventing an intruder from gaining entry by smashing a window and reaching inside the vehicle to operate the door handles.

Note that locking with the key will not activate superlocking.

WARNING

For safety, NEVER use Superlocking if passengers are to remain inside the vehicle - in an emergency they would not be able to escape.

Anti-theft alarm indicator light

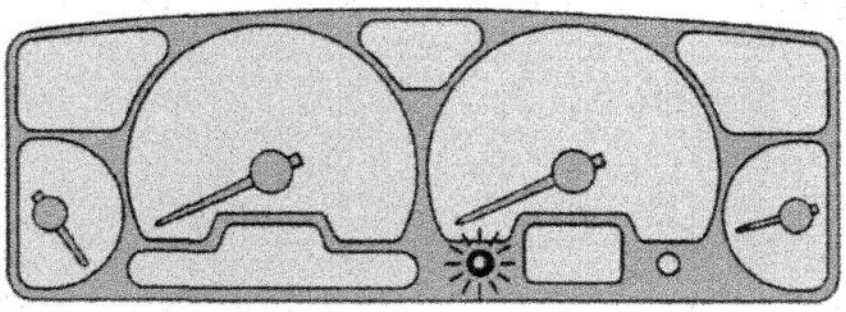

H2546

This light provides information about the status of the alarm system, as follows:

When the vehicle is locked:
The light flashes rapidly while the alarm is arming itself. After ten seconds, the light adjusts to a slower frequency and continues to flash as an anti-theft deterrent until the alarm is disarmed.

If the engine is immobilised *(even though the alarm has been disarmed):*
The light flashes slowly until the engine is remobilised.

If the alarm has been triggered:
The light will flash rapidly when the alarm is disarmed until the starter switch is turned to position II.

If the remote handset battery power is low:
The light will flash rapidly for ten seconds after the handset has been used when the driver's door is opened.

Mislock

If the driver's door is not fully closed when the handset lock button is pressed, the alarm sounder or vehicle horn will sound once, indicating a mislock. In this case, none of the doors will lock and the alarm system will not be armed.

If a passenger door or other aperture is not fully closed when the handset lock button is pressed, the alarm sounder or vehicle horn will sound once, indicating a mislock. However, the 'partial arming' attributes of the security system will enable as much of the system to be armed as possible (all fully closed door or bonnet apertures will be protected, but an open door will not!). As soon as the open aperture is closed, the system will automatically revert to a fully armed state.

NOTE: *If a mislock occurs as a result of an open door, the superlocking and interior space protection* features will not be activated.*

The mislock audible warning can be disabled by a Land Rover dealer.

If the alarm sounds

If the alarm is triggered, the alarm sounder or vehicle horn will sound for 30 seconds before switching off and resetting itself to the same protection status that existed prior to the alarm being triggered.

To silence the alarm, press either button on the remote handset.

Headlight courtesy delay
When locking the vehicle, the remote handset can be used to illuminate the headlights for 30 seconds. At night this will make it easier for you to unlock the garage, or walk to your house in safety. Operate this feature at the same time as you lock the car, by keeping the handset LOCK button pressed for more than 2 seconds (the doors lock and alarm system arms in the usual way).

To extinguish the lights before the 30 second illumination period has expired, press the lock button again.

The headlight courtesy delay can be disabled by a Land Rover dealer.

Single point entry
This is a personal security feature, which enables the driver's door only to be unlocked, leaving the other doors in a locked state. It can be operated by the remote handset as follows:

- press the unlock button once to unlock the driver's door.
- press a second time (within one minute) to unlock the remaining doors.

Single point entry can be disabled by a Land Rover dealer.

*

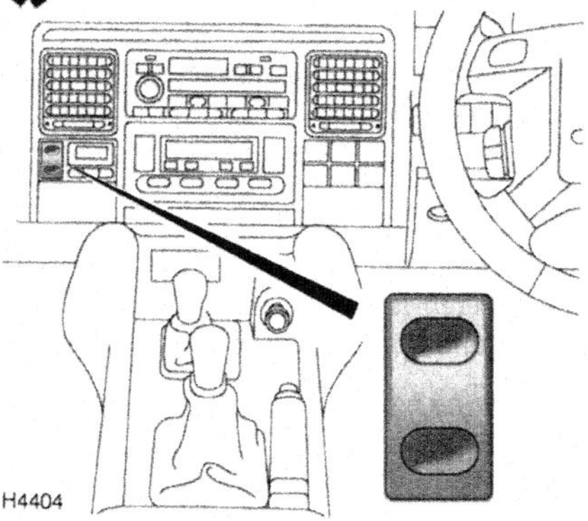

H4404

Interior locking switch

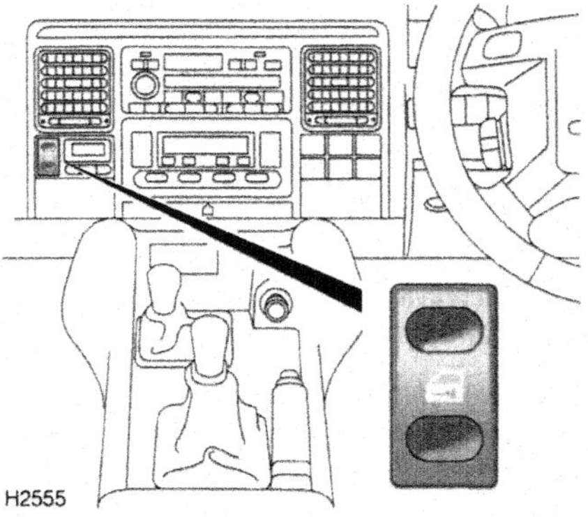

H2555

This is a personal security feature which allows the driver to lock (or unlock) all the doors from inside the vehicle (while driving or with the vehicle stationary). Press the lower part of the switch to lock (the alarm will not be armed), and the upper part to unlock.

NOTE: *If the locks have already been superlocked, the switch will not release the locks.*

Interior door handles and door sill locking buttons
From inside the vehicle, each door can be individually locked by depressing the appropriate door sill button. However, doors cannot be unlocked by raising the sill button.

Use the door handles to unlock, as follows:

- First operation of the door handle unlocks the door.
- Second operation of the door handle opens the door.

Interior space protection*

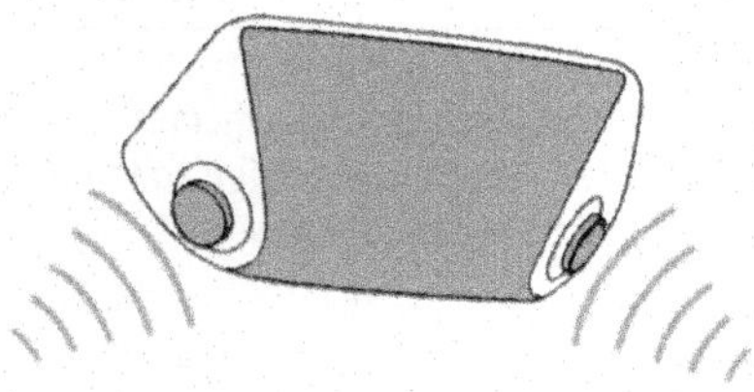

H2468

Interior space protection is designed to protect the interior of the vehicle from intrusion (entry by a thief through a smashed window, for example). Two pairs of sensors monitor the interior space and activate the alarm if air movement is detected in the passenger compartment.

Using the handset:
Interior space protection is activated automatically whenever the remote handset is used to set the alarm and can ONLY be deactivated with the handset.

Key operation:
Using the key will NOT activate (or deactivate) interior space protection.

NOTE: *Interior space protection cannot be activated if a door is open, or if the starter switch is turned on.*

WARNING

Never activate interior space protection if windows or sunroof are to be left open, or if passengers or animals are to be left inside the vehicle - any movement will activate the alarm.

Speed-related locking*
This security feature locks all the doors automatically when the vehicle speed exceeds 4 mph (7 km/h), and unlocks the doors as soon as the starter switch is turned off (provided the doors had previously been locked by the speed related feature).

Note speed-related locking is not selectable by the driver, and that operation of the door locks by any other means (interior locking switch on the fascia panel, for example) will disable the speed-related locking function for the remainder of the journey, or until the starter switch is turned off and on again.

Speed related locking can be selected or deselected by a Land Rover dealer.

ENGINE IMMOBILISATION

Engine immobilisation is an important aspect of the security system and includes a feature known as 'passive immobilisation'. This is designed to safeguard the vehicle from theft, should the driver forget to lock the doors and prevents the engine from being started unless the GENUINE handset key is inserted into the starter switch. Engine immobilisation is automatic whenever any of the following conditions occur.

- The vehicle is locked using handset or key.
- Thirty seconds after the starter switch has been turned off AND the driver's door opened.
- Five minutes after the starter switch is turned off, or the alarm system is disarmed.

NOTE: *The engine will be re-mobilised automatically whenever the genuine handset key is inserted into the starter switch and turned to position 'II'.*

Emergency key access

If the handset is damaged, or fails to operate, the engine can be re-mobilised by using the key to enter a unique four number emergency key access code. The code is recorded on the Security Information card and is entered as follows:

IMPORTANT INFORMATION
When entering a code: • ENSURE each key movement is carried out with care and precision and turned to the full extent of its travel. • After turning the key to either the lock or unlock positions, make sure it is FULLY returned to the centre (vertical) position. • An interval of 10 seconds or more between key turns, or the key being held in a locked or unlocked position for 5 seconds or more will cancel an entry attempt, in which case you must start again with operation 1.

1. Ensure that all doors are closed, then using the key turn the driver's door lock to the UNLOCK position (towards the front of the car) and hold in this position for at least 5 seconds until the alarm sounder sounds once). Then return the key to the centre position. It is now possible to use the key to enter the separate numerical values of the four numbers that make up the emergency key access code.

2. Enter the FIRST number of the code. If the first number is 4, turn the key (towards the front of the car) to the UNLOCK position 4 times. Ensure the key is FULLY returned to the centre position after each turn.

3. Enter the SECOND number of the code. If the second number is 3, turn the key (towards the rear) to the LOCK position 3 times. Remember; the key must be FULLY returned to the centre position after each turn.

4. Enter the THIRD number of the code. If the third number is 12, turn the key to the UNLOCK position twelve times, ensuring that the key is FULLY returned to the centre position after each turn.

5. Enter the FOURTH number of the code. If the fourth number is 1, turn the key to the LOCK position once. Ensure the key is FULLY returned to the centre position.

6. Finally, turn the key to the unlock position once more. If the code has been entered correctly, a double 'bleep' will sound (a single 'bleep' indicates that the code has been entered incorrectly).

NOTE: *If the Mislock audible warning has been deselected (by a Land Rover dealer), the alarm sounder will not sound when an EKA code has been entered. Instead, the alarm indicator light on the instrument panel will flash once (for one second) to indicate a successful code entry.*

There is now a **five minute delay** before the alarm and engine immobiliser are deactivated. **DO NOT OPEN THE DOOR OR ATTEMPT TO ENTER THE VEHICLE YET!**

7. Through the driver's door window, observe the anti-theft alarm indicator light on the instrument panel. If code entry was successful, this light will continue flashing (once every two seconds) for the five minute delay period.

DO NOT OPEN THE DOOR OR ATTEMPT TO ENTER THE VEHICLE until the full delay period has elapsed - this will be indicated by the anti-theft alarm indicator light extinguishing.

8. Now open the door, insert the key into the starter and turn the switch to position 'II' IMMEDIATELY! If the starter switch is not turned to position 'II' within 30 seconds of the indicator light extinguishing, the engine will automatically immobilise again.

If an incorrect code has been entered:

If an incorrect code has been entered, the alarm sounder will sound once and the anti-theft alarm indicator light will continue to flash. In this case, return to operation '1' and re-enter the code.

After three failed entry attempts, the security system invokes a delay period of ten minutes during which the system will not accept any further attempts to enter a code.

IMPORTANT INFORMATION
Memorise the emergency key access code or keep the Security card on your person in case of emergencies. NEVER leave the card in the vehicle.

REMOTE HANDSET BATTERY

The battery should last for approximately three years dependent upon use. When the battery needs replacing it will be apparent from the following symptoms:

- A gradual deterioration in range and performance.
- The alarm indicator light in the instrument panel will flash rapidly for 10 seconds after the driver's door is opened.

Always fit a Land Rover YWX10003L or a Panasonic CR2032 replacement battery (available from a Land Rover dealer).

WARNING

The handset contains delicate electronic circuits and must be protected from impact and water damage, high temperatures and humidity, direct sunlight and the effects of solvents, waxes and abrasive cleaners.

Battery replacement

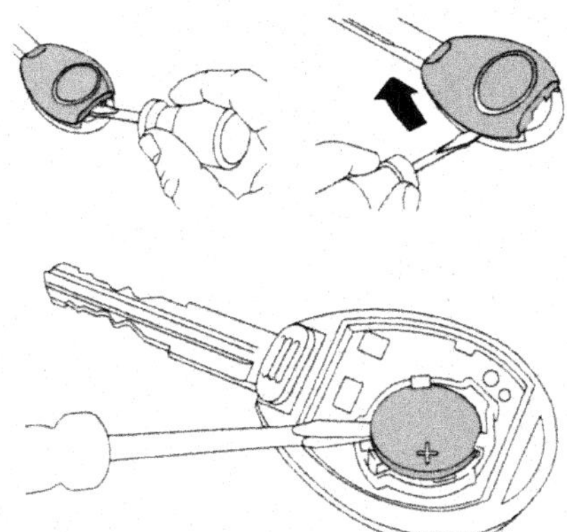

H2794

1. With the handset face down, insert the blade of a small flat-bladed screwdriver into the slot at the rear of the handset (see inset) and prise the back upwards.
2. Insert the screwdriver blade as shown in the right hand inset and then carefully slide it along the joint towards the key to release the back of the handset.
3. Use a small flat-bladed screwdriver to prise the battery from its mounting (see illustration), taking care to avoid touching the circuit board or the metal battery contacts.
4. Fit the new battery, ensuring that correct polarity is maintained ('+' side facing up). Finger marks will adversely affect battery life; if possible, avoid touching the flat surfaces of the battery and wipe them clean before fitting.
5. Press the two halves of the handset firmly together and ensure that both halves are fully joined to prevent dirt or moisture from entering the handset.

The handset is now ready for use.

CHILD-PROOF LOCKS

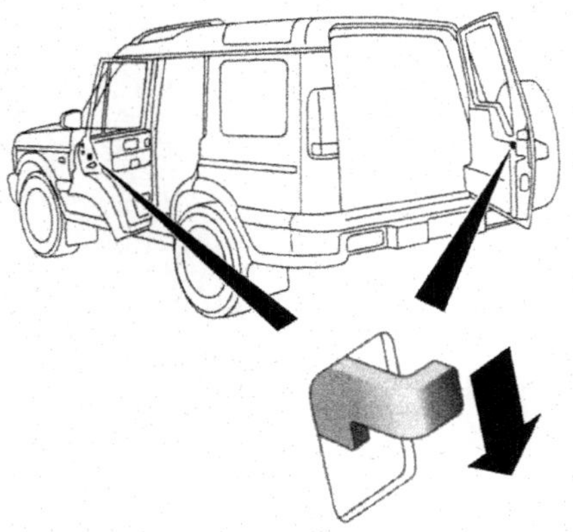

H2464

Move the locking levers on the rear doors and taildoor down to engage the child locks.

With the child-proof locks engaged, neither the rear doors nor the taildoor can be opened from inside the vehicle, thereby avoiding the risk of a door being opened accidentally while the vehicle is moving.

WARNING

NEVER leave children unsupervised in the vehicle.

DOOR LOCKING CUT-OFF SWITCH

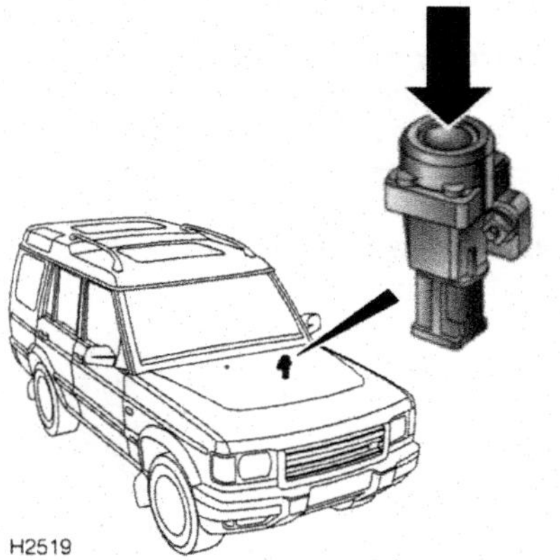

H2519

An inertia switch, operational only with the starter switch in position 'II' and the alarm disarmed, prevents the doors centrally locking (or if the doors are locked, will unlock them) in the event of an accident or sudden impact.

When the switch operates, the direction indicator lights flash (if market permits), until the system is reset by turning the starter switch on and off, and opening and closing the driver's door.

Note that doors cannot be locked again until the switch is reset.

The inertia switch also cuts off the fuel supply (see *'FUEL CUT-OFF SWITCH', page 108*).

WARNING

Always check for fuel leaks before resetting the switch!

MANUALLY OPERATED FRONT SEATS

WARNING

To avoid the risk of loss of control and personal injury, DO NOT adjust the driver's seat while the vehicle is in motion.

Forward/backward adjustment

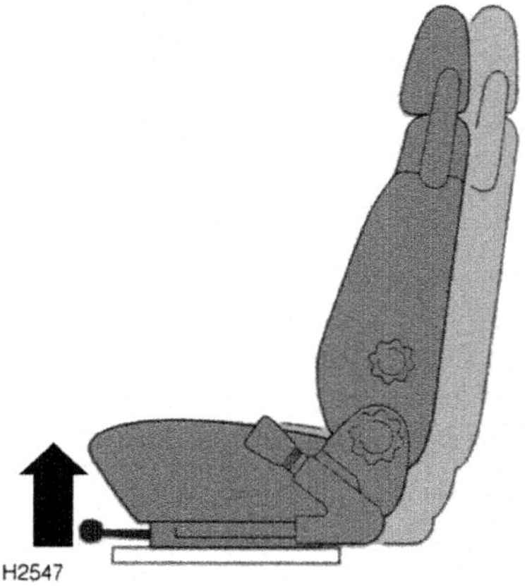

H2547

Lift the lever to slide the seat forward or back. Ensure the seat is locked in position before driving.

Seat back adjustment

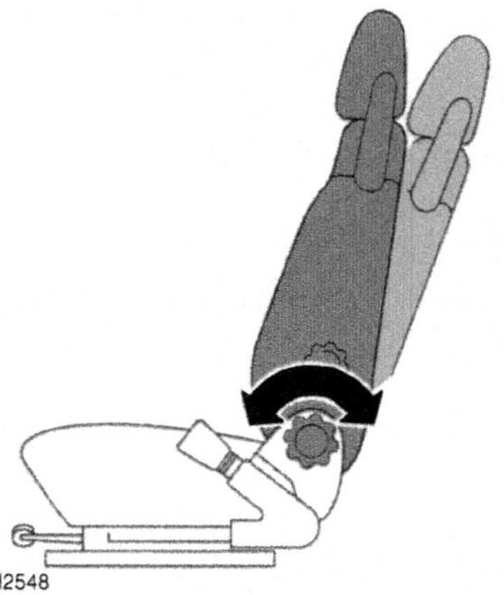

H2548

Rotate the handwheel to achieve the desired backrest angle.

WARNING

DO NOT travel with the seat backs reclined steeply rearwards. Optimum benefit is obtained from the seat belt with the seat back angle set to approximately 25° from the upright (vertical).

Lumbar support adjustment*

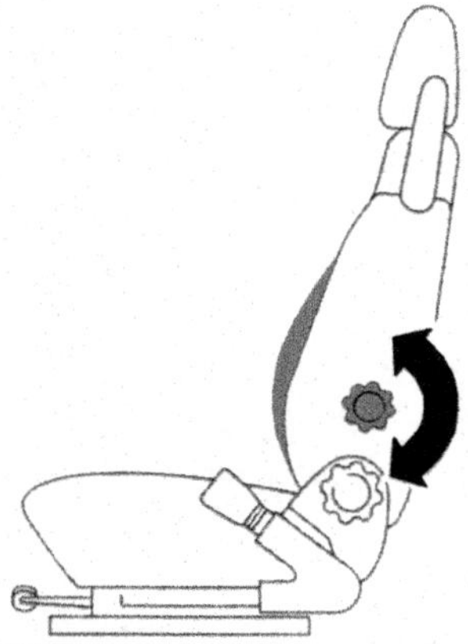

H2590

Rotate the handwheel to increase or decrease support to the lumbar region of the back.

POWER OPERATED FRONT SEATS*

WARNING

To avoid the risk of loss of control and personal injury, DO NOT adjust the driver's seat while the vehicle is in motion.

The seat adjustment controls are situated on the side of the centrally mounted cubby box.

Seat adjustment is only possible when the starter switch is turned to position 'II' or for 45 seconds after opening the driver's door.

Forward/backward adjustment

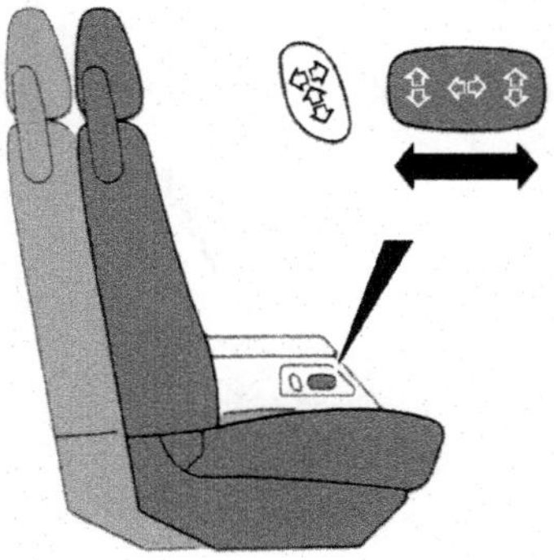

H2469

Push and hold the switch forwards or backwards to move the seat to the desired position.

Seat cushion angle adjustment

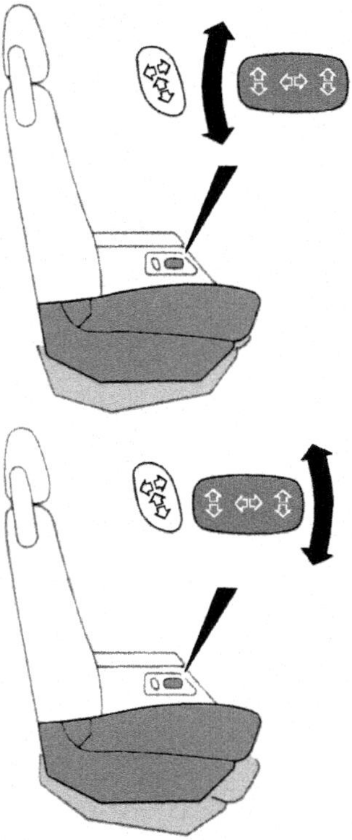

H2470

Twist the switch to tilt the seat cushion to the desired position. Note that the front and rear of the switch work independently - the front raising or lowering the front of the cushion, the rear of the switch similarly controlling the rear of the seat cushion.

Seat cushion height adjustment*

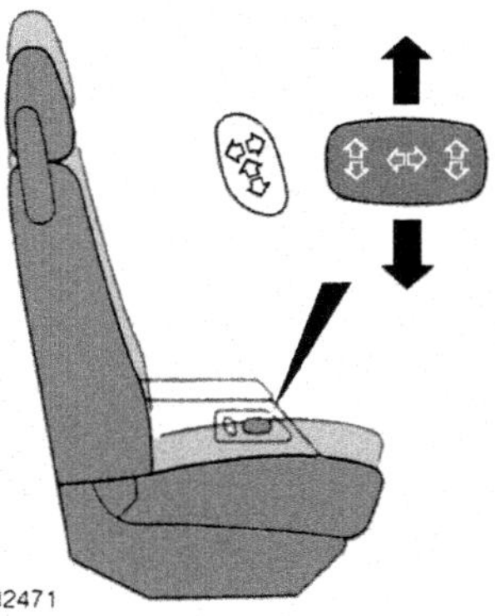

H2471

On some vehicles, the height of the seat cushion can be adjusted. Push the switch up or down to raise or lower the cushion.

Lumbar support adjustment

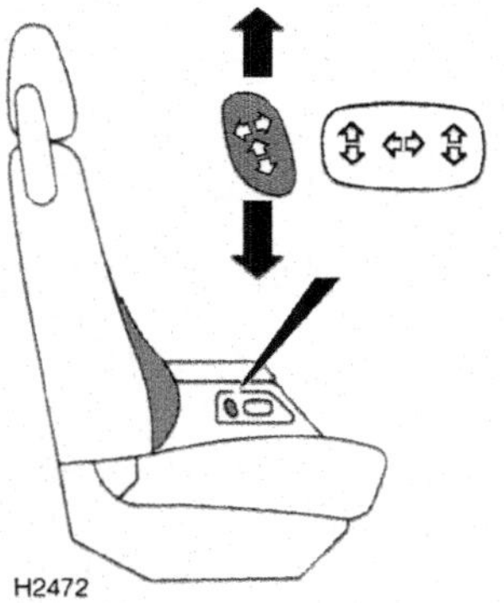

H2472

Push the switch up to increase support to the lumbar region of the back. Lower the switch to reduce lumbar support.

Seat back adjustment

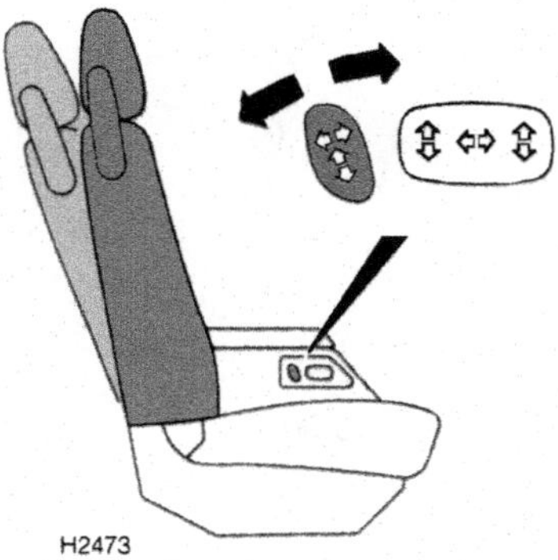

H2473

Twist the switch forward or backward until the desired seat back angle is achieved.

WARNING

DO NOT travel with the seat backs reclined steeply rearwards. Optimum benefit is obtained from the seat belt with the seat back angle set to approximately 25° from the upright (vertical).

HEAD RESTRAINTS

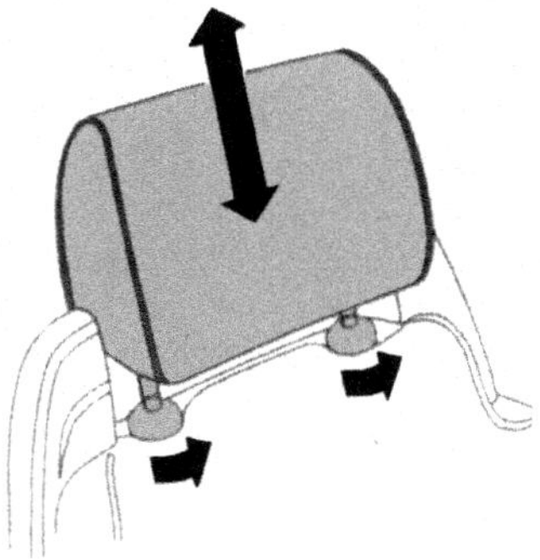

H2465

Pull the head restraint up or down until the cushion is level with the back of the head.

WARNING

Head restraints are designed to support the back of the head (NOT THE NECK), and to restrain rearward movement of the head in the event of a collision. The restraint must be positioned level with the head to be effective.

Head restraint removal

Turn both mounting collars fully anti-clockwise and pull the restraint upwards to remove.

After replacing a head restraint turn the mounting collars clockwise.

FOLDING ARMRESTS*

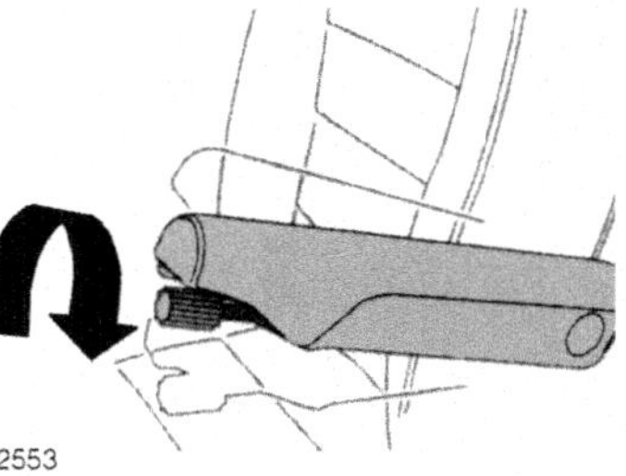

H2553

Some vehicles are fitted with adjustable front seat armrests, which can be either; stowed vertically in line with the seat backrest when not required, or folded horizontally to serve as an arm/elbow rest.

The height/angle of each armrest can be adjusted by turning the knob set into the end of the armrest: clockwise to raise and anti-clockwise to lower.

HEATED FRONT SEATS*

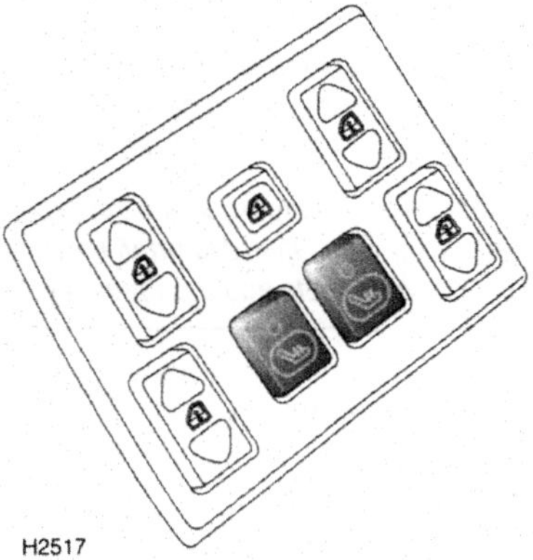
H2517

With the starter switch turned on and the engine running, press the switches to operate the heating elements in either the driver's or front passenger seat (the indicator light in the switch illuminates). Press a second time to switch off.

The seat heaters are thermostatically controlled and operate intermittently to achieve and then maintain a predetermined temperature between 79°F and 97°F (26° - 36°C).

IMPORTANT INFORMATION
The seat heaters consume considerable power from the battery. For this reason, they should ONLY be operated while the engine is running.

FOLDING THE REAR SEATS

H2493

WARNING

DO NOT adjust any part of a seat while the vehicle is in motion.

One or both parts of the split rear seat can be either partially or fully folded to further increase the rear loadspace.

1. To release either part of the backrest, lift the lever shown in the inset, and then fold the backrest onto the seat base.
2. Ensure the outer head restraints are fully lowered, the armrest is stowed and the centre head restraint* is removed.
3. To release the seat base, pull the release strap upward (arrowed in illustration). With backrest and seat base released, the assembly can be folded forward as shown.

Returning the seat to the upright position

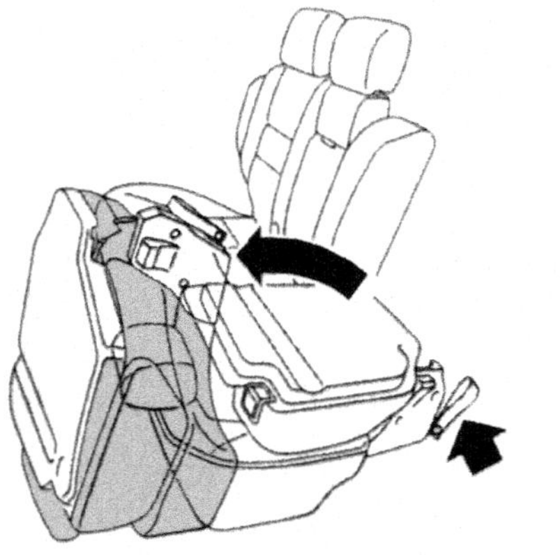

H2549

Push the seat assembly back onto the floor - the floor catches should latch with the base of the seat. Then raise the backrest.

If the backrest cannot be raised easily, DO NOT force it. This indicates that the seat base has not fully engaged with the floor catches (note that the seat assembly is designed to prevent the backrest from being raised unless the seat is properly secured to the floor).

With the seat base secure, the backrest can be raised and locked in position (none of the RED panel on the release lever should be visible when the backrest is correctly latched).

WARNING

After the seat is returned to the upright position, the latching mechanism should be checked and physically tested to ensure that both the seat base and backrest are secure before driving.

OCCASIONAL REAR SEATS

WARNING

Before driving with passengers seated in the occasional rear seats, for safety ensure that the floor latches are fully engaged.

Do not carry passengers in the occasional rear seats if a dog guard is fitted between the second row of seats and the loadspace.

Erecting the seats

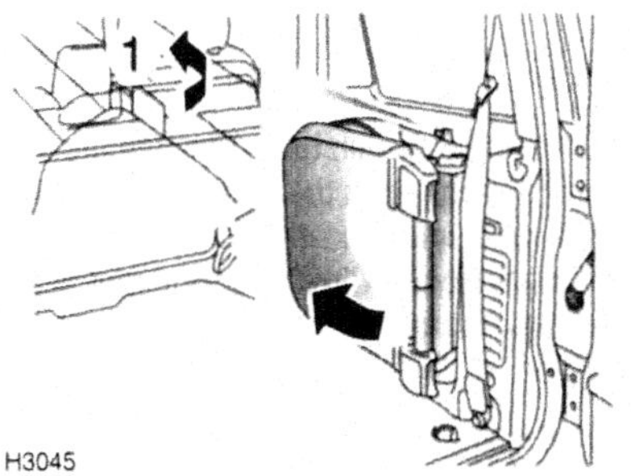

H3045

1. Push the lever (shown in inset) and hold to release the seat from its stowed position.

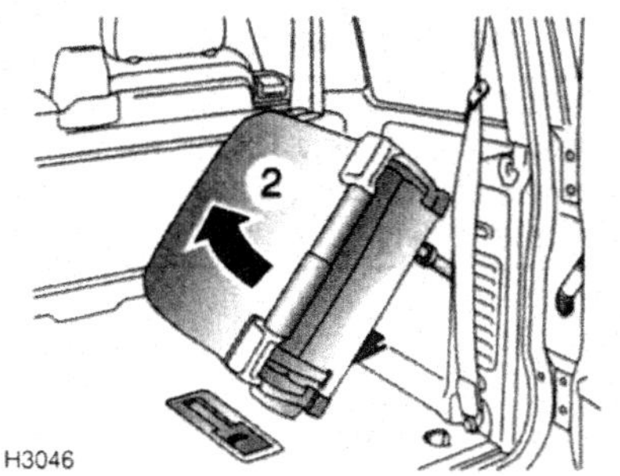

H3046

2. Swing the seat away from the vehicle side, at the same time lifting and turning it towards the horizontal.

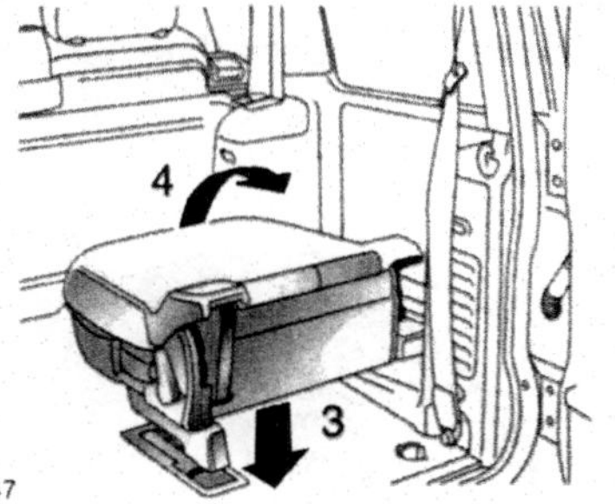

H3047

3. Lower the seat to the loadspace floor, PUSHING DOWN FIRMLY to ensure that the floor latch has fully engaged.
4. Pull the backrest into the upright position.

NOTE: *The backrest cannot be raised unless the seat is securely latched to the floor.*

IMPORTANT INFORMATION
Remember to unfold the head restraints from the roof before driving.

Stowing the seats

NOTE: *Before stowing a seat, ensure that the drinks tray to the side of the seat has been emptied, and that the seat belt buckle is folded down to prevent it from becoming trapped between the backrest and cushion.*

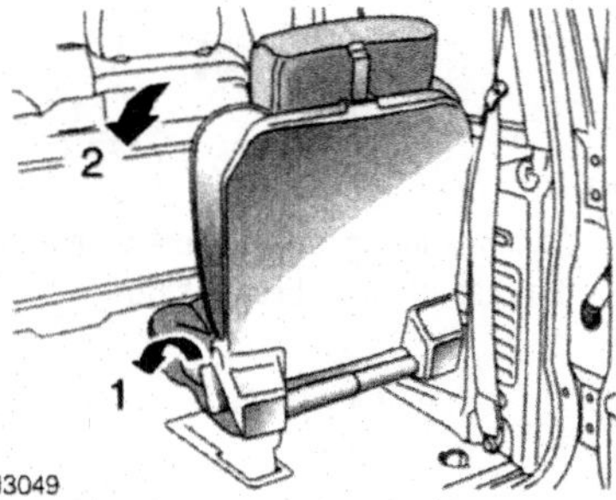

H3049

1. Push the backrest release lever forward to unlock the backrest.
2. Fold the backrest fully forward.

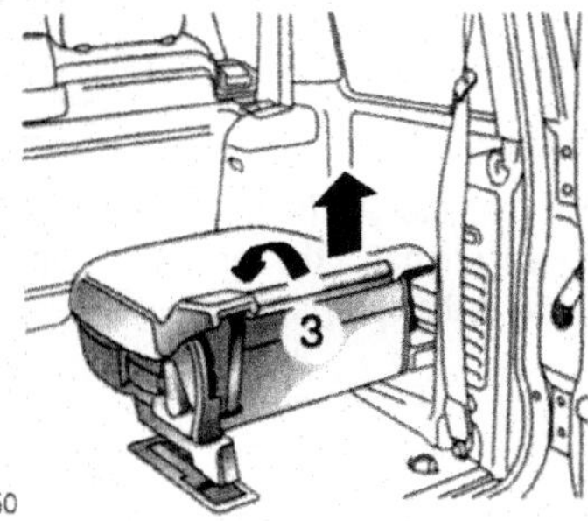

H3050

3. Turn the twist grip (moving part of the bar on the back of the seat) fully forward to release the floor latch, and start to lift the seat from the loadspace floor.

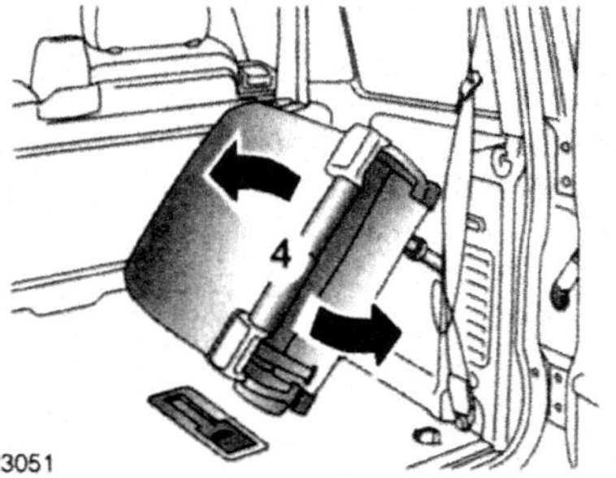

H3051

4. Continue lifting, at the same time turning the seat into a vertical position.

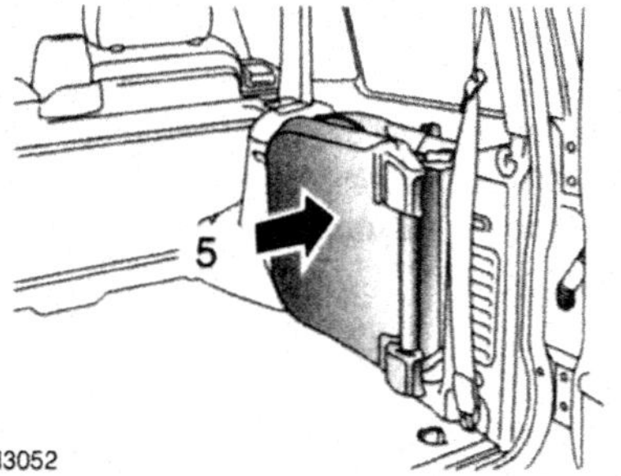

H3052

5. Push the seat firmly into the vehicle side, ensuring that the seat has engaged fully with the securing catch.

Head restraints

NOTE: *The head restraints for use with the occasional rear seats are hinged from the roof.*

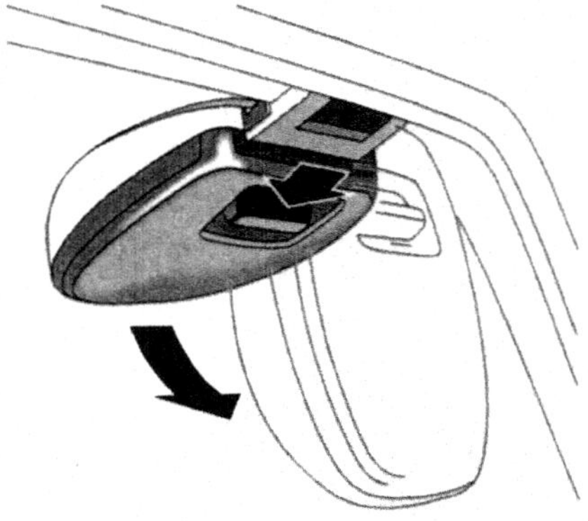

H3544

1. To unfold a head restraint, pull the handle (arrowed in illustration) forward and swing the restraint down from the roof. Stow the head restraint when not in use by pushing it back flush with the roof.

WARNING

DO NOT drive with occupants in the occasional rear seats unless the head restraints are unfolded.

SEAT BELT SAFETY

The seat belts fitted to the front and second row seats are intended for use by adult sized occupants. Each belt should be used by one occupant only.

Observe the following precautions:

- DO make sure ALL passengers are securely strapped in at all times - even for the shortest journeys.
- ALWAYS adjust seat belts to eliminate any slack in the webbing. DO NOT slacken the webbing by holding the belt away from the body - to be fully effective, the seat belt must remain in full contact with the body at all times.
- ALWAYS fit the lap strap as low on the hips as possible (never across the abdomen), and ensure that the diagonal belt passes across the shoulder without slipping off or pressing on the neck.
- DO NOT wear seat belts over hard, sharp or fragile items in clothing, such as pens, keys, spectacles etc.
- Always replace a seat belt assembly that has withstood the strain of a severe vehicle impact, or if the webbing shows signs of fraying.
- Where possible use the seat belts to secure large items of luggage that are to be carried on the seats - in the event of an accident, insecure items become flying missiles capable of causing serious injury.
- DO NOT use a seat belt that is twisted or obstructed in any way that could impede its smooth operation.
- DO NOT allow front seat occupants to travel with the seat backs reclined steeply rearwards. Optimum benefit is obtained from the seat belt with the seat back angle set to approximately 25° from the upright (vertical) position.
- DO NOT allow foreign matter (particularly sugary food and drink particles) to enter the seat belt locks - such substances can render the locks inoperative.
- In most countries, all occupants are required by law to wear a seat belt, unless they have been issued with a medical exemption certificate.
- During pregnancy, women should wear the lap belt across the hips below the baby, with the diagonal belt passing across the shoulder, between the breasts and to one side of the baby - if in doubt, consult a doctor.

WARNING

The airbag supplementary restraint system (SRS) is designed to add to the overall effectiveness of the seat belts. It does not replace them. SEAT BELTS MUST ALWAYS BE WORN!

Ensure that all seat belts are worn correctly - an improperly worn seat belt increases the risk of death or serious injury in the event of a collision.

SEAT BELTS

To minimise injury in the event of an accident, it is important that seat belts are worn correctly. Read the instructions below and the advice contained under the heading *'SEAT BELT SAFETY'.*

Fastening the seat belts

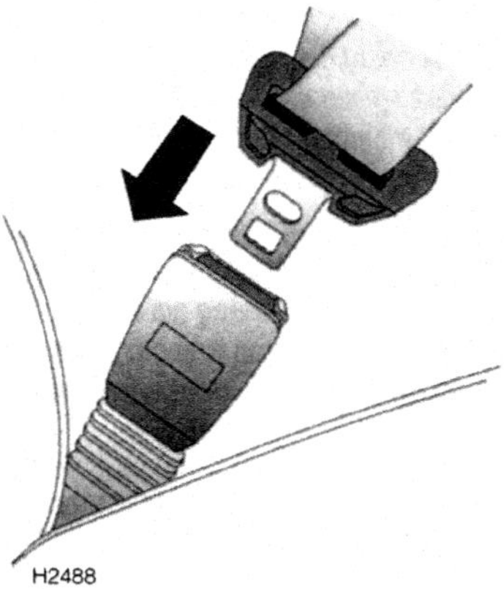
H2488

Inertia reel belts are fitted to all front and rear seating positions, and also to the occasional rear seats*.

Pull the belt over the shoulder and across the chest and, ensuring that the webbing is not twisted, insert the metal tongue plate into the buckle nearest the wearer - a 'CLICK' indicates that the belt is securely locked.

Seat belts are designed to bear upon the bony structure of the body (pelvis, chest and shoulders) and can only be worn safely with the seats in a normal upright position - DO NOT allow front seat occupants to travel with the seat steeply reclined.

Releasing the belt

Press the RED button on the seat belt buckle.

Upper anchorage adjustment (front seats only)

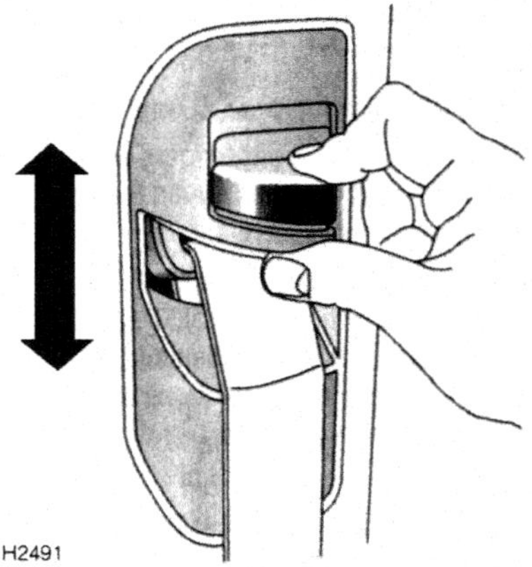
H2491

The height of the seat belt upper anchorage can be adjusted for comfort AND safety. Squeeze the control between finger and thumb to raise or lower the anchorage. For safety, the seat belt should always be worn with the webbing crossing the shoulder MIDWAY BETWEEN THE NECK AND THE EDGE OF THE SHOULDER.

Ensure the anchorage has 'clicked' into one of the locked positions before driving and DO NOT adjust the height once the vehicle is in motion.

Where possible, rear seat passengers should adjust their position on the seat to enable the seat belt webbing to cross the shoulder without pressing on the neck.

SEAT BELT PRE-TENSIONERS

The seat belt pre-tensioners activate in conjunction with the airbag SRS and provide additional protection in the event of a severe frontal impact on the vehicle (see *'HOW THE AIRBAG SRS WORKS', page 39*). The pre-tensioners automatically retract the seat belts fitted to the front seats. This reduces any slack in both the lap and diagonal portions of the belts, thereby reducing forward movement of the belt wearer in the event of a severe frontal collision.

The airbag SRS warning light on the instrument panel will alert you to any malfunction of the seat belt pre-tensioners.

If the pre-tensioners have been activated, the seat belts will still function as restraints, and must be worn in the event that the vehicle remains in a driveable condition.

NOTE: *The seat belt pre-tensioners will NOT be activated by rear, side or minor frontal impacts.*

IMPORTANT INFORMATION
The seat belt pre-tensioners will only be activated once and then MUST BE REPLACED by a Land Rover dealer. Failure to replace the pre-tensioners will reduce the efficiency of the vehicle's front restraint systems. After any frontal impact, always have the seat belts and pre-tensioners checked and, if necessary, replaced by a Land Rover dealer. In the interests of safety, it is recommended that removal or replacement of the front seats and seat belts should only be carried out by a Land Rover dealer.

CARING FOR SEAT BELTS

Regularly inspect the belt webbing for signs of fraying, cuts and wear; also pay particular attention to the condition of the fixing points and adjusters.

DO NOT bleach or dye the webbing and avoid contaminating the webbing with polish, oil or chemicals (see *'CLEANING THE INTERIOR', page 171*).

Testing inertia reel belts

- With the seat belt fastened, give the webbing near the buckle a quick upward pull. The buckle must remain securely locked.
- With the seat belt unfastened, unreel the webbing to the limit of its travel. Check that unreeling is free from snatches and snags and then allow the belt to FULLY retract.
- Partially unreel the webbing, then hold the tongue plate and give it a quick forward pull. The mechanism must lock automatically and prevent any further unreeling.

If a seat belt should fail any of these tests, contact your dealer immediately.

WARNING

Always replace a seat belt that shows signs of webbing damage or has withstood the strain of a severe vehicle impact.

CHILD SAFETY SEATS

Seat belts fitted to your vehicle are designed for adults and larger children. For their safety, it is very important that all infants and children under 12 are restrained in a suitable child safety seat appropriate to their age and size (see table). Child safety seats approved for use in your vehicle are available from Land Rover dealers.

Only fit a child safety seat of a type approved for the specific seating positions in your vehicle (see table), and ensure the seat manufacturer's fitting instructions are followed exacly.

Vehicles fitted with a passenger airbag

For optimum safety, children should travel in the rear of the vehicle at all times; front passenger seat travel is NOT recommended. However, if a passenger airbag is fitted and it is essential that a child travel in the front, set the seat fully rearward and seat the child in an approved, FORWARD FACING child seat. DO NOT use a rear facing child seat - an inflating airbag could impact with the seat and cause serious injury to the child!

The above symbol affixed to the passenger side fascia panel of your vehicle, warns against the use of a REAR FACING child seat in the front passenger seat, when a passenger airbag is fitted. This type of child seat could cause serious injury to a child in the event of an airbag deployment.

WARNING

DO NOT install a rearward facing child seat in a passenger seat equipped with an airbag system. Failure to follow this advice could result in serious injury, or even death for the child in the event of airbag deployment.

Mass Group	Seating Positions			
As indicated on child safety seat packaging.	Front Passenger	Second Row Outboard	Second Row Centre	Third Row Seats*
0 = Up to 10 kg (0-9 months)	X	U	U	X
0+ = Up to 13 kg (0-18 months)	X	U	U	X
I = 9 to 18 kg (9 months - 4 years)	X	U	U	X
II & III =15 to 36 kg (4-12 years)	X	U	U	X

U = Suitable for 'universal' category restraints approved for this mass group.
X = Seat position not suitable for children in this mass group.
* = Unsuitable for use with many child restraints due to the limited space between the 2nd and 3rd row seats. Smaller forward facing restraints and booster cushions may safely be used in these positions if a good fit of the child restraint can be achieved following the manufacturers instructions.

Seat belt locking mechanism

All front passenger and second row seat belts have a special locking mechanism which aids the retention of child seats. The procedure to install a child seat is as follows:

1. Install the child seat in the vehicle, attach the seat belt and secure the buckle in accordance with the manufacturers fitting instructions.
2. Pull on the shoulder section of the belt to unreel all of the remaining webbing to the limit of its travel. This will engage the automatic locking feature, which then acts as a ratchet, allowing the webbing to retract ONLY.
3. Allow the seat belt to retract onto the child seat (a 'clicking' sound will confirm that the ratchet has engaged), firmly pushing the child seat into the seat.
4. Ensure there is no slack in the seat belt by pulling upwards on the shoulder belt immediately above the child restraint. The seat belt should now be locked and the child seat held firmly in position.

Once the child seat is removed and all the seat belt webbing is allowed to retract, the seat belt locking mechanism reverts to normal operation.

NOTE: *The automatic locking mechanism should also be used when securing large items of luggage to a seat.*

Child Restraints

ISOFIX CHILD RESTRAINTS*

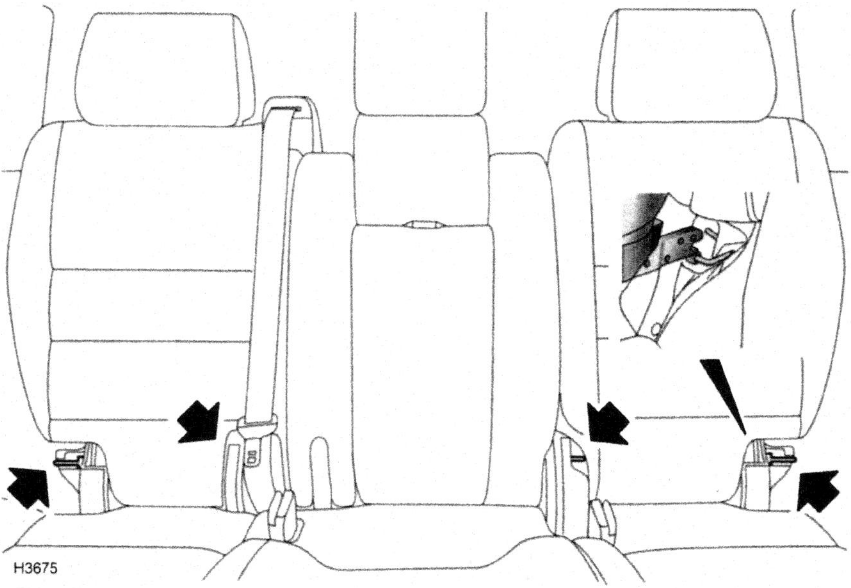

In some markets, child restraint systems complying with International Standard Organisation (ISO) regulations and approved for fitting in your vehicle may be available. These restraints are different to conventional child seats, requiring anchor bars built into the vehicle seat in order to accept the ISOFIX locking mechanism.

Both outer, rear (second row) seating positions in your vehicle are equipped to accept ISOFIX restraints.

WARNING

DO NOT attempt to fit ISOFIX restraints to the centre seating position - the anchor bars are not designed to hold an ISOFIX restraint in this position.

Fitting ISOFIX child restraints

ISOFIX child restraints should only be fitted in the two outer seating positions of the second row seats. Anchor bars built into the rear seat frame enable the ISOFIX restraints to be securely attached to the vehicle seat in these positions only. The anchor bar locations are shown in the illustration above.

When fitting ISOFIX child restraints, always follow the instructions supplied by the manufacturer of the restraint.

Once the ISOFIX restraint is installed, you are recommended to test the security of the installation before seating the child. Attempt to twist the restraint from side to side and to pull the restraint away from the vehicle seat; then check that the anchors are still securely in place.

WARNING

If the restraint is not correctly anchored, there is a significant risk of injury to the child in the event of a collision or emergency braking.

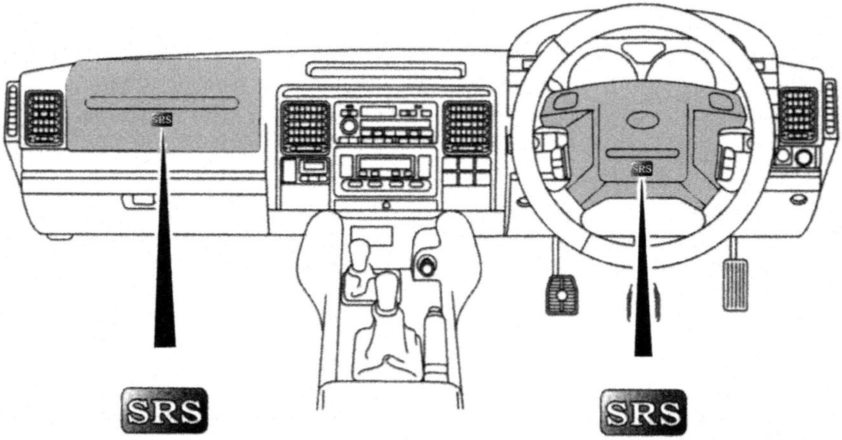

H2551

AIRBAG SRS

The airbag supplementary restraint system (SRS) provides additional protection for either the driver, or the driver and front seat passenger, in the event of a severe frontal impact on the vehicle.

WARNING

The airbag is a supplementary restraint system that provides ADDITIONAL protection in a severe frontal impact only - it does NOT replace the need to wear a seat belt. For maximum safety protection in all crash situations, a seat belt must be worn.

Provided the front seat occupants are correctly seated, with seat belts properly worn, the airbags will provide additional protection to the chest and facial areas in the event of the car receiving a severe frontal impact.

NOTE: *Inflation and deflation of the airbags takes place very quickly and will not protect against the effects of secondary impacts that may occur.*

The airbag(s) are located in the centre pad of the steering wheel and, where fitted, in the fascia panel above the glovebox.

WARNING

Do not allow a front seat passenger to obstruct the operation of the airbag by placing feet, knees or any other part of the person, or any other objects in contact with, or in close proximity to, an airbag module.

To ensure correct deployment of the airbags, it is essential that obstructions are not allowed to intervene between an airbag and the occupant. The following are examples of the type of obstructions that could either, impede correct operation of the airbags, or jeopardise personal safety in the event of an airbag deployment:

- Accessories attached to or obscuring an airbag cover.
- Items of hand luggage, or other objects placed on an airbag cover.
- Feet, knees or any other part of the anatomy in contact with, or in close proximity to, an airbag cover.

WARNING

DO NOT attach or position items on or to an airbag cover (steering wheel centre pad or fascia panel), which could interfere with the inflation of the airbag or, if the airbag inflates, be propelled inside the car causing injury to the occupants.

Seating positions

In order to provide optimum protection in the event of a severe frontal impact, it is necessary for the airbags to deploy with considerable speed.

An inflating airbag can cause facial abrasions and other injuries if the occupant is too close to the airbag at the time of its deployment.

WARNING

To minimise the risk of accidental Injury from inflating airbags, seat belts should be correctly worn at all times. In addition, both driver and front seat passenger should adjust their seat to provide the maximum practical distance from the airbags.

HOW THE AIRBAG SRS WORKS

In the event of a severe frontal impact, the airbag control unit monitors the rate of deceleration or acceleration induced by the collision, to determine whether the airbags should be deployed.

Operation of the airbag SRS is dependent entirely on the rate at which the vehicle's passenger compartment changes speed as a result of a collision. The circumstances affecting different collisions (vehicle speed, angle of impact, type and size of object hit, for example), vary considerably and will affect the rate of acceleration or deceleration accordingly.

NOTE: *The airbag SRS is not designed to operate as a result of rear collisions, minor frontal or side Impacts, roll over accidents; nor will it operate as a result of heavy braking or driving over bumps and potholes.*

It follows, therefore, that significant superficial damage can occur without the airbags deploying or, conversely, that a relatively small amount of structural damage may cause the airbags to be deployed.

Airbags will only deploy when they are required to supplement the restraining force of the seat belts.

In the case of a severe frontal collision, both front airbags and seat belt pre-tensioners will be deployed.

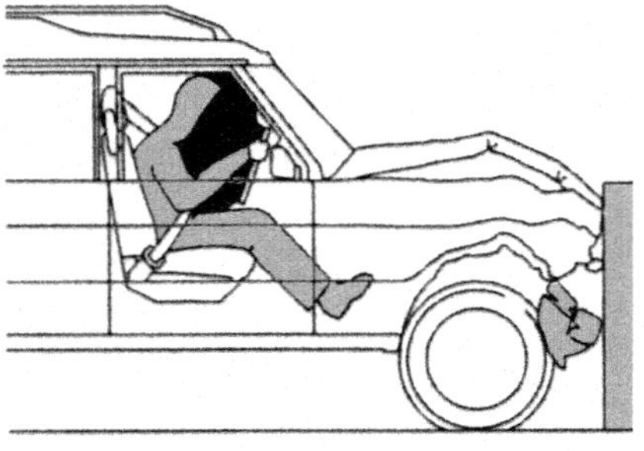

H2638

Airbag inflation is virtually instantaneous and occurs with considerable force, accompanied by a loud noise. The inflated bag, together with the seat belt restraint system, limit the movement of a front seat occupant, thereby reducing the risk of injury to the head and upper torso.

WARNING

An inflating airbag can cause facial abrasions and other injuries. Minimise the risk of injury by ensuring that front seat occupants are wearing their seat belts and are seated correctly, with the seat as far back as is practical.

When an airbag inflates, a fine powder is released. This is not an indication of a malfunction, however, the powder may cause irritation to the skin and should be thoroughly flushed from the eyes and any cuts or abrasions of the skin. After inflation the airbags deflate immediately. This provides a gradual cushioning effect for the occupant and also ensures that the driver's forward vision is not impaired.

NOTE: *After inflation, some airbag components are hot - DO NOT touch until they have cooled.*

Airbag SRS warning light

A warning light mounted on the instrument panel will alert you to any malfunction of the airbag SRS. The airbag SRS should always be checked by a dealer if any of the following symptoms occur:

- The warning light fails to illuminate when the starter switch is turned to position 'II'.
- The warning light fails to extinguish within approximately four seconds after the starter switch is turned to position 'II'.
- The warning light illuminates after the engine is started, or while the vehicle is being driven.

SERVICE INFORMATION

WARNING

DO NOT attempt to service, repair, replace, modify or tamper with any part of the airbag SRS, or wiring in the vicinity of an airbag SRS component; this could cause the system to activate, resulting in personal injury.

After ten years from the original date of registration (or the installation date of a replacement airbag SRS), some components will need to be replaced by a Land Rover dealer (note the 'airbag module replacement date' shown on page 2 of the Service Portfolio book).

In addition, ALWAYS contact your dealer if:

- an airbag inflates.
- the front of the vehicle is damaged, even if the airbag has not inflated.
- any part of an airbag module cover (the steering wheel centre pad or fascia panel) shows signs of cracking or damage.

IMPORTANT INFORMATION

The components that make up the airbag SRS are sensitive to electrical or physical interference, either of which could easily damage the system and cause inadvertent operation or a malfunction of the airbag.

For your safety it is recommended that you seek the assistance of a Land Rover dealer to carry out any of the following:

- Removal or repair of any wiring or component in the vicinity of any of the SRS components (yellow wiring harness), including the steering wheel, steering column, instrument and fascia panels.
- Installation of electronic equipment such as a mobile phone, two-way radio or in-car entertainment system.
- Modification to the front of the vehicle, including the bumper and chassis.
- Attachment of accessories to the front of the vehicle.

Disposing of vehicles

If you sell your vehicle, be sure to inform the new owner that the vehicle has an airbag SRS. In addition, make sure the new owner is aware of the airbag module replacement date shown on page 2 of the Service Portfolio book.

If your vehicle is to be scrapped; uninflated airbags are potentially very dangerous and must be safely deployed in a controlled environment by qualified personnel, before a vehicle is scrapped.

STEERING COLUMN ADJUSTMENT

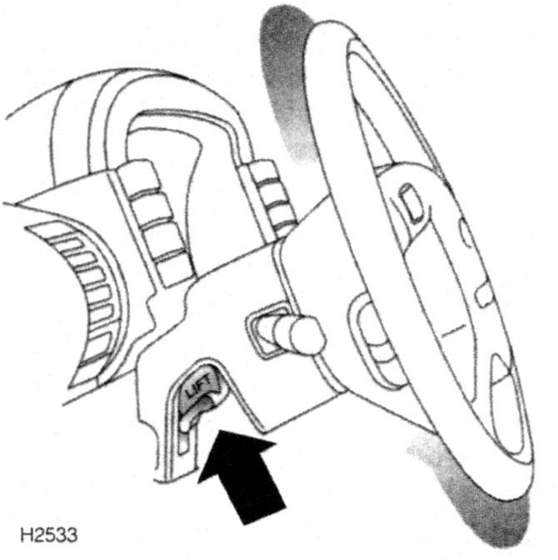

H2533

The angle of the steering column can be adjusted to suit your driving position:

1. With the vehicle stationary, push the locking lever up and hold in this position.
2. Move the steering wheel (up or down) into the desired position, making sure the instrument panel is clearly visible.
3. When adjustment is complete, release the locking lever to lock the steering column in position.

WARNING

DO NOT adjust the steering column while the vehicle is in motion. This is extremely dangerous!

EXTERIOR MIRRORS

NOTE: *Objects viewed in exterior mirrors may appear further away than they actually are.*

Manually adjustable mirrors

Manually adjustable mirrors are fitted to some vehicles - move the mirror glass to the required position.

Electrically adjustable mirrors

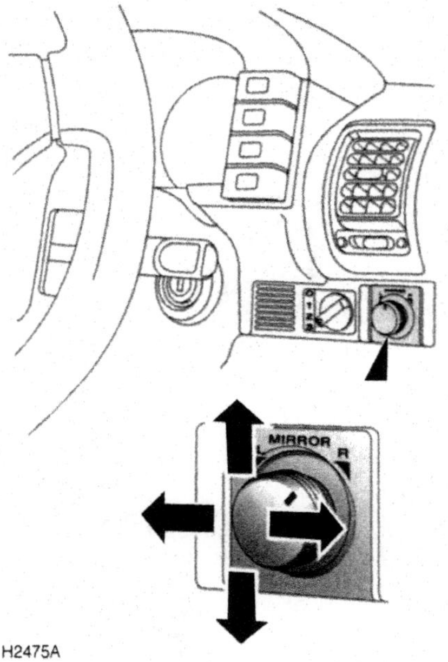

H2475A

- Turn the control to the '**L**' or '**R**' position to select either the left or right hand mirror.
- With the starter switch turned to position 'II', push the control in the appropriate direction to tilt the mirror glass up/down/left or right.
- When adjustment is complete, return the control to the OFF position (midway between '**L**' and '**R**').

NOTE: *In some markets the door mirrors have integral heating elements which disperse ice or mist from the glass. These will operate in conjunction with the heated rear window.*

Door Mirrors

Folding the mirror body

The door mirrors are designed to fold forwards or rearwards on impact. They can also be folded back towards the side windows into a 'park' position to enable the vehicle to negotiate narrower openings.

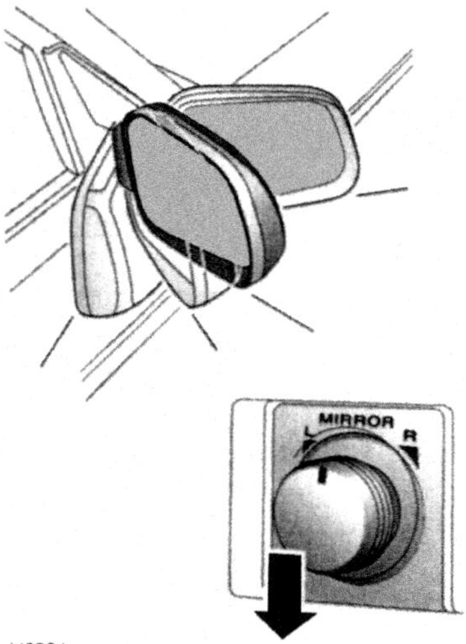

H2981

Manual operation: On some vehicles this operation can be carried out manually, by physically pushing the mirror bodies back towards the side windows, and then pulling them back into the normal (extended) positions.

Electric operation: On some vehicles mirror folding can be carried out electrically as follows:

1. Ensure the mirror control is turned to the centre position.
2. With the starter switch turned to position 'II', push the control down once to fold the mirrors back towards the side windows.
3. Before driving, push the control down a second time to return the mirrors to their normal (extended) position.

If the mirrors are accidentally knocked out of position (i.e. with one mirror extended and the other in the 'parked' position), an additional operation of the switch will re-synchronise them.

INSTRUMENT PANEL

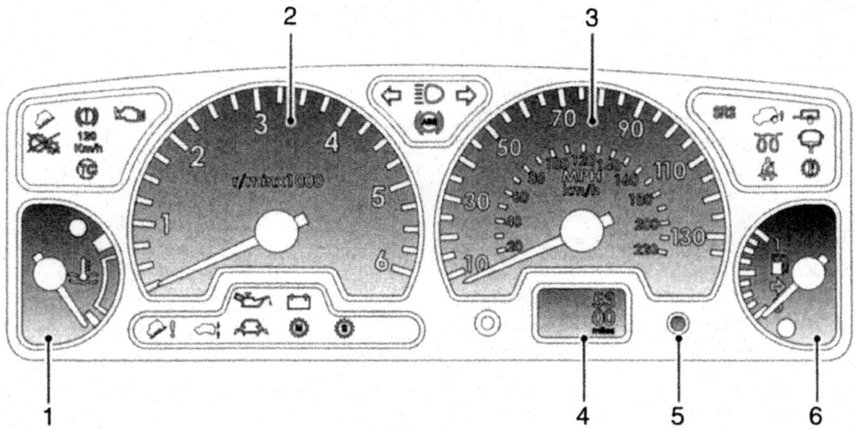

H2581b

1. Temperature gauge

Once the engine coolant has reached its normal operating temperature, the pointer will rise to a position within the WHITE segment of the gauge (the precise position will vary according to climatic conditions).

If the pointer moves towards the RED segment, this indicates that the engine coolant is becoming too hot. Should the pointer move INTO the RED segment and the RED warning light within the gauge illuminates, severe engine damage could occur (under these circumstances, the air conditioning may switch off and engine performance may reduce in order to minimise engine load).

Stop the vehicle as soon as safety permits and allow the engine to idle for five minutes in order to cool down - DO NOT SWITCH OFF. Seek qualified assistance before continuing.

2. Tachometer

Indicates engine speed in revolutions per minute (x 1000). In normal driving conditions the engine is most fuel efficient between 2000 and 3000 rev/min.

Vehicles equipped with a catalytic converter are fitted with a system which automatically restricts the number of engine revolutions per minute once the engine's maximum 'governed' speed has been reached.

3. Speedometer

Indicates road speed in miles per hour and/or kilometres per hour.

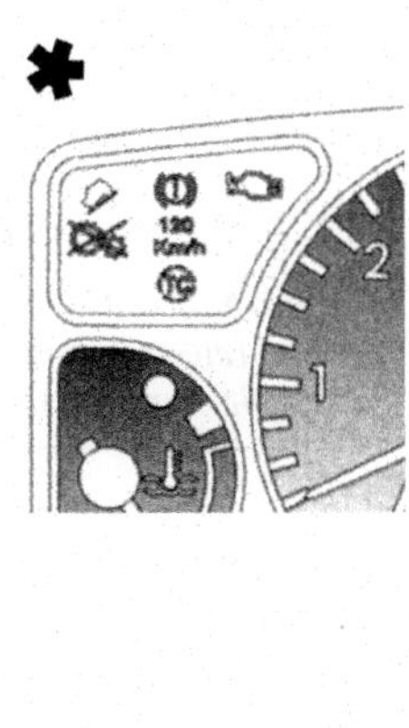

4. Total distance (odometer) and trip recorder
With the starter switch turned to position 'II', the display indicates the total distance travelled by the vehicle, and also shows the most recent individual journey distance.In some markets, the display can be set to show either miles or kilometres. To convert from one to another, press and hold the trip recorder reset button for more than two seconds.

NOTE: *On automatic gearbox vehicles the display also indicates which selector position is selected.*

5. Trip recorder reset button
Press briefly to return the trip recorder display to zero.

6. Fuel gauge
The pointer drops to zero when the starter switch is turned off, but quickly rises to show the level of fuel in the tank when the switch is turned to position 'II'. After refuelling, the gauge rapidly rises to reflect the increase of fuel in the tank.

When the fuel remaining in the tank is a minimum of 3 gallons (14 litres) on petrol vehicles, or 2 gallons (9 litres) on diesel vehicles, the AMBER low fuel warning light in the fuel gauge illuminates. If the light illuminates, refuel at the first opportunity.

The small arrow visible below the fuel pump symbol on the gauge indicates the side of the vehicle on which the fuel filler is located - a useful reminder to help you position the vehicle on the correct side of the forecourt pumps before refuelling.

WARNING

NEVER allow petrol engined models to run out of fuel (the resultant misfire may destroy the catalytic converter).

INSTRUMENT PANEL

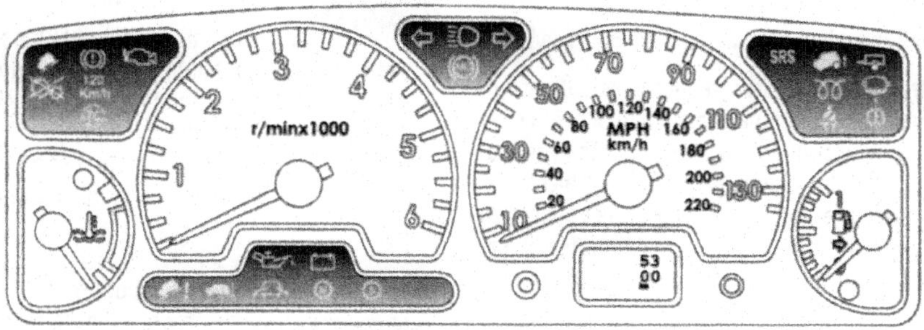

H2483b

The location and specification of the warning lights may vary according to model and market requirements.

Check engine - AMBER*

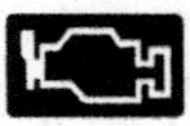

The light illuminates as a bulb and system check when the starter switch is turned on, and extinguishes as soon as the engine is started. Illumination at any other time indicates an engine fault - if the light illuminates while driving, avoid high speeds and seek qualified assistance urgently.

Airbag SRS - RED

The light illuminates when the starter switch is turned to position 'II' and extinguishes after about 4 seconds. If the light illuminates at any other time, the system is faulty - seek qualified assistance urgently.

Handbrake, brake fluid - RED

The light illuminates for about 3 seconds as a bulb check when the starter switch is turned on. It also illuminates when the handbrake is applied with the starter switch in position 'II'.

The light should extinguish when the handbrake is fully released or shortly after the electrical circuits are switched on. If the light illuminates whilst driving, a fault with the braking system is indicated. Stop the vehicle as soon as safety permits and seek qualified assistance before continuing.

Low oil pressure - RED

The light illuminates as a bulb check when the starter switch is turned to position 'II' and extinguishes when the engine is started. If the light remains on, flashes on and off, or illuminates whilst driving, stop the vehicle as soon as safety permits and SWITCH OFF THE ENGINE IMMEDIATELY. Seek qualified assistance before driving. Always check the oil level when this light illuminates.

Transmission oil temperature - RED*

Illuminates as a bulb check when the starter switch is turned to position 'II' and extinguishes after 3 seconds approx. If the light illuminates while driving, the gearbox oil temperature is too high (most likely to occur in very hot weather during continuous high speed driving, or whilst towing heavy loads on steep inclines or if the handbrake has been applied while driving).

If the light illuminates, reduce speed. If the light remains on, stop the vehicle and allow the gearbox to cool. Do not drive until the light has extinguished. (Depending on the ambient temperature and the carrying loads imposed on the vehicle, it may take several minutes before the light extinguishes and it is safe to drive).

Anti-lock braking system - AMBER

The light illuminates as a bulb and system check when the starter switch is turned to position 'II'. If the light illuminates whilst driving or remains illuminated after the starter switch is turned on, a fault has occurred. This means that full ABS control may not be available and you should seek qualified assistance urgently.

NOTE: *Faults which cause the ABS light to illuminate after the initial system checks, or whilst driving, will be accompanied by a warning chime sounding 3 times.*

Headlight main beam - BLUE

Illuminates when the headlights are switched to main beam.

Direction indicators - GREEN

The left or right warning light flashes in time with the corresponding left or right direction indicator lights whenever they are operated. If the warning light fails to flash, or flashes very rapidly, this may indicate a bulb failure in one of the direction indicator lights.

If the hazard switch is pressed, both warning lights will flash in conjunction with the direction indicator lights.

Trailer direction indicators - GREEN

The light illuminates briefly as a bulb check when the starter switch is turned to position 'II'. If a trailer is attached, the light illuminates in conjunction with the vehicle direction indicator lights to show that all trailer indicator lights are functioning correctly. In the event of a bulb failure on the trailer, the warning light remains off.

Glow plug - AMBER (diesel only)

Illuminates when the starter switch is turned to position 'II'. Wait for the light to extinguish before starting the engine.

Battery charging - RED

The light illuminates as a bulb check when the starter switch is turned to position 'II' and extinguishes once the engine is running. If it remains on, or illuminates whilst driving, a fault is indicated. Seek qualified assistance urgently.

Warning Lights

Seat belt - RED*

The light illuminates when the starter switch is turned to position 'II' and extinguishes after approximately 6 seconds, even if the driver's seat belt remains unfastened. In some markets illumination of the light will be accompanied by a warning chime (see *'AUDIBLE WARNINGS', page 52*)

Hill descent control (HDC) 'information' - GREEN

Illuminates briefly as a bulb and system check when the starter switch is turned to position 'II' and also when HDC is selected.

If HDC is selected when Low Range gears are engaged the light will illuminate continuously indicating that HDC is active.

When HDC is selected and non-operating gears are engaged (i.e. High range), the light will flash to inform the driver that HDC is selected, but will not operate.

If the light starts to flash while HDC is active, normal functionality may seize and HDC 'fade out' may be induced (see *'HILL DESCENT CONTROL', page 121*).

Hill descent control (HDC) 'failure' - AMBER

Illuminates briefly as a bulb and system check when the starter switch is turned to position 'II'.

If the light illuminates at any other time, either a fault has occurred which affects the functionality of the system, or over-use of the system has been detected, in which case HDC may 'fade out' (see *'HILL DESCENT CONTROL', page 121*).

***NOTE:** Faults which cause the HDC 'failure' light to illuminate after the initial system checks, or whilst driving, will be accompanied by a warning chime sounding 3 times.*

Traction Control - AMBER

Illuminates as a bulb check when the starter switch is turned to position 'II' and extinguishes after approximately 3 seconds. The light illuminates for a minimum of 2 seconds, whenever traction control is operating.

If the light illuminates continuously, and remains illuminated when the vehicle is stationary, a fault with the system is indicated; seek qualified assistance.

***NOTE:** Faults which cause the light to illuminate after the initial system checks, or whilst driving, will be accompanied by a warning chime sounding 3 times.*

Active cornering enhancement (ACE) - RED/AMBER*

The light illuminates RED when the starter switch is turned to position 'II'. After two seconds, the RED illumination changes to AMBER, and after a further two seconds, the light extinguishes.

If illumination occurs while driving, a fault with the system is indicated, as follows:

- ***If the light shows RED*** *(a flashing red light which changes to constant illumination after two minutes, and is accompanied by a warning chime):* This indicates a system fault that may result in serious damage to vehicle components and reduced ACE performance. Stop the vehicle as soon as safety permits and switch off the engine. DO NOT CONTINUE DRIVING! Seek qualified assistance immediately.
- ***If the light shows AMBER*** *(constant illumination):* This indicates a system fault that will result in reduced ACE performance but will not leave the vehicle in a dangerous condition. You may continue driving, but reduce speed, take additional care, and consult a Land Rover dealer at the earliest opportunity.

Fuel filter - AMBER (diesel only)

Illuminates as a bulb check when the starter switch is turned to position 'II' and extinguishes after 3 seconds approximately. If the light illuminates while driving, this indicates the presence of excessive amounts of water in the fuel. You may continue driving but should seek qualified assistance at the earliest convenient time.

Off Road - AMBER*

Illuminates briefly as a bulb and system check when the starter switch is turned to position 'II' and then extinguishes.

If the off-road switch is pressed:
The light flashes continually while the rear of the vehicle is either; rising to off-road height, or returning to standard ride height. The light illuminates constantly while the suspension remains at off-road height.

In addition, the light will flash if extended mode is induced.

Manual mode - GREEN (Auto only)

Illuminates for 3 seconds as a bulb check when the starter switch is turned to position 'II'. Illuminates constantly while Manual mode is selected.

NOTE: *If both the Manual and Sport mode lights (shown below) flash together, this indicates an electrical fault with the automatic gearbox. If the lights continue flashing after the vehicle has been brought to a halt and the starter switch has been turned off and then on again, you should seek qualified assistance urgently.*

Sport mode - GREEN (Auto only)

Illuminates for 3 seconds as a bulb check when the starter switch is turned to position 'II'. Illuminates constantly while Sport mode is selected.

Self-levelling suspension - AMBER*

Illuminates briefly as a bulb and system check when the starter switch is turned to position 'II' and then extinguishes.

If the remote handset is operated:
The light flashes continually while the rear of the vehicle is being lowered, or raised.

If the light illuminates constantly:
A fault with the suspension is indicated. Seek qualified assistance as soon as possible.

While it is possible to continue driving the vehicle in this condition, there is a considerable risk of causing further damage to the suspension. Preferably, the vehicle should be brought to a halt as soon as conditions allow. Further travel should be limited to reaching the nearest Land Rover dealer, or driving to a place of safety while awaiting recovery. In any event, speed must be restricted to a rate that will guarantee a smooth, and totally bump-free, ride at all times, ideally traversing only smooth, metalled roads.

*

Hi/Lo range- AMBER

Illuminates briefly as a bulb and system check when the starter switch is turned to position 'II' and then extinguishes.

Illuminates continuously while the transfer gearbox lever is in the neutral position.

Differential lock warning light - AMBER*

Illuminates when the differential lock is selected and remains illuminated while the differential lock is engaged.

It will only extinguish when the differential lock actually disengages.

There will be a slight delay between differential lock disengagement and the warning light being extinguished, and is quite normal.

NOTE: *If the warning light is obviously reluctant to extinguish after the differential lock has disengaged, some transmission 'wind-up' may be present.*

Reversing the vehicle for a short distance and then moving forward will usually 'unwind' the transmission and the warning light will extinguish, The vehicle can then be driven as normal.

However, if after two or three attempts to 'unwind' the transmission, the light remains on, consult your dealer AS SOON AS POSSIBLE.

AUDIBLE WARNINGS

The market specification will determine which of the following audible warnings are appropriate to your vehicle.

Lights on reminder

If the lights are left on after the starter switch is turned off, a warning chime will sound when the driver's door is opened. The chime will cease as soon as the lights are switched off or when the driver's door is closed.

Transfer box reminder

A warning will chime continuously while the transfer gearbox is in neutral.

Self-levelling suspension warning

- A single warning will chime whenever the off-road switch is operated to raise the vehicle to off-road height, or to return it to standard ride height.
- A warning will chime continuously while the remote handset is used to lower the vehicle from standard ride height, and also while returning the vehicle to standard ride height.
- A warning chime will sound 3 times if changes to or from off-road height are requested but not permitted.

ABS warning

If a fault with the anti-lock braking system is detected, a warning will chime three times. You may continue driving, but should understand that full ABS control may not be available. Consult your dealer at the earliest opportunity.

ACE warning

A single warning will chime if a fault with the active cornering enhancement system is detected. The chime will coincide with the ACE warning light flashing RED.

HDC warnings

- A warning will chime continuously in conjunction with the HDC warning light flashing green, whenever HDC has been selected but the system's operating criteria have not been met.
- A warning will chime continuously and the HDC failure warning light will illuminate (amber), whenever a fault is detected with the HDC system.
- A single warning will chime when HDC is deselected.

Starter key reminder

If the key is left in the starter switch while the driver's door is open, a warning will chime continuously. The chime stops as soon as the door is closed or the key is removed from the starter switch.

Seat belt reminder

In some markets, if the driver's seat belt has not been fastened when the starter switch is turned on, a warning chime will sound (one second frequency). The chime operates in conjunction with the seat belt warning light and sounds for 6 seconds, or until the seat belt is fastened (whichever occurs first).

In Gulf States markets, either; the chime will continue sounding indefinitely until the seat belt is fastened, or; the chime will sound for 6 seconds whenever the driver's door is opened and closed with the starter switch turned on.

DIRECTION INDICATORS

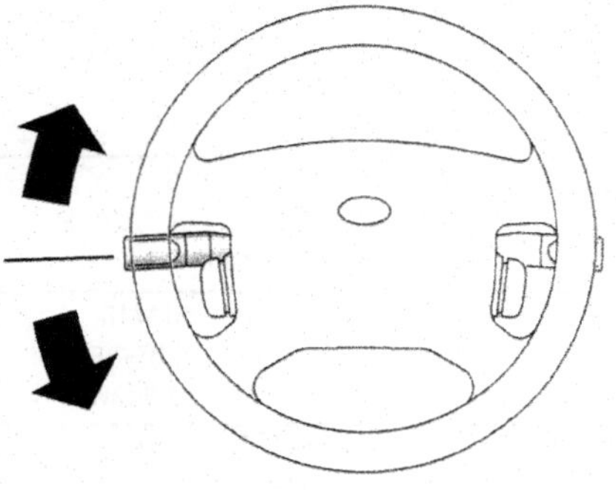

H2582

Move the lever DOWN to indicate a LEFT turn, and UP to indicate a RIGHT turn (the appropriate GREEN warning light on the instrument panel will flash in time with the direction indicators).

Hold the lever part-way up or down against spring pressure to indicate a lane change.

LIGHTS

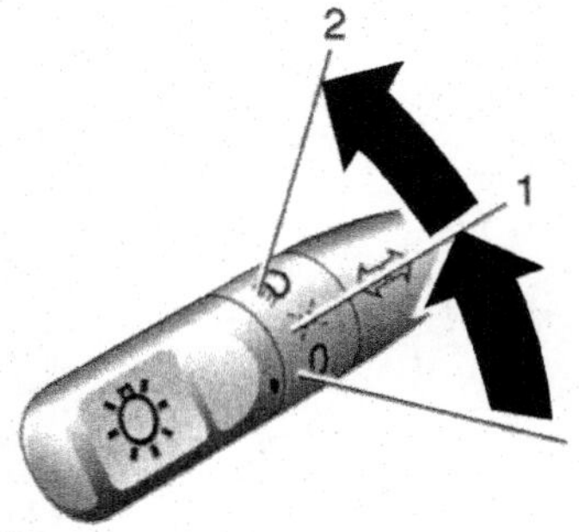

H2448

Side, tail and instrument panel lights
Turn lighting switch to position 1.

Headlights
Turn lighting switch to position 2.

Headlight main and dipped beams

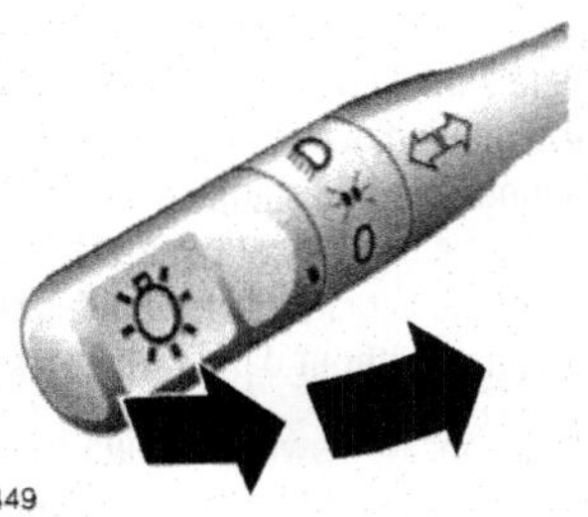

H2449

Pull the lever fully towards the steering wheel to change headlight beams (BLUE warning light glows when the headlights are on main beam).

To flash the headlights, pull the lever part way towards the steering wheel and release.

Headlight levelling*

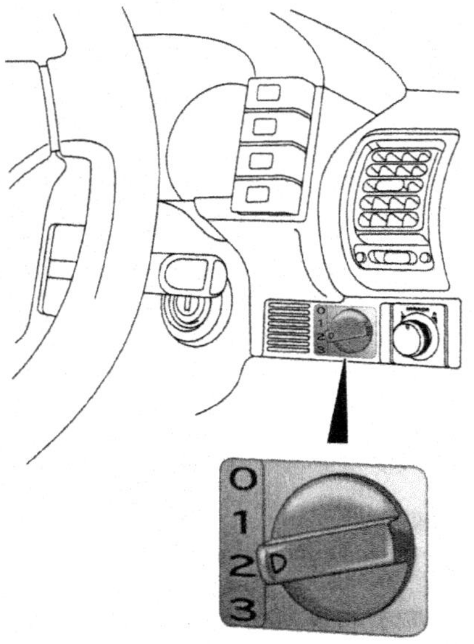

H2476

The angle of the headlight beams is affected by the distribution of weight inside the vehicle. The headlights should be adjusted so that the point at which the beams meet the road surface ahead of the vehicle provides adequate illumination without dazzling other road users.

The four-position switch should be used to adjust the headlight beams in relation to the vehicle loadings identified opposite.

Note that the loading criteria differs for vehicles with conventional coil spring suspension, compared with those fitted with air suspension (if in doubt, air suspension vehicles can be identified by the fascia-mounted off-road switch).

Models with Coil suspension

Position	Loading Condition
0	Driver, or driver and front passenger only (loadspace empty).
1	All seats occupied (loadspace and occasional rear seats empty)
2	All seats occupied with loadspace loaded to max. permissible rear axle weight.
3	Driver only with loadspace loaded to max. permissible rear axle weight.

Models with Air suspension

Position	Loading Condition
0	Driver, or driver and front passenger only (loadspace empty).
1	All seats occupied (loadspace and occasional rear seats empty)
2	All seats occupied with loadspace loaded to max. permissible rear axle weight.
2	Driver only with loadspace loaded to max. permissible rear axle weight.

FOG LIGHTS

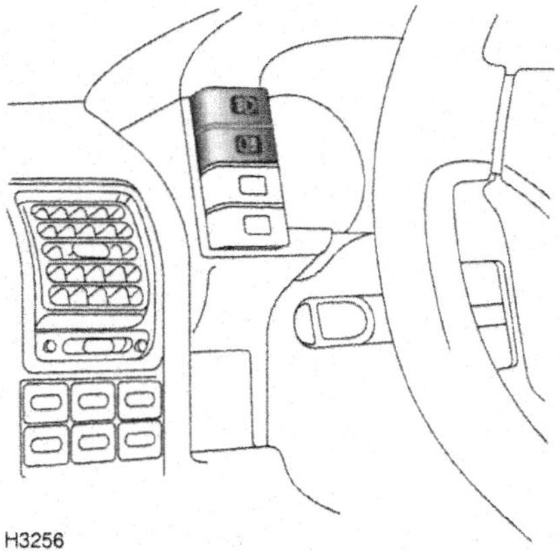

H3256

Front fog lights*

Press to operate, press a second time to switch off (the indicator light in the switch illuminates when the fog lights are switched on).

The fog lights can be operated ONLY when the starter switch is at position 'II' and the side or headlights are also switched on. The fog lights extinguish automatically when the side lights or the starter switch is turned off.

Rear fog guard lights

Press to operate, press a second time to switch off (the indicator light in the switch illuminates when the fog guard lights are switched on). The rear fog guard lights illuminate ONLY when the headlights (or front fog lights) are also switched on, and the starter switch is turned to position 'II'. Switching off the headlights, or front fog lights, or turning the starter switch to position '0' will automatically extinguish the rear fog guard lights too (the lights will not illuminate again unless switched on).

ALWAYS remember to switch the fog guard lights off as soon as visibility permits; in clear conditions fog guard lights can dazzle other road users!

*

Models with Coil suspension (5 & 7 seater)

Position	Loading Condition
0	Driver, or driver and front passenger only (loadspace empty).
N/A (5 Seat) 1 (7 Seat)	Driver, front passenger and rear occasional seats (loadspace empty).
1 (5 Seat) 2 (7 Seat)	All seats occupied (loadspace empty).
2	All seats occupied with loadspace loaded to max. permissible rear axle weight.
3	Driver only with loadspace loaded to max. permissible rear axle weight.

Models with Air suspension (5 & 7 seater)

Position	Loading Condition
0	Driver, or driver and front passenger only (loadspace empty).
0	Driver, front passenger and rear occasional seats (loadspace empty).
0	All seats occupied (loadspace empty).
0	All seats occupied with loadspace loaded to max. permissible rear axle weight.
2	Driver only with loadspace loaded to max. permissible rear axle weight.

HAZARD WARNING LIGHTS

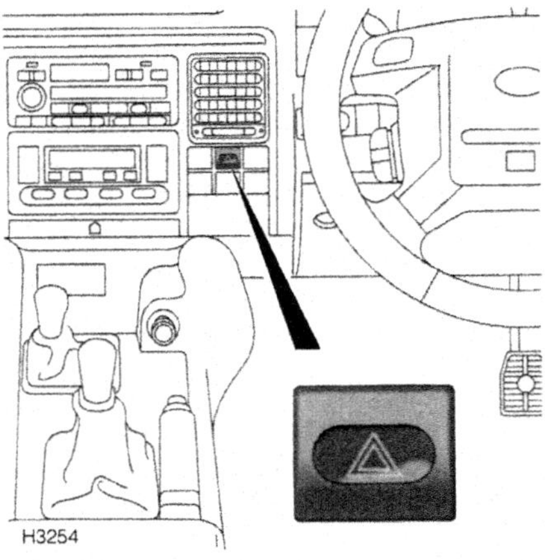

H3254

Press to operate; all the direction indicator lights (including those fitted to a trailer) will flash together. Use ONLY in an emergency to warn other road users when your stationary vehicle is causing an obstruction, or is in a hazardous situation. Remember to switch off before moving away.

Wipers & Washers

OPERATING

The wipers and washers will only operate when the starter switch is turned to position 'I' or 'II'.

IMPORTANT INFORMATION
• DO NOT operate the wipers on a dry screen. • In freezing or very hot conditions, ensure that the blades are not frozen or stuck to the glass. • In winter, remove any snow or ice from around the arms and blades, including the wiped area of the windscreen and the heater air intakes.

NOTE: *If the wiper blades have stuck to the glass, a thermal cut-out may temporarily prevent the wiper motor from operating. If this is the case, switch the wipers off, free them from the obstruction and then switch on again.*

WINDSCREEN WIPERS

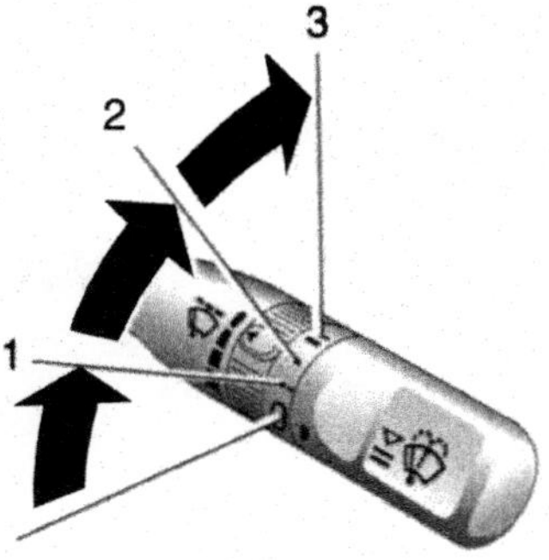

Intermittent wipe

Turn switch to position 1.

Normal speed wipe

Turn switch to position 2.

Fast speed wipe

Turn switch to position 3.

NOTE: *If the front screen wipers are operating (in either intermittent or continuous mode), the rear wiper operates automatically whenever reverse gear is selected.*

Single wipe

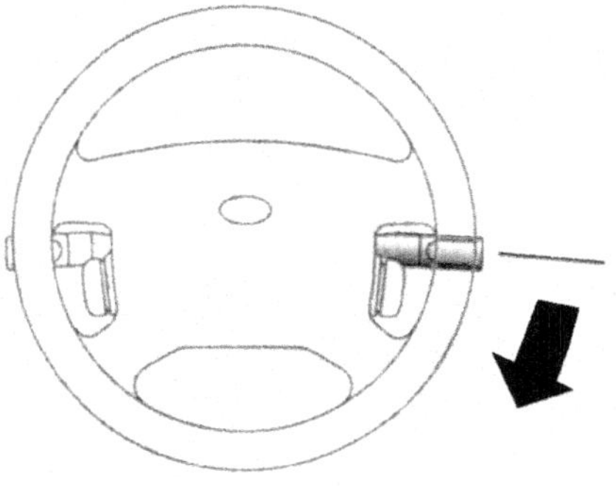

H2583

Pull the lever down and release immediately.

NOTE: *With the lever held down, the wipers will operate at high speed until the lever is released.*

Variable delay (intermittent wipe)

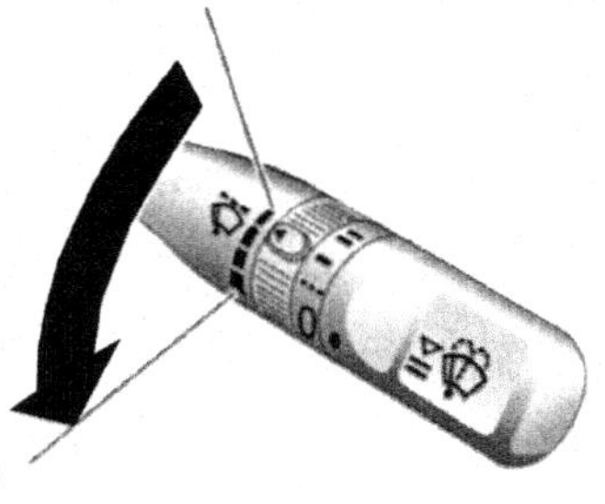

H2451

Rotate the switch to vary the delay between wipes.

WINDSCREEN WASHER

H2452

Pull the lever towards the steering wheel. The windscreen wipers will operate in conjunction with the washers for as long as the lever is held in this position, the wipers continuing for a further 4 seconds after the lever is released.

HEADLIGHT WASHERS*

When the headlights are illuminated, the headlight washers operate automatically in conjunction with every third operation of the windscreen washers.

REAR WINDOW WIPER AND WASHER

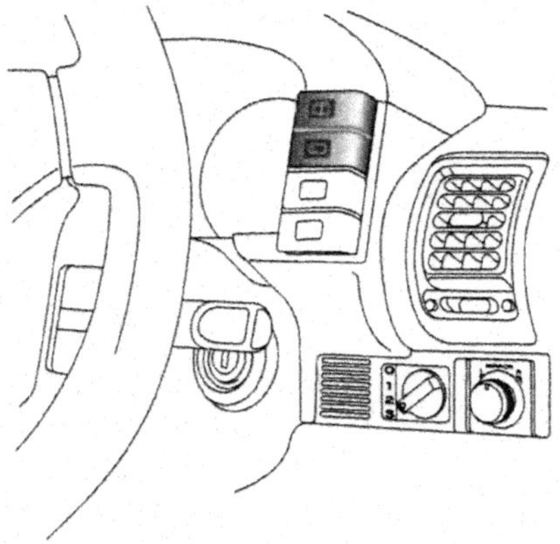

H2584

Rear window wash/wipe

Press and hold switch for the required duration of window washing. The wiper operates automatically during washing and continues for a further 3 wipes after the switch is released.

Rear window wiper

Press to operate: after continuously wiping 3 or 4 times, the wiper operates intermittently until switched off.

NOTE: *When reverse gear is selected, the rear wiper will operate either continuously or intermittently in tandem with the front wipers.*

HORN

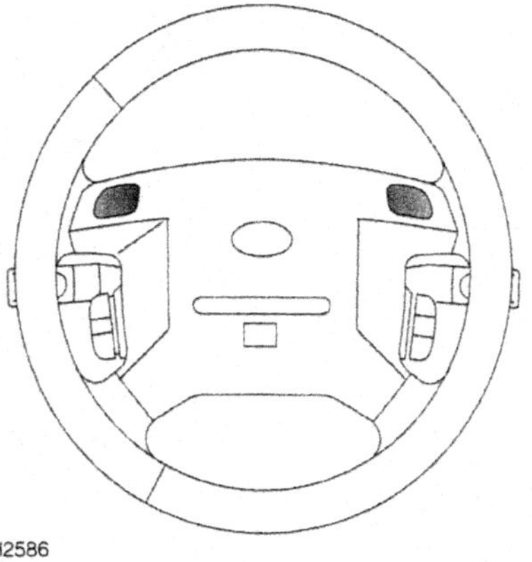

H2586

To operate, press either of the horn switches set into the steering wheel pad.

Electric Windows

ELECTRIC WINDOW CONTROLS

WARNING

Accidental closing of an electrically operated window on fingers, hands or any vulnerable part of the body, can result in serious injury. Always observe the following precautions:

- ***ENSURE the windows are not obstructed when opening or closing.***
- ***DO NOT allow passengers to extend an part of their bodies through the windows while the vehicle is moving - injury from flying debris, branches of trees or other obstructions could occur.***
- ***ALWAYS close the windows when the vehicle is left unattended.***

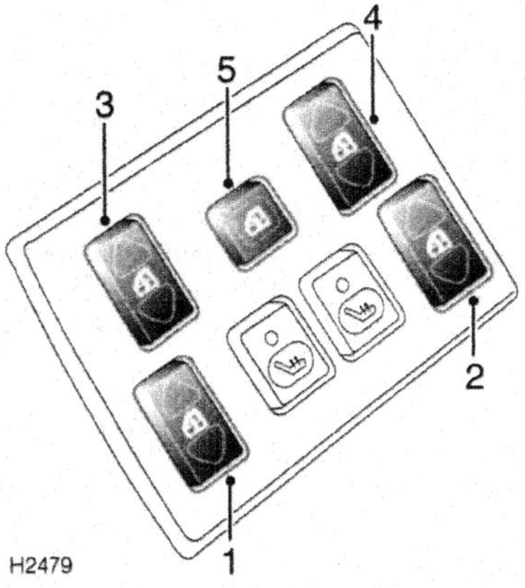

The switches on the centre console operate the windows as follows:

1. Right hand front window.
2. Left hand front window.
3. Right hand rear window.
4. Left hand rear window.
5. Isolating switch for rear door window switches.

NOTE: *Rear windows can also be operated by the individual switches mounted on each rear door, provided the isolation switch has not been activated.*

Operating the windows

The electric windows can be operated when the starter switch is at position 'II' and for up to 45 seconds after the starter switch is turned to position '0' (provided a door is not opened in the meantime).

Press and HOLD the bottom of a switch to lower and the top of a switch to raise. The window will stop moving as soon as the switch is released.

WARNING

ENSURE children are kept clear whilst raising or lowering windows.

NOTE: *Ensure that all adult passengers are familiar with the controls and the potential dangers of electrically operated windows.*

'One touch' down (Front windows only)

By briefly pressing (and then releasing) the bottom of a switch, a front window will open fully at a single touch. Window movement can be stopped at any time by BRIEFLY pressing the top of the switch.

Rear window isolation switch

Press once to isolate the rear window switches; press a second time to restore independent control.

WARNING

ISOLATE the rear window switches when carrying children.

MANUAL SUNROOF*

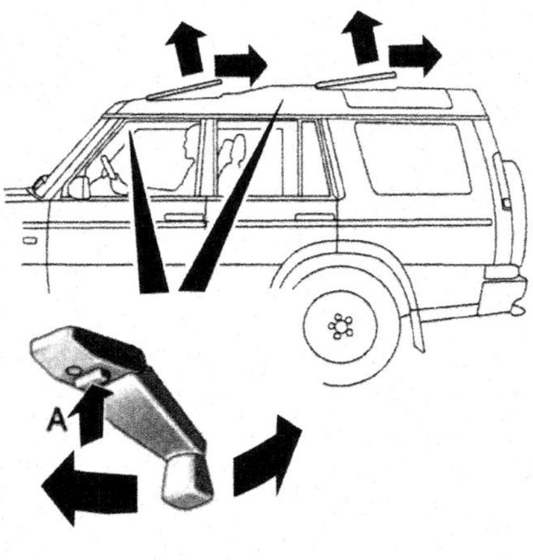

H2453

Pull the operating handle from its recess until it locks in position (see inset). The roof can be opened in two separate phases as follows:

- ***To tilt the roof:*** depress the locking button 'A' and rotate the handle clockwise ONE COMPLETE TURN.
- ***To fully open the roof:*** depress the button again and continue turning clockwise.

To close the roof: rotate the handle anti-clockwise.

WARNING

ENSURE the sunroof is not obstructed when opening or closing.

DO NOT allow passengers to extend any part of their bodies through the sunroof aperture while the vehicle is moving - injury from flying debris, branches of trees or other obstructions could occur.

ALWAYS close the roof when the vehicle is unattended.

Sunroof roller blind

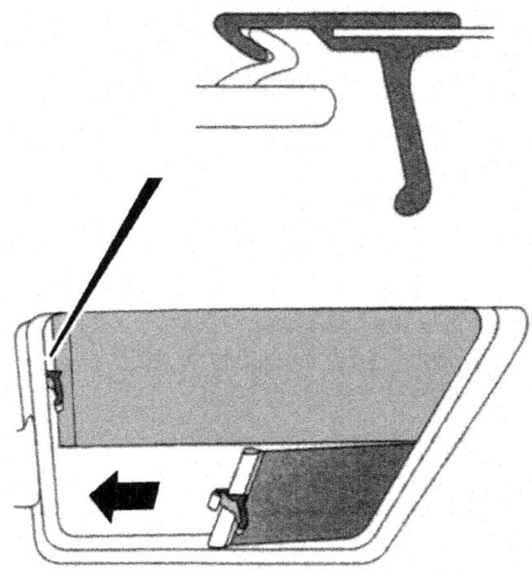

H2477

Pull the sunroof blind across the sunroof aperture and secure the hook on the blind to the front edge of the sunroof cassette.

NOTE: *The sunroof can still be opened and closed with the sunroof blind in position.*

ELECTRIC SUNROOF*

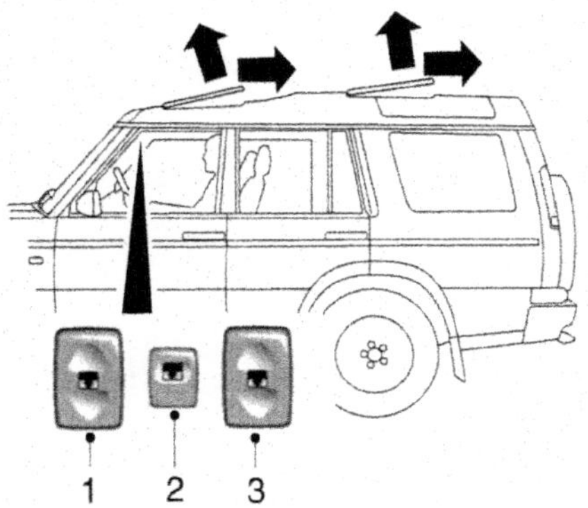

1. Front sunroof operating switch
2. Rear sunroof disable switch. (Always disable the rear sunroof when driving with children in the rear of the vehicle).
3. Rear sunroof operating switch.

   NOTE: *Vehicles fitted with a rear sunroof have an additional operating switch set into the roof lining forward of the rear sunroof.*

The electric sunroof can be operated when the starter switch is at position 'II', and for up to 45 seconds after the starter switch is turned off (provided a door is not opened in the meantime).

The roof opens in two separate phases as follows:

- ***To tilt the roof:*** press the upper part of the switch once BRIEFLY - the rear edge of the roof automatically rises to the tilted position.
- ***To open the roof:*** press the upper part of the switch BRIEFLY a second time - the roof remains tilted and slides towards the rear until it is fully open or until movement is stopped by briefly pressing the lower part of the switch.

To close the roof: press and hold the lower part of the switch until the roof has moved to the required position.

The roof will pause momentarily when it reaches the tilt position.

NOTE: *If the roof is obstructed for more than 7 seconds whilst opening or closing, an automatic cut-out will prevent the sunroof motor from operating. After a period, operation of the motor will be restored.*

WARNING

Accidental closure of a sunroof on fingers, hands or any vulnerable part of the body, can result in serious personal injury. Always observe the following precautions:

ENSURE the sunroof is not obstructed when opening or closing.

ENSURE that all adult passengers are familiar with the controls and the potential dangers of operating an electrically operated sunroof.

DO NOT allow passengers to extend any part of their bodies through the sunroof aperture while the vehicle is moving - injury from flying debris, branches of trees or other obstructions could occur.

ALWAYS close the roof when the vehicle is unattended.

Sunroof roller blind

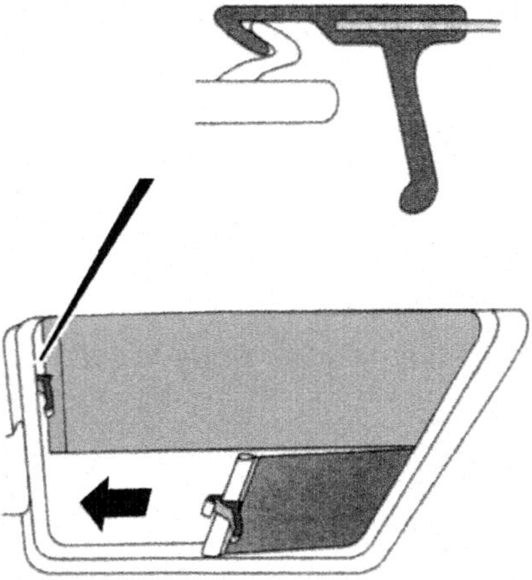

H2477

Pull the sunroof blind across the sunroof aperture and secure the hook on the blind to the front edge of the sunroof cassette.

NOTE: *The sunroof can still be opened and closed with the sunroof blind in position.*

VENTILATION

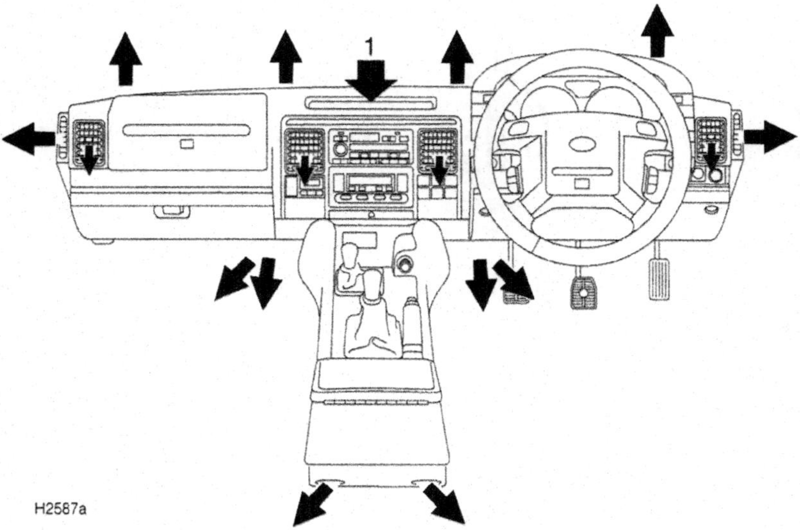

H2587a

The ventilation system provides fresh or heated air to the interior of the vehicle from the air intake grille in front of the windscreen.

NOTE: *Always keep the air intake grille clear of obstructions such as leaves, snow or ice.*

Air outlets are provided to the windscreen, face and feet - the location of those vents is shown in the illustration above. The temperature of the air supplied to the vents is controlled by the heater.

NOTE: *Vent (1) is designed to keep the audio unit cool, there is no air flow from this vent.*

Information concerning the operation of the heating and ventilation system, appear on the following pages.

Face level vents

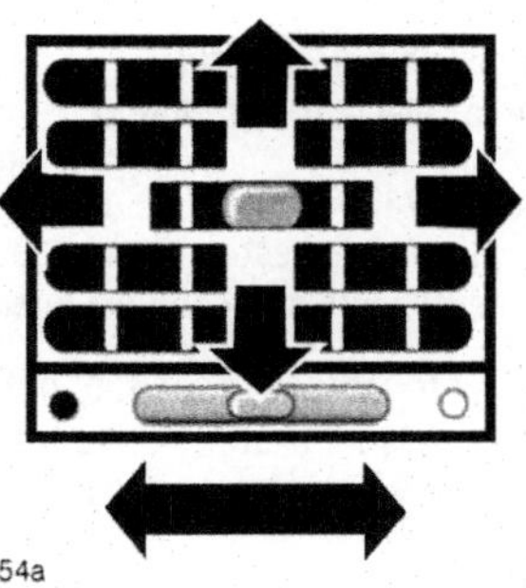

H2454a

Each vent can be opened or closed by rotating the thumbwheel: left to open, right to close. Direct the flow of air by moving the control in the centre of the louvres.

To ensure best ventilation and minimum noise, the vents should be fully open when the air distribution control is set to face level.

HEATER CONTROLS

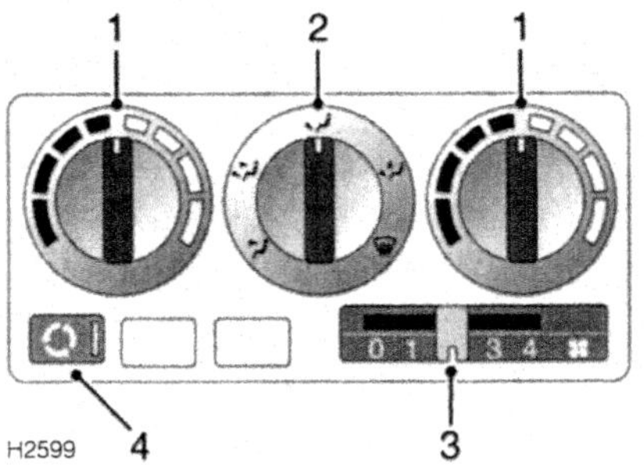

1. Temperature controls
The left hand control varies air temperature from the vents on the left side of the vehicle. The right hand control adjusts air temperature from the vents on the right side.Rotate each control clockwise (towards the RED segments) to increase the air temperature, or anti-clockwise (towards the BLUE) to reduce the temperature.

2. Air distribution control
Rotate to select air distribution:

Air to face vents (to ensure best performance, the face level vents must be fully open)

Air to face vents and foot outlets (to ensure best performance, the face level vents must be fully open)

Air to foot outlets

Air to foot outlets and windscreen (recommended for clearing mild windscreen misting)

All air to windscreen (recommended for clearing heavy windscreen misting)

3. Air blower control
Move the control to the right to progressively increase the fan speed.

With the control at '**0**' the fan is stationary and the volume of air entering the passenger compartment is solely dependent upon the ram effect of the vehicle moving through the air.

4. Air recirculation control
Press to recirculate air inside the vehicle (indicator light illuminates).

The air recirculation mode prevents the heating system from taking in fresh air from outside the vehicle. Instead, the air already inside the vehicle is recirculated, thus preventing the entry of traffic fumes. In cold weather air recirculation also enables warmer air to be used to defrost the windscreen when the engine is still cold.

WARNING

The air recirculation mode can cause the windscreen to mist. If this happens, switch off air recirculation immediately.

NOTE: *The air blower switch and air recirculation control will only operate with the starter switch at position 'II'.*

VENTILATION

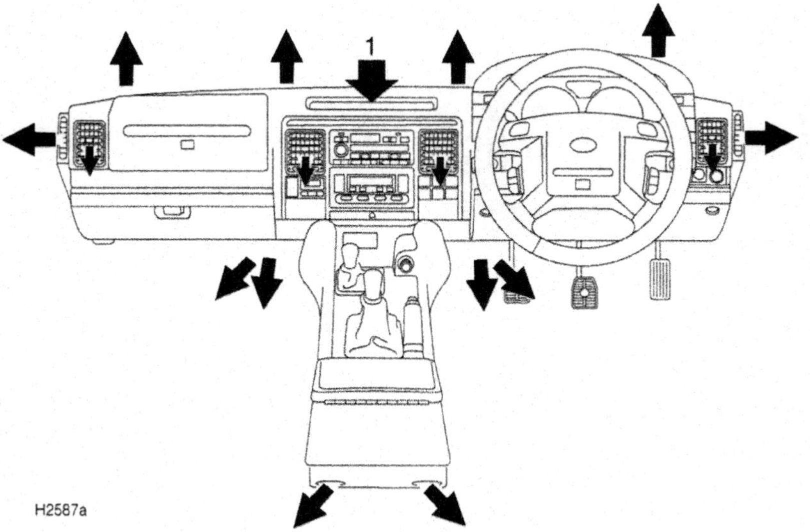

H2587a

The ventilation system provides fresh or heated air to the interior of the vehicle from the air intake grille in front of the windscreen.

NOTE: *Always keep the air intake grille clear of obstructions such as leaves, snow or ice.*

Air outlets are provided to the windscreen, face and feet - the location of those vents is shown in the illustration above. The temperature of the air supplied to the vents is controlled by the heater.

NOTE: *Vent (1) is designed to keep the audio unit cool, there is no air flow from this vent.*

Information concerning the operation of the heating and ventilation system, appear on the following pages.

Face level vents

H2454a

Each vent can be opened or closed by rotating the thumbwheel: left to open, right to close. Direct the flow of air by moving the control in the centre of the louvres.

To ensure best ventilation and minimum noise, the vents should be fully open when the air distribution control is set to face level.

HEATER CONTROLS

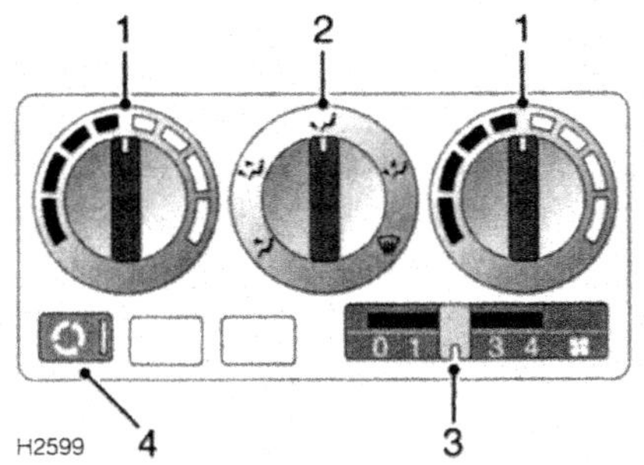

1. Temperature controls
The left hand control varies air temperature from the vents on the left side of the vehicle. The right hand control adjusts air temperature from the vents on the right side.Rotate each control clockwise (towards the RED segments) to increase the air temperature, or anti-clockwise (towards the BLUE) to reduce the temperature.

2. Air distribution control
Rotate to select air distribution:

Air to face vents
(to ensure best performance, the face level vents must be fully open)

Air to face vents and foot outlets
(to ensure best performance, the face level vents must be fully open)

Air to foot outlets

Air to foot outlets and windscreen
(recommended for clearing mild windscreen misting)

All air to windscreen
(recommended for clearing heavy windscreen misting)

3. Air blower control
Move the control to the right to progressively increase the fan speed.

With the control at '**0**' the fan is stationary and the volume of air entering the passenger compartment is solely dependent upon the ram effect of the vehicle moving through the air.

4. Air recirculation control
Press to recirculate air inside the vehicle (indicator light illuminates).

The air recirculation mode prevents the heating system from taking in fresh air from outside the vehicle. Instead, the air already inside the vehicle is recirculated, thus preventing the entry of traffic fumes. In cold weather air recirculation also enables warmer air to be used to defrost the windscreen when the engine is still cold.

WARNING

The air recirculation mode can cause the windscreen to mist. If this happens, switch off air recirculation immediately.

NOTE: *The air blower switch and air recirculation control will only operate with the starter switch at position 'II'.*

USING YOUR HEATER

Fresh air enters the heater unit through the grille in front of the windscreen and stale air is drawn out through vents in the rear of the vehicle. Ducts along the transmission tunnel provide heating for rear seat passengers - these must not be obstructed.

The following examples of basic heater settings are intended as a general guide; the air distribution, temperature and blower controls can then be further adjusted to suit your comfort requirements.

Always remember that full heating is not available until the engine has reached its normal operating temperature.

Maximum heating

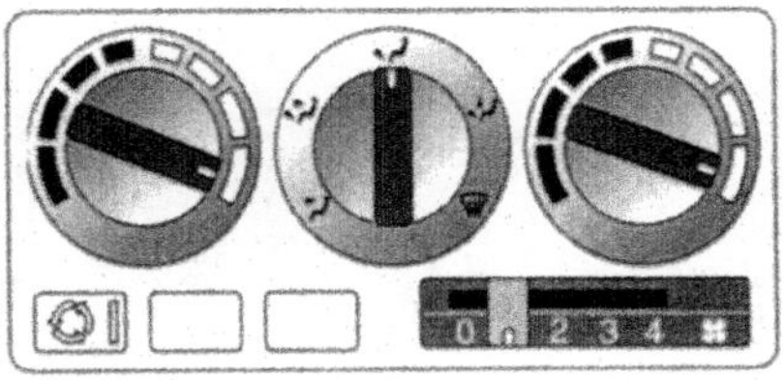

H2601

Set the controls as shown, with the blower at the slowest speed (position 1) until the temperature gauge indicates that the engine is warming up - the blower speed can then be increased.

Demisting

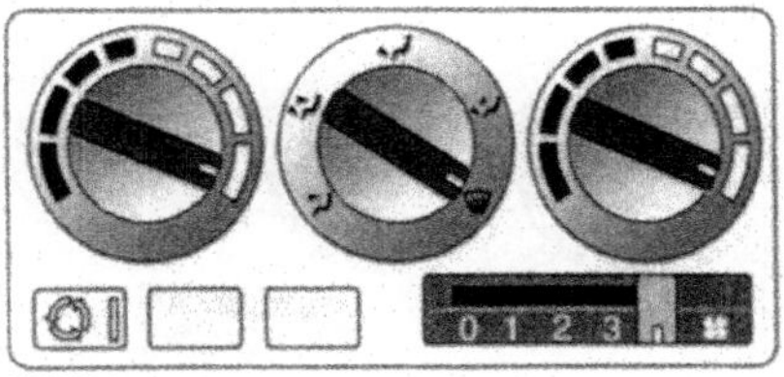

H2603

Set the controls as shown to obtain the maximum flow of heated air from the windscreen and side window vents.

Opening a window may improve ventilation.

Defrosting

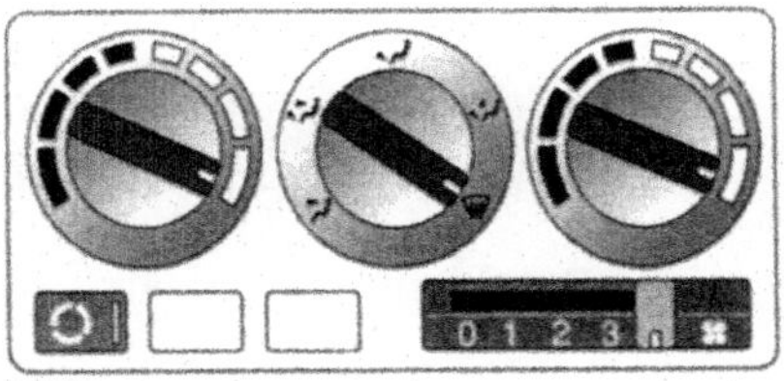

H2604

Set the controls as shown and switch on air recirculation to prevent cold air from being drawn into the vehicle. Turn air recirculation off as soon as the windscreen is clear to prevent any possibility of the windscreen misting.

Maximum ventilation

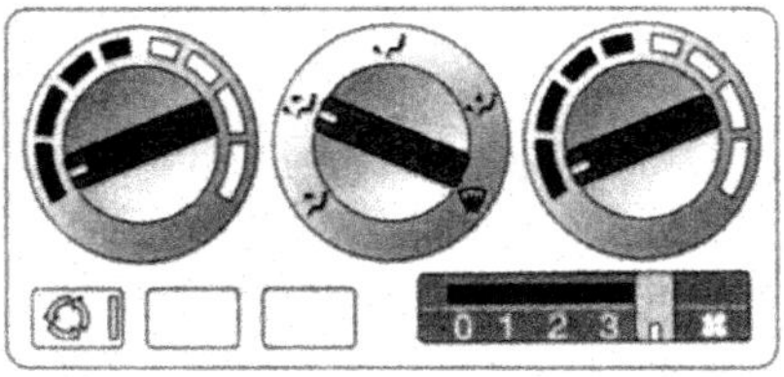

H2602

Set the controls as shown, with the face level vents open.

Adjust the blower speed as required.

VENTILATION

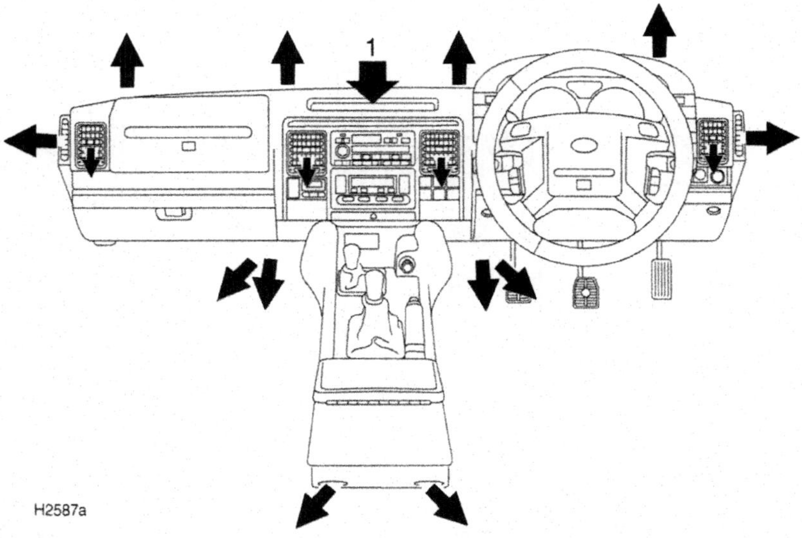

H2587a

The ventilation system provides fresh or heated air to the interior of the vehicle from the air intake grille in front of the windscreen.

NOTE: *Always keep the air intake grille clear of obstructions such as leaves, snow or ice.*

Air outlets are provided to the windscreen, face and feet - the location of those vents is shown in the illustration above. The temperature of the air supplied to the vents is controlled by the heater.

NOTE: *Vent (1) is designed to keep the audio unit cool, there is no air flow from this vent.*

Information concerning the operation of the air conditioning system, appear on the following pages.

Face level vents

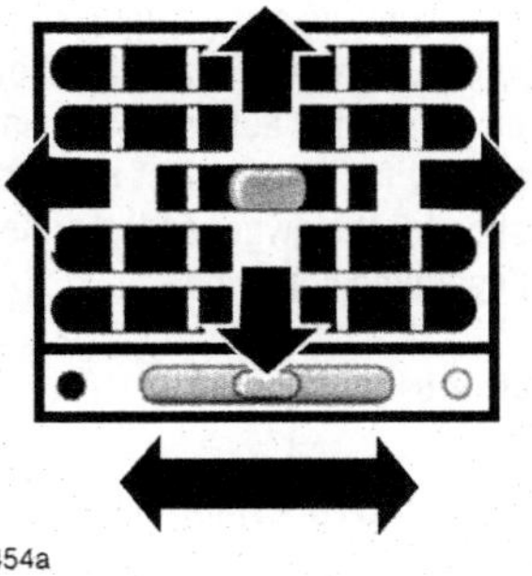

H2454a

Each vent can be opened or closed by rotating the thumbwheel: left to open, right to close. Direct the flow of air by moving the control in the centre of the louvres.

To ensure best ventilation and minimum noise, the vents should be fully open when the air distribution control is set to face level.

AIR CONDITIONING CONTROLS

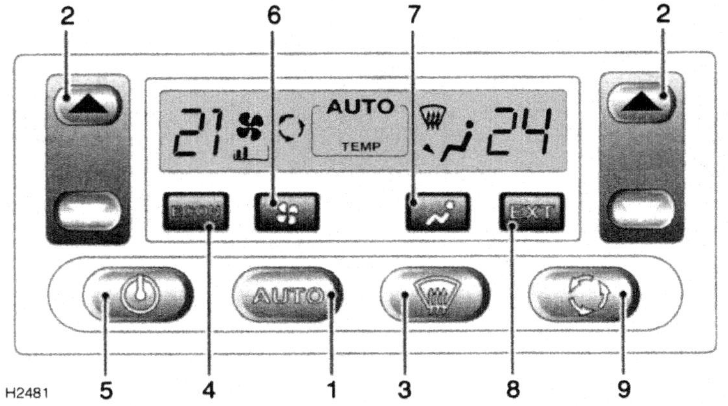

The air conditioning system features automatic temperature and air distribution control, which is programmed to maintain optimum levels of comfort within the vehicle in all but the most severe climatic conditions.

While the controls can be adjusted manually to satisfy individual requirements, allowing the system to function automatically (in Auto mode) is by far the simplest method of operation for the owner and is preferable in most operating conditions.

1. Auto mode

- Press 'AUTO' (1) for fully automatic operation.
- Press the temperature control switches (2) on either side of the display to select the required temperature.
- Let the automatic temperature control system do the rest.

In Auto mode, air distribution and blower speeds are adjusted automatically to achieve and then maintain the desired temperature. (*An enclosed area in the centre of the display will show 'AUTO' together with the air distribution and blower speed settings*).

Both the air distribution and blower controls can be operated independently to override the automatic setting. In this case, the relative symbols will move outside the enclosed area in the centre of the display to indicate that they are no longer being controlled automatically.

NOTE: *If the air distribution and blower controls are operated independently, the system may not be able to achieve or maintain the required temperature settings.*

2. Temperature controls

Operate the rocker switches on either side of the display to set the required temperature for the corresponding side of the passenger compartment (left hand switch for the left side of the vehicle, and right hand switch for the right side).

Temperatures above 28°C (82°F) and below 16°C (61°F) cannot be set. Above or below these maximum and minimum settings 'HI' or 'LO' will appear in the display.

The temperatures shown on the display are relative, target, temperatures only and are not reflective of any specific temperature measured within the vehicle interior.

NOTE: *The system will not achieve temperatures on the passenger side of the vehicle that are more than 5°C (9°F) greater or less than the temperature set for the driver's side.*

3. Defrost mode

If the windscreen is misting or covered in ice, press the 'SCREEN' button; the system will immediately direct its output to achieve maximum screen clearing by:

- setting the blower speed to maximum
- distributing air flow to the screen only.

In addition, the rear and front screen heaters* will be switched on (or their timed operating cycle will recommence if they are already switched on).

NOTE: *The temperature and blower speed controls can be adjusted and air recirculation selected manually if required.*

Press the 'SCREEN' button a second time (or select 'AUTO') to leave the Defrost mode - the system will default automatically to Auto mode.

4. Economy mode

ECON

Press the 'Econ' button to operate (the display shows 'ECON').

In economy mode the air conditioning compressor is switched off and the system functions as a conventional heating and ventilation system. This reduces the load on the engine, thereby reducing fuel consumption.

Select Economy mode whenever air conditioning is not required i.e. in cold weather when the external temperature is lower than the temperature required for the passenger compartment.

The air distribution, blower and recirculation controls can be operated independently.

Pressing the 'Econ' button a second time will switch the air conditioning compressor on and return the system to Auto mode.

NOTE: In Economy mode, it is possible to switch the blower off (no segments showing in the display).

5. On/off button

Press to switch on or off.

When switching on, note that the system automatically recalls the mode and control settings that were last used.

6. Blower button

Press the button to adjust the blower speed. The blower speed increases incrementally with each press of the button, until maximum fan speed is reached (the display shows five segments and the word 'MAX').

Once the maximum fan speed has been reached, another press of the button returns the blower to its slowest speed (one segment shows in the display).

7. Air distribution control

Press the button to adjust. Air distribution changes incrementally with each press of the switch in the following sequence:

Face level vents

Foot and face level vents

Foot level vents

Foot level, windscreen and side window vents

Windscreen and side window vents

A further operation of the button returns to the start of the sequence.

NOTE: *If the button is pressed for more than one second, air distribution will automatically default to foot and face level vents.*

8. External temperature

Press the button to display. The external temperature is displayed for approximately 6 seconds, after which the display reverts to its previous state.

NOTE: *While the air conditioning system is switched off, the external temperature can be displayed briefly by pressing the button.*

9. Air recirculation

The air recirculation feature can be used to prohibit the entry of air from outside the vehicle, alternatively recirculating the air inside the vehicle instead. This is useful to prevent the entry of traffic fumes.

The feature also significantly influences the dehumidifying and cooling performance of the air-conditioning system. Therefore, in Auto mode, air recirculation is controlled automatically to enable the air-conditioning system to achieve its optimum performance.

However, the feature is also manually selectable in Auto, Defrost and Economy modes, as follows:

In Auto mode:

- Press the button briefly *(display shows recirculation symbol):*

  Air recirculation operates until the control is pressed a second time to switch off.

- Press and hold for 2 seconds *(two bleeps will sound, display shows recirculation symbol):*

  Air recirculation operates for a pre-timed period of 4-6 minutes only.

In Defrost and Economy modes:

- Press the control briefly *(display shows recirculation symbol):*

  Air recirculation operates for a pre-timed period of 4-6 minutes only.

- Press and hold for 2 seconds *(two bleeps will sound, display shows recirculation symbol):*

  Air recirculation operates until the control is pressed a second time to switch off.

NOTE: *Prolonged recirculation may cause the windows to mist.*

Temperature conversion (°F - °C)

The temperature displays can be converted to or from Fahrenheit and Centigrade, as follows:

- Press and hold the air recirculation button.
- At the same time, press and hold the on/off button for 3 seconds.
- A 'bleep' will sound to indicate that the conversion has taken place.

Rear air conditioning controls

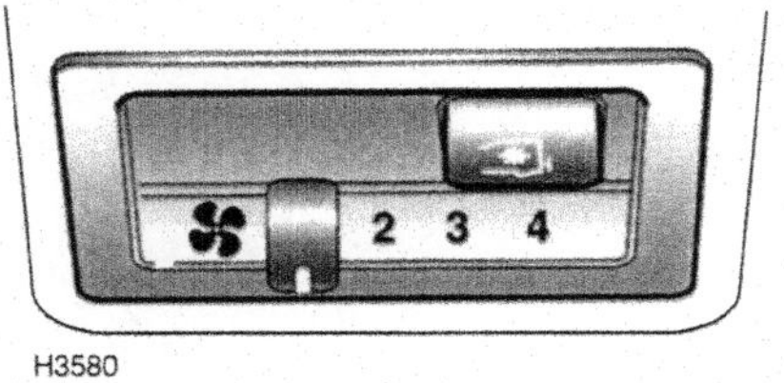

H3580

Some vehicles are equipped with a supplementary air conditioning system, which supplies cooled, dried air to the rear passenger compartment through air vents set into the rear roof lining. The rear air conditioning will only operate when the front air conditioning is switched on. In all other respects, however, it is controlled independently using the controls set into the roof lining. To operate:

1. With the front air conditioning switched on, press the on/off switch in the rear air conditioning control panel (illustrated).
2. Adjust the slider control to increase or reduce the air conditioning fan speed.
3. Always switch off the rear air conditioning after use, otherwise operation will start automatically again when the vehicle is next used.

During cold weather, when the air conditioning is not in use, the rear air conditioning controls can be used to supply recirculated air to the rear passenger compartment.

GENERAL NOTES

- For optimum operating efficiency, ensure all the air vents (including those in the rear of the vehicle) are open.
- For the automatic temperature control system to function efficiently, all windows (and the sunroof) should be closed, and the air intake vents free from ice, snow, leaves or other debris.
- In very humid conditions, slight screen misting may be experienced when the air conditioning system is turned on. This is a natural occurrence on most automotive air conditioning systems. It is not a fault and misting will clear after a few seconds once the air conditioning system is operating.
- The air conditioning compressor will not function unless the engine is running.
- Surplus water produced by the dehumidifying process is expelled from the system via drain tubes beneath the vehicle. This may result in a small pool of water forming on the road when the vehicle is stationary and is not a cause for concern.
- If desired, the system's audible information chimes can be deactivated, as follows:
  1. Press 'Auto' button and hold.
  2. Press 'On/off' button and hold pressed for 3 seconds, then release.
  3. Press 'On/off' button again for a further 3 seconds, and release.
  4. Release 'Auto' button.

Heated Screens

HEATED FRONT SCREEN AND REAR WINDOW

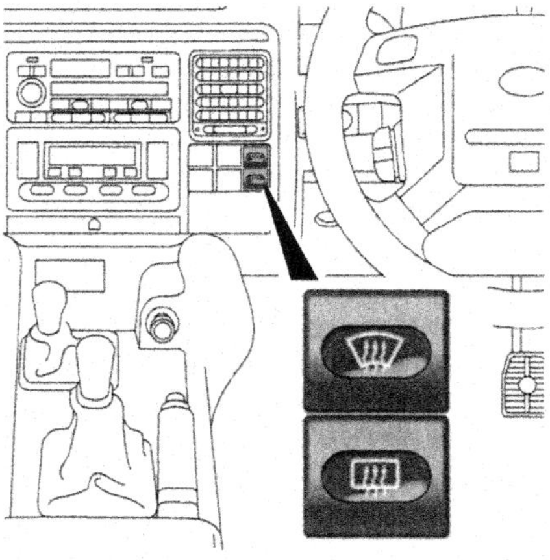

WARNING

DO NOT stick labels over the heating elements, and DO NOT scrape or use abrasive materials to clean the inside of the window.

Heated front screen*

Press to operate (the indicator light in the switch illuminates); press a second time to switch off (the indicator light extinguishes). The heated screen operates only with the engine running. After 5 minutes continuous operation, the heater switches off automatically.

Heated rear window

Press to operate; press a second time to switch off. The indicator light in the switch illuminates while the heating elements are switched on and extinguishes when they are turned off. Note that the heating elements operate only with the engine running.

After 15 minutes continuous operation, the heater switches off automatically.

FRONT INTERIOR & LOADSPACE LIGHTS

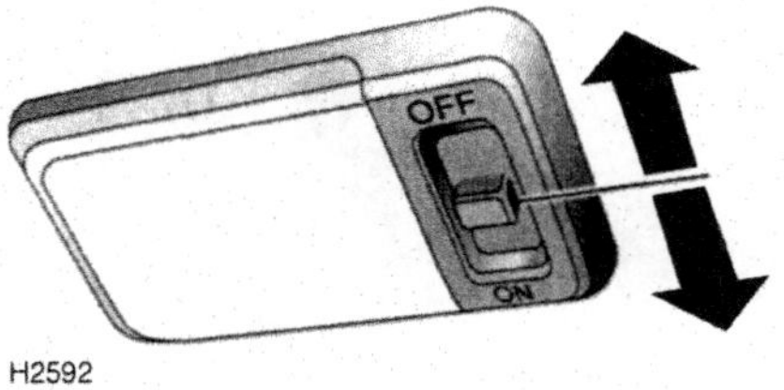

H2592

Switch positions:

- **'OFF'** - Light permanently off.
- **'ON'** - Light illuminates continuously.

With the switch in the centre position, the interior light illuminates automatically whenever the vehicle is unlocked, when the starter switch is turned off (to position '0'), or when a door or taildoor is opened. The light remains illuminated for 15 seconds after the doors and taildoor are closed, or until the starter switch is turned on.

After driving, the interior lights will fade and then extinguish as soon as the vehicle is locked or when the last door is closed.

NOTE: *When the light is switched for automatic operation (switch in centre position), a 'time-out' function extinguishes the lights after 8 minutes approx. if a door is left open, to prevent the battery from discharging.*

REAR INTERIOR LIGHTS

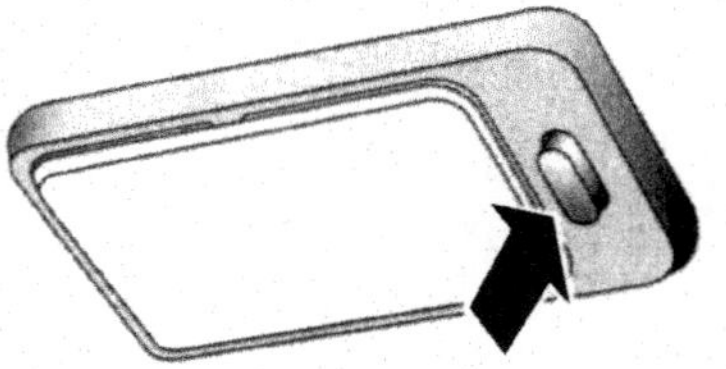

H2593

Press the switch to illuminate (or extinguish) the lights manually.

Lights illuminate automatically when the vehicle is unlocked or whenever a door or taildoor is opened, and extinguish approximately 15 seconds after ALL the doors are closed, or as soon as the starter switch is turned on.

GLOVEBOX LIGHT

Illuminates automatically whenever the glovebox is opened, provided the sidelights are switched on, and extinguishes when the glovebox is closed.

CLOCK

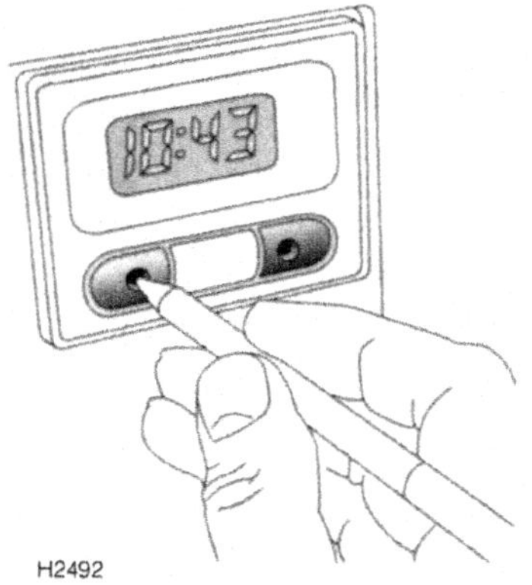

H2492

The digital clock display illuminates constantly and dims automatically for night time viewing, when the side lights are illuminated.

To adjust the time, use a ballpoint pen or similar probe to press the hour (left hand) and minute (right hand) controls, until the correct time is displayed.

NOTE: *The clock will need to be reset if the battery is disconnected.*

Pressing both hour and minute controls simultaneously 'zeroes' the display.

COIN TRAY

H2600

Push the front to open. To remove the tray, open fully, then press down on the release plate (arrowed in illustration) and pull to remove.

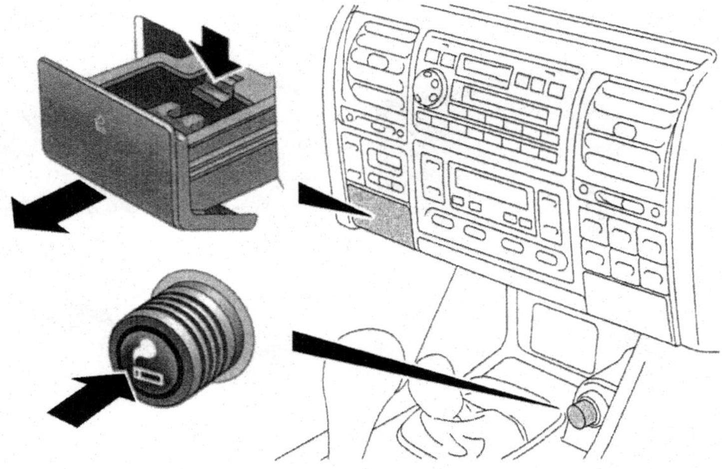
H2503

CIGAR LIGHTER*

With the starter switch turned on, press the lighter in to heat up. When it has reached the correct temperature it will partially eject and can then be withdrawn for use.

- ONLY hold the cigar lighter by the handle.
- DO NOT plug accessories into the cigar lighter socket unless they are approved by Land Rover (see *'AUXILIARY POWER SOCKET', page 79*, for more information).

***NOTE:** On vehicles not fitted with a cigar lighter, the power socket is protected by a removable blank cover.*

ASHTRAYS

WARNING

DO NOT use the ashtrays for disposing of waste paper or other combustible items.

Front

Push the front of the ashtray to open. To remove the ashtray, open fully, then press down on the release plate (arrowed in illustration) and pull to remove.

Rear

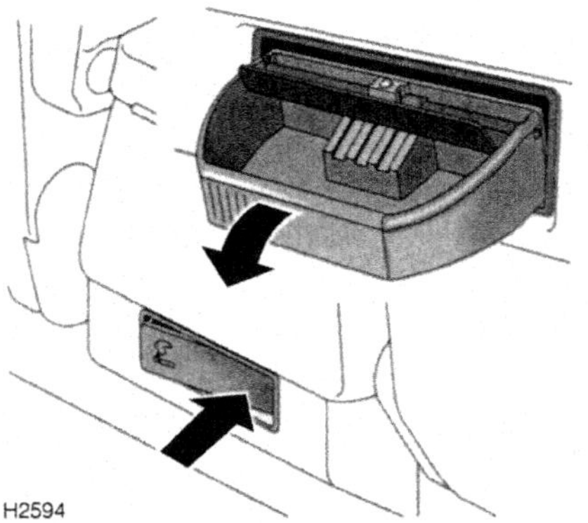

H2594

Push the front of the ashtray on the right hand side to open. To remove, open the ashtray and then carefully lever the tray downwards to disengage the upper pivot.

Refit by locating the upper pivot and then easing the ashtray into a position whereby the lower pivot can also be engaged.

UNDER SEAT STOWAGE BOX

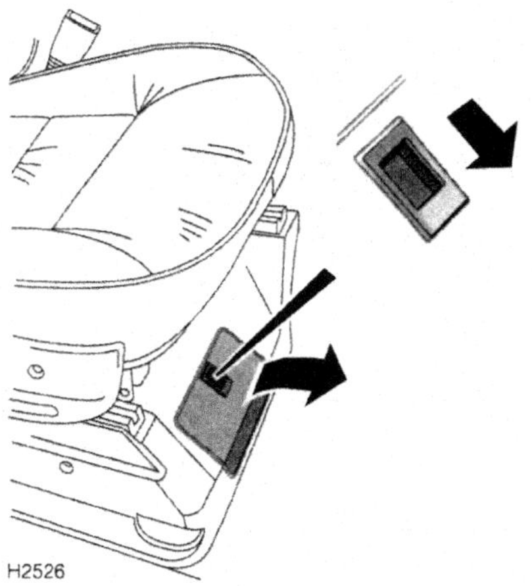

H2526

To gain access, depress the catch (arrowed in illustration) and open the lid.

NOTE: *On some models the stowage box provides the location for a CD autochanger.*

AUXILIARY POWER SOCKET

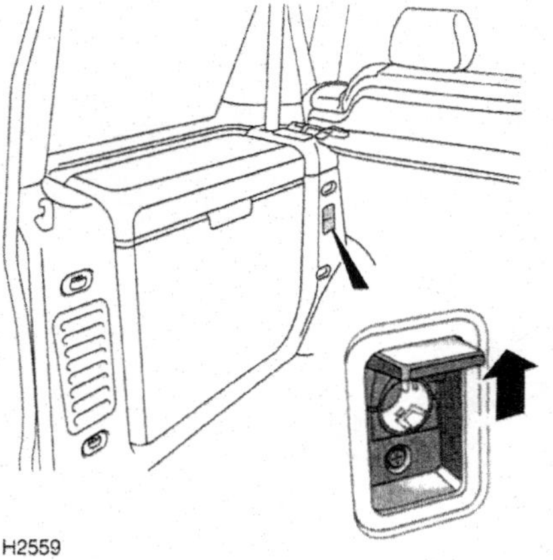

H2559

An auxiliary power socket is mounted immediately behind the rear seat on the left hand side of the loadspace. This can be used to power Land Rover approved accessories that use a maximum of 180 watts.

Always run the engine during prolonged use of electrical accessories, otherwise the battery may become discharged.

WARNING

NEVER plug non-approved accessories into the power socket - damage to the vehicle's electrical systems could occur.

CUP HOLDERS

WARNING

The driver should not drink and should not use the cup holder while driving.

If the cup holder is retractable, it should be kept closed when not in use.

DO NOT place anything other than suitable drinks containers in the cup holder, because such items may be thrown about in the compartment and possibly injure occupants in the event of an accident or emergency manoeuvre.

Do not carry open-top drink containers in the cup holders while the vehicle is in motion; a spilled hot drink could cause personal injury. Spilled drinks can also damage upholstery, carpeting and electrical components.

Use only for soft containers. DO NOT use to hold cups made of glass, china or hard plastic, as these may cause injury in the event of an accident or emergency manoeuvre. Unopened, sealed containers (drinks cans, for example) are hard objects and may also cause injury.

Front*

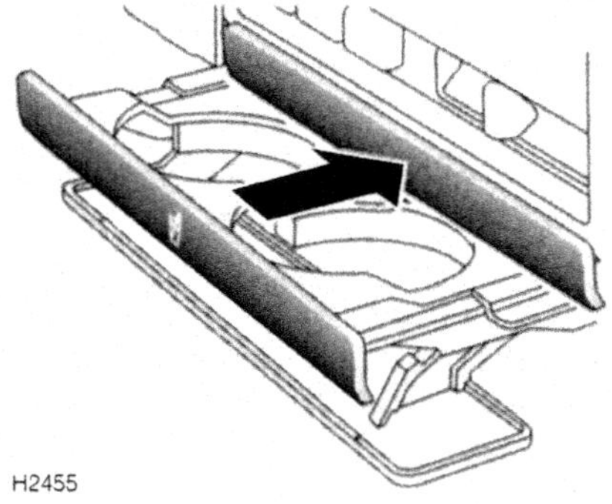

Push leading edge of tray to open.

Rear (2nd row seats)*

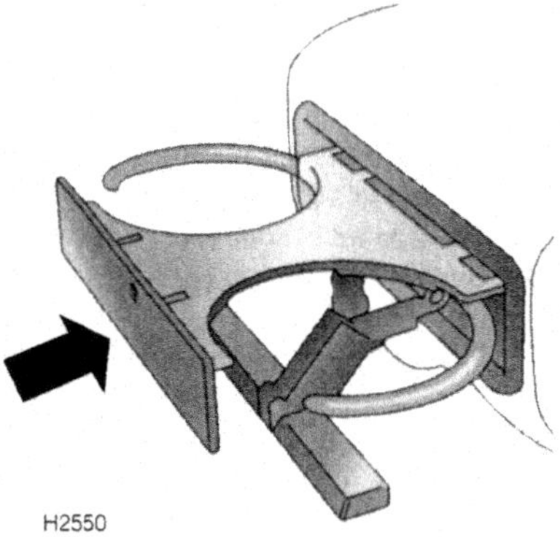

With the centre armrest lowered, press the front of the cup holder tray to open.

Rear (occasional 3rd row seats)*

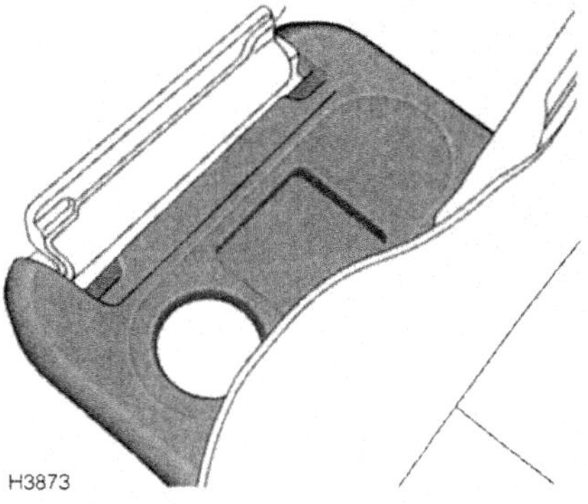

The cup holder and trinket tray are fitted to the individual seats and are accessible when the third row occasional rear seats are erected for use (see *'OCCASIONAL REAR SEATS', page 28*). The cup holder and trinket tray are located on the outboard side of the seat.

WARNING

Remove any drink containers or personal belongings from the cup holders and trinket trays, BEFORE returning the occasional rear seats to their stowed position - damage to the seats could occur.

NOTE: *If rear air conditioning is fitted to the vehicle, only the right-hand seat is equipped with a cup holder and trinket tray.*

CUBBY BOX

WARNING

Do not carry open-top drink containers in the cup holders while the vehicle is in motion; a spilled hot drink could cause personal injury. Spilled drinks can also damage upholstery, carpeting and electrical components.

Use only for soft cups. DO not carry cups made of glass, china or hard plastic, because these may cause injury in the event of an accident or emergency manoeuvre.

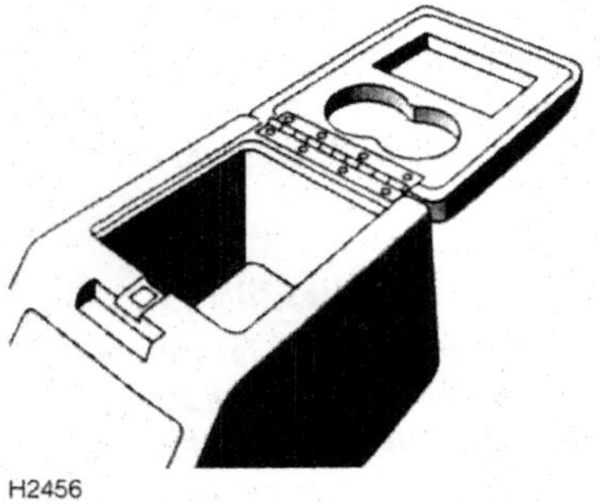

H2456

Lift front of lid to open.

NOTE: *The recesses in the underside of the lid can be used to hold cups or drink cans.*

SUN VISOR VANITY MIRROR ILLUMINATION*

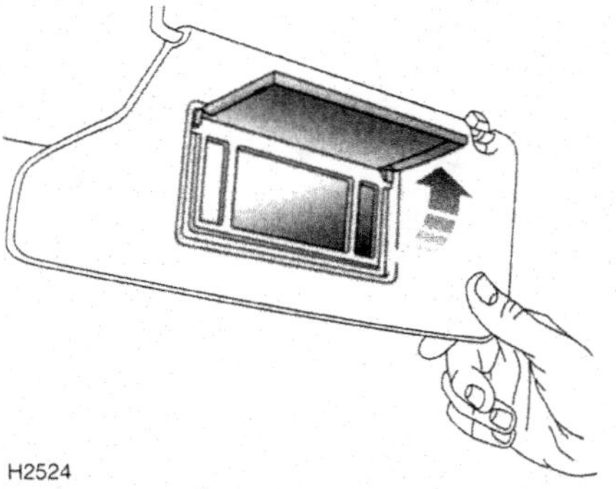

H2524

With the starter switch turned to position 'II', pivot the sun visor downward and raise the cover on the vanity mirror to illuminate the mirror. Close the cover to extinguish the lights.

INTERIOR REAR-VIEW MIRROR

Automatic mirror

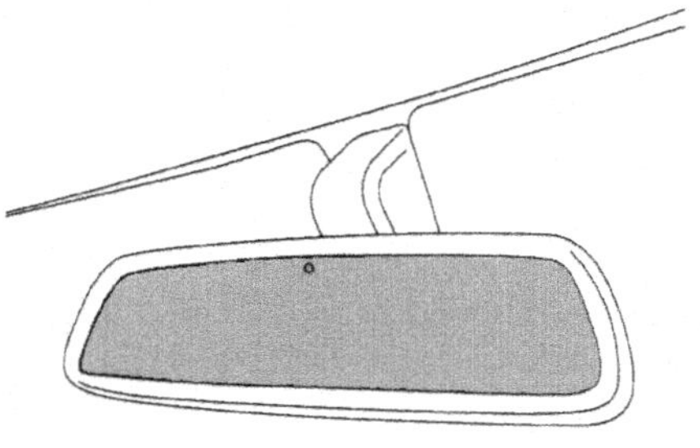

H3585

The automatic rear view mirror is equipped with an automatic dimming function which operates whenever the starter switch is turned to position 'II'. When powered, the mirror will automatically reduce glare from the headlights of following vehicles in dark or low light conditions.

Manual mirror

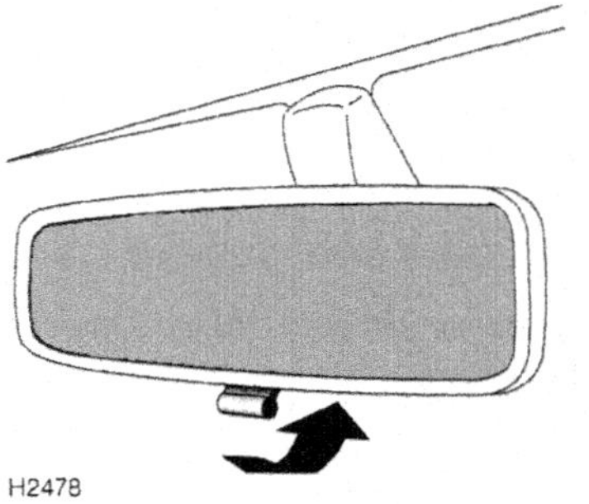

H2478

The manual rear view mirror can be dipped to reduce glare from the headlights of following vehicles. At night, move the lever at the base of the mirror forward to 'dip' the mirror. Normal visibility is restored by pulling the lever back again.

WARNING

In some circumstances the view reflected in a 'dipped' manual mirror can confuse the driver as to the precise location of following vehicles. Remember to take additional care!

COMPASS MIRROR*

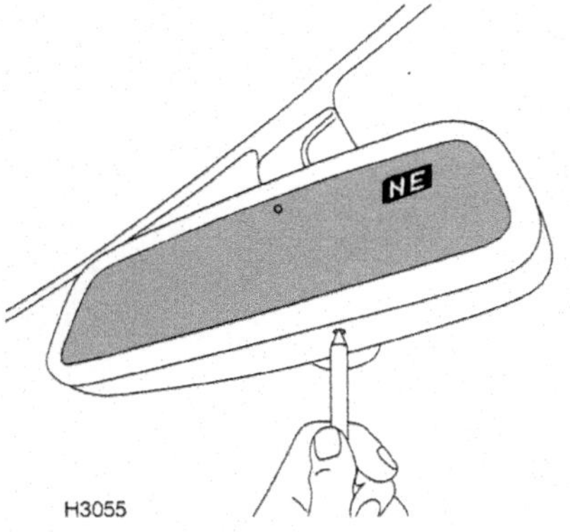

H3055

WARNING

The compass is a direction aid only. While drivers may wish to observe the compass display while driving, it must not be allowed to distract from proper observation of traffic, road conditions and other hazards, either on the public highway or while driving off-road.

Whenever the starter switch is turned to position 'II', the vehicle's direction of travel - 'N', 'NE', 'E', 'SE', 'S'. 'SW', 'W' or 'NW' - will be displayed in the mirror display. The display will change whenever the vehicle direction changes by more than 22.5° from the midpoint of each compass segment (a short time delay is incorporated to prevent nuisance changes occurring).

To ensure accuracy, the compass must be calibrated and also set to the compass set zone in which the vehicle is to be used (see the appropriate map page that follows). Both operations will have been carried out before the vehicle was delivered. Re-calibration will not normally be necessary unless the battery has been disconnected for a period of time.

Calibrating the compass

1. Turn the starter switch to position 'II'. The mirror display should show the letter 'C'.
2. If 'C' is not displayed, use a ballpoint pen or similar probe to press the button on the underside of the mirror for six seconds, until 'C' is displayed. The button can then be released and the compass calibrated as follows.
3. Calibrate the compass by driving the vehicle in circles at 5 mph (3 km/h) or less - two circles should be sufficient - until the mirror display shows a direction ('N', 'NE', 'E', 'SE', 'S', 'SW', 'W' or 'NW').

   Alternatively, the compass will eventually calibrate itself during normal vehicle use, but depending upon the type of driving that is undertaken, this may take considerably longer.

Setting the compass

Variations in the earth's magnetic field cause changes to occur in the compass reading, as the vehicle is driven from one set zone to another. However, it should be noted that magnetic variation between adjacent zones is only 4°, and for most motoring situations, resetting the compass should only be necessary if the vehicle has crossed more than one zone, or calibration was carried out in any zone other than zone 8.

Note that the precise points at which the set zones change cannot be accurately plotted and that drivers situated in an area where zones merge, should not need to reset the compass every time the vehicle crosses from one to another.

Compass

To set the compass:

1. Identify the appropriate zone for your location (see maps on the following pages).
2. Turn the starter switch to position 'II'.
3. Using a ballpoint pen or similar probe, press and hold the button on the underside of the mirror until a zone number appears in the display. This will take approximately 3 seconds (note that the compass automatically defaults to zone 8).
4. Release the button, then continue pressing and releasing the button alternately, until the required zone number appears in the display.
5. Once the set zone has been selected, the display reappears (after approximately 10 seconds) and the compass is correctly set for the required zone.

Compass Set Zones

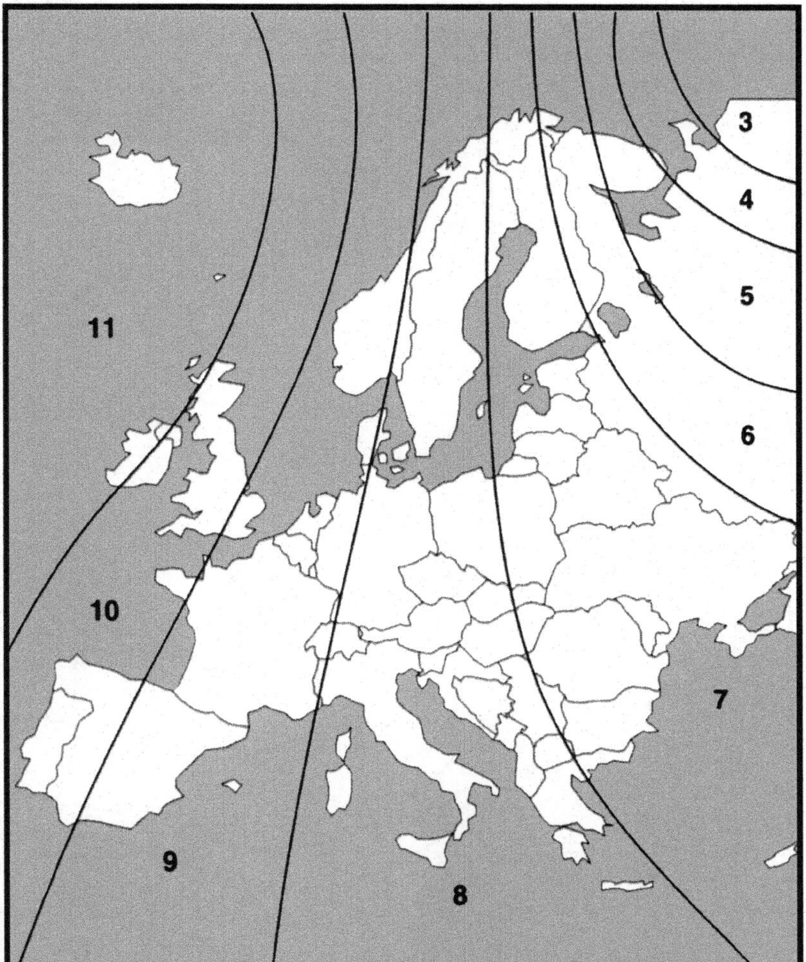

Europe

Compass Set Zones

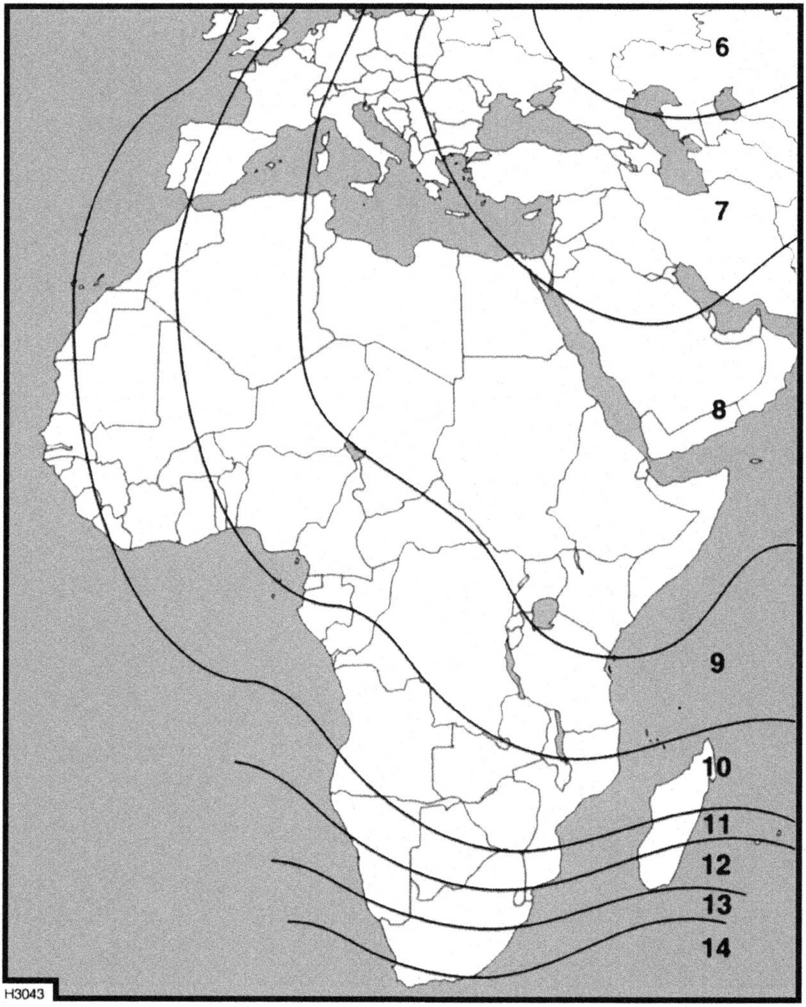

Africa

Compass Set Zones

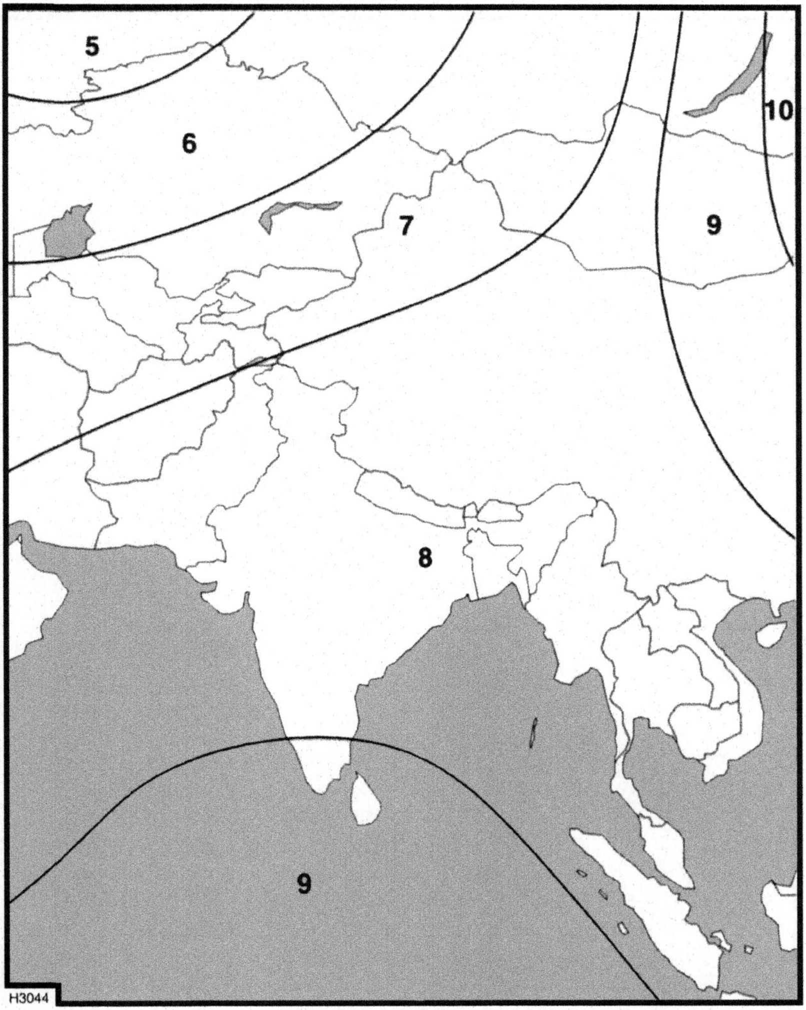

India & Middle East

Compass Set Zones

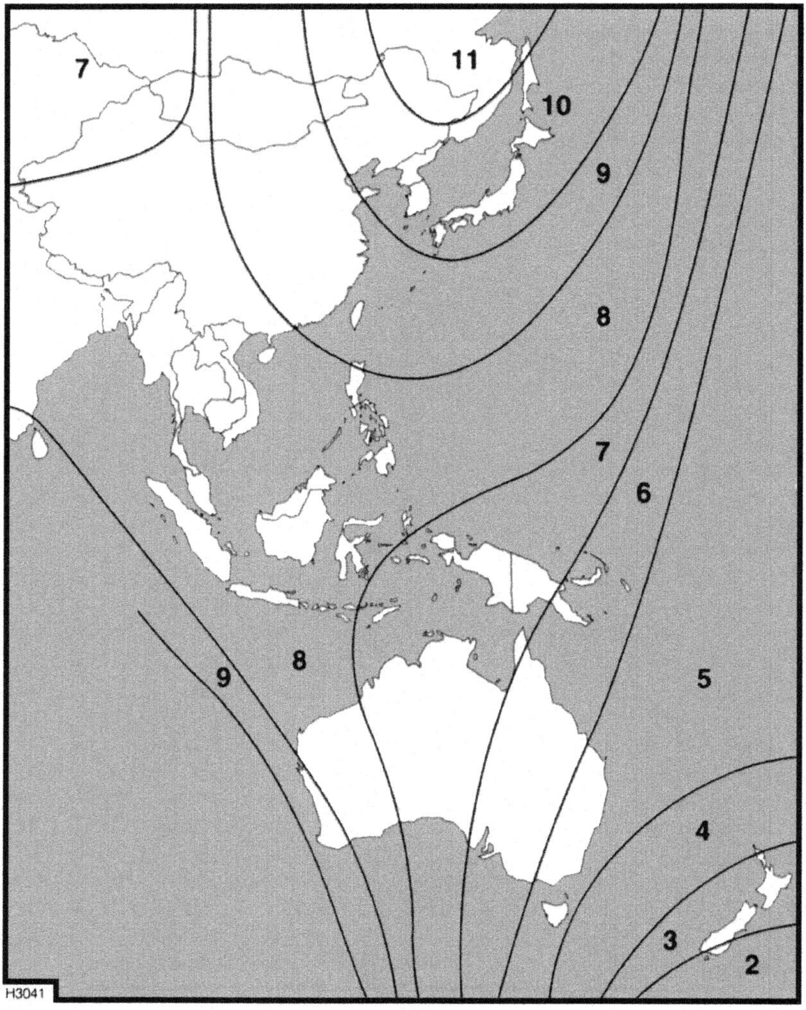

Ausralasia & Far East

REAR STEP

H2482

Press down with your foot to lower the step. The step will automatically return to its stowed position after use.

REAR DOOR

*

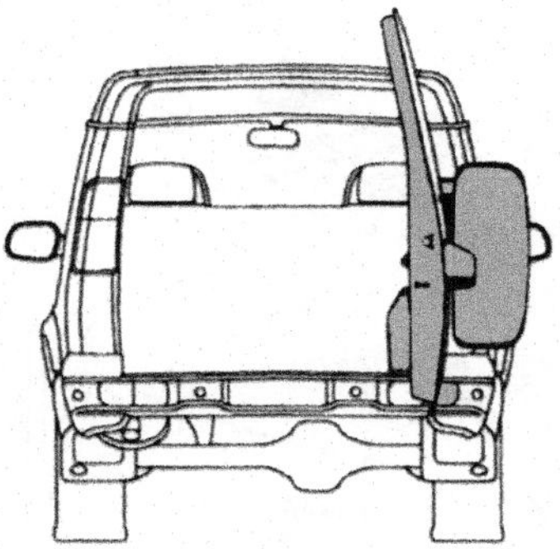

H4524

WARNING

Lights located on the same side of the vehicle as the rear door hinges will be obscured when the door is fully open. Owner should be mindful of and considerate to local traffic/environmental conditions.

LOADSPACE COVER*

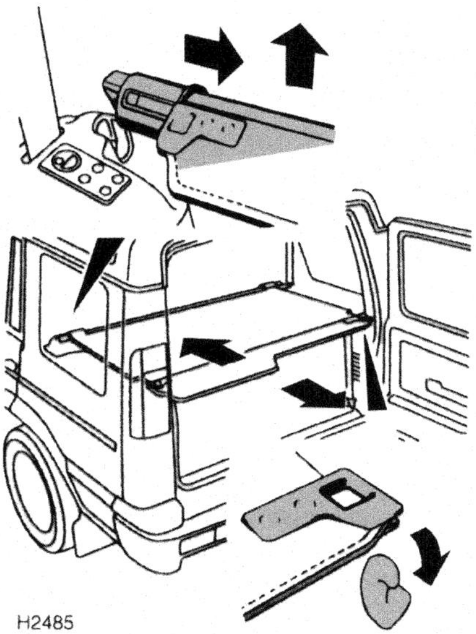

H2485

The rear loadspace cover is a spring loaded roller blind, which can be retracted when not in use by detaching the cover from the hooks at the rear of the vehicle (see lower inset).

To remove the loadspace cover:

1. Slide the retracted cover firmly to the right.
2. Lift the left hand end of the cover from its location.
3. Carefully manoeuvre the cover from the rear of the vehicle.

Refitting the loadspace cover is the reverse of the removal procedure.

NOTE: *Removal of the loadspace cover may be eased by folding the rear seat backrest forward.*

WARNING

DO NOT carry loose items of luggage on top of the loadspace cover - these may obscure vision and could become dangerous projectiles in the event of a sudden stop or collision.

All equipment, luggage or tools carried in the loadspace should be secured to minimise the risk of injury to the driver and passengers in the event of an accident or emergency manoeuvre.

DO NOT store the loadspace cover loose in the vehicle.

*

LOADSPACE COVER*

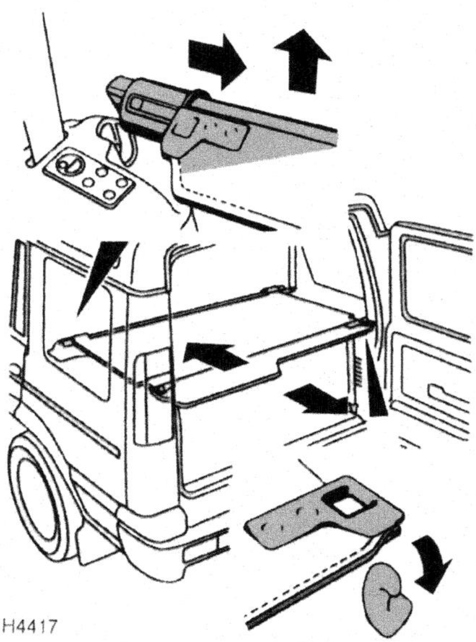

H4417

IN-CAR TELEPHONES

For your safety, always note the following precautions before fitting an in-car telephone, or any mobile communication equipment.

- Only use an installation kit incorporating an aerial external to the vehicle.
- Ensure that the installation is carried out by a competent installer.

For your safety

WARNING

Using any hand-held appliance while driving can be dangerous. Always stop the vehicle before making a call and ensure the telephone is switched off while you are driving.

RADIO AERIAL

A single aerial (or twin aerials on some models) is etched onto the surface of the glass of one (or both) rear side windows.

No maintenance is possible, however it is important to ensure that the interior surface of the glass is protected from possible damage caused by contact with hard objects or from the injurious effects of abrasive cleaners.

IN-CAR ENTERTAINMENT

Radio cassette player

Full operating instructions for any audio equipment fitted as standard to your vehicle, are contained in the *'In-Car Entertainment'* book in the vehicle literature pack.

CD autochanger*

The CD autochanger is located under the right hand front seat. Full operating instructions are contained in the *'In-Car Entertainment'* book.

WARNING

DO NOT insert or eject the magazine while driving.

HEADPHONE CONTROLS*

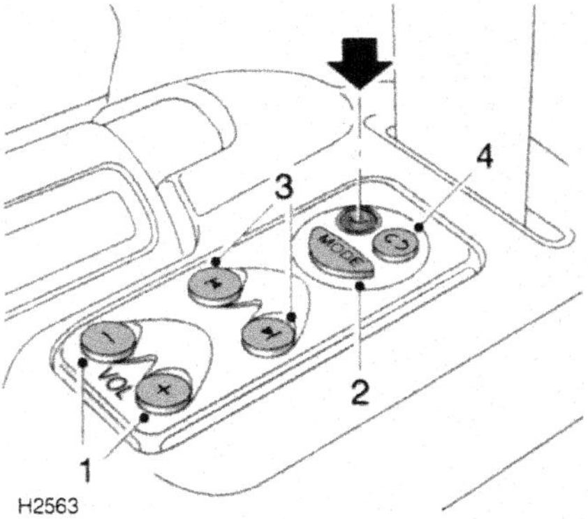

The control panel (illustrated) is for the convenience of rear seat passengers and can be used with headphones only.

The controls include:

1. Volume
2. Mode (for changing between radio, cassette tape and CD)
3. Auto search (to search up or down the selected waveband, or skip forward or back between tracks of a tape or CD).
4. Multi-function control (selects the next radio pre-set, reverses the direction of tape play, or selects the next CD in the autochanger).

Full operating instructions are included in the *'In-Car Entertainment'* book.

NOTE: *Where a conflict arises between operation of the vehicle's audio unit and the headphone controls, the audio unit takes priority.*

RADIO REMOTE CONTROLS *

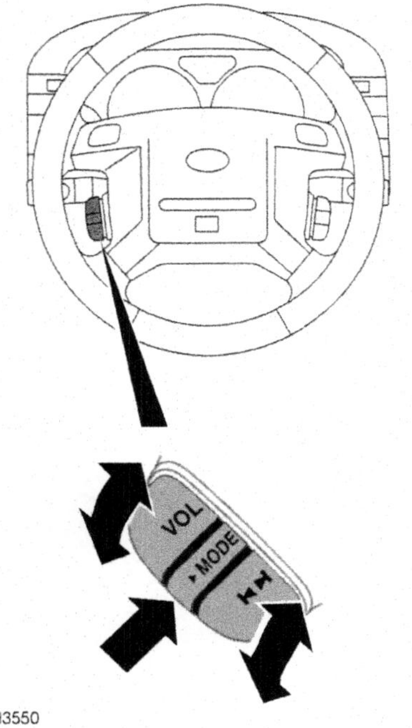

H3550

Volume control

VOL Lift or press to increase or decrease the volume.

Mode select control

MODE Press to change to cassette tape or compact disc play, or to return to radio tuner mode. The mode change will only be affected if a tape or disc has been loaded in the autochanger.

Search control

Lift or press to change to the next or previous radio station on the selected waveband.

During tape or CD play, lift the control to move forward to the next track on the tape or disc, or press to return to the start of the current track. Operate the control repeatedly to move forward or back through several tracks at a time.

Driving & Operating

Driving & Operating

STEERING COLUMN LOCK

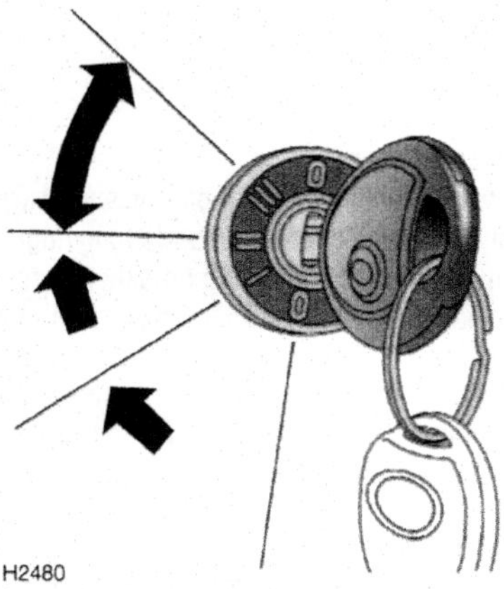

To unlock the steering column

Insert the key FULLY and turn the starter switch to position 'I'. A small movement of the steering wheel may be necessary to disengage the steering lock while turning the switch.

To lock the steering column

Turn the key to position '**0**' and withdraw it from the starter switch. Turn the steering wheel slightly until the lock engages.

WARNING

Once the steering lock is engaged, it is impossible to steer the vehicle. DO NOT remove the key or turn the starter switch to position '0' while the vehicle is in motion.

STARTER SWITCH

The starter switch is located to the right of the steering column, and uses the following sequence of key positions to operate the steering lock, electrical circuits and starter motor:

Position '0'

- Steering locked (if key is removed).
- Most lighting circuits are operational, including: sidelights, headlights and hazard warning lights.

Position 'I'

- Steering unlocked.
- Clock, radio/cassette player and cigar lighter can now be operated.

Position 'II'

- All instruments, warning lights and electrical circuits are operational.

Position 'III'

- Starter motor operates.

  Release the key immediately the engine starts (the key will automatically return to position 'II'). Note that operation of position 'I' electrical functions will be interrupted during engine cranking.

NOTE: *On automatic models gear selector position 'P' or 'N' must be selected before the engine will start.*

STARTING - Petrol models

WARNING

Never start or leave the engine running in an unventilated building - exhaust gases are poisonous and contain carbon monoxide, which can cause unconsciousness and may even be fatal.

Before starting the engine and driving, ENSURE you are familiar with the precautions shown under *'CATALYTIC CONVERTER*', page 103.*

In particular, you should be aware that if the engine fails to start, continued use of the starter may result in unburnt fuel damaging the catalytic converter.

1. Check that the handbrake is applied and that the gear lever is in neutral ('P' or 'N' for automatic transmission).
2. Switch off all unnecessary electrical equipment.
3. Turn the starter switch to position 'II' and then on to position 'III' to operate the starter motor. DO NOT press the accelerator pedal while starting, and RELEASE THE KEY as soon as the engine is running.

In temperate climates DO NOT operate the starter for longer than 10 seconds. If the engine fails to start, switch off and wait 10 seconds before re-using the starter.

NOTE: *Continued use of the starter will not only discharge the battery, but may cause damage to the starter motor and the catalytic converter.*

NOTE: *The battery charging and oil pressure warning lights should extinguish as soon as the engine is running.*

In cold weather, or when the battery is in a low state of charge, on manual gearbox vehicles depress the clutch pedal while starting and hold it down until the engine is running. This will reduce the load on the battery.

Cold climates

In very cold climates the oil pressure warning light may take several seconds to extinguish. Similarly, engine cranking times will also increase; at -13°F (-25°C) the starter motor may need to be operated continuously for as long as 30 seconds before the engine will start. For this reason, ensure that all non-essential electrical equipment is switched off.

Block heaters

Only approved block heaters restricted to a maximum of 400 W should be used. Block heaters that exceed this output may damage the emission control components.

Automatic gearbox vehicles

After starting, ensure that the handbrake and foot brake are firmly applied and the accelerator pedal is not depressed while moving the gear selector lever from 'N' or 'P', otherwise, the vehicle may move immediately the selector lever is moved to one of the drive positions (1,2,3,D or R). This is particularly important when the engine is cold, because the engine will be idling at a faster speed than normal.

STEERING COLUMN LOCK

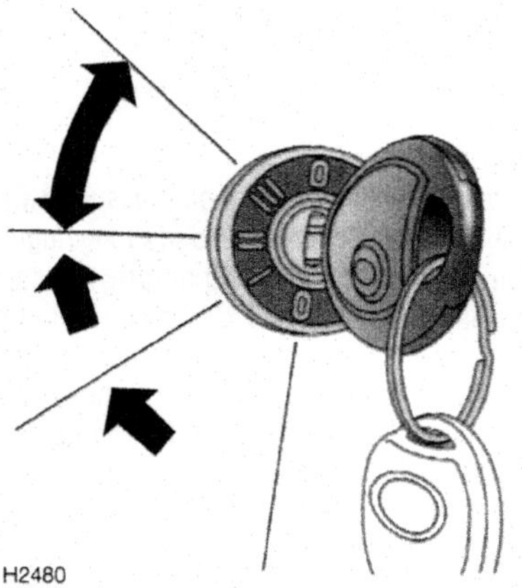

H2480

To unlock the steering column

Insert the key FULLY and turn the starter switch to position 'I'. A small movement of the steering wheel may be necessary to disengage the steering lock while turning the switch.

To lock the steering column

Turn the key to position '**0**' and withdraw it from the starter switch. Turn the steering wheel slightly until the lock engages.

WARNING

Once the steering lock is engaged, it is impossible to steer the vehicle. DO NOT remove the key or turn the starter switch to position '0' while the vehicle is in motion.

STARTER SWITCH

The starter switch is located to the right of the steering column, and uses the following sequence of key positions to operate the steering lock, electrical circuits and starter motor:

Position '0'

- Steering locked (if key is removed).
- Most lighting circuits are operational, including: sidelights, headlights and hazard warning lights.

Position 'I'

- Steering unlocked.
- Clock, radio/cassette player and cigar lighter can now be operated.

Position 'II'

- All instruments, warning lights and electrical circuits are operational.

Position 'III'

- Starter motor operates.

  Release the key immediately the engine starts (the key will automatically return to position 'II'). Note that operation of position 'I' electrical functions will be interrupted during engine cranking.

NOTE: *On automatic models gear selector position 'P' or 'N' must be selected before the engine will start.*

STARTING - Petrol models

WARNING

Never start or leave the engine running in an unventilated building - exhaust gases are poisonous and contain carbon monoxide, which can cause unconsciousness and may even be fatal.

Before starting the engine and driving, ENSURE you are familiar with the precautions shown under *'CATALYTIC CONVERTER*', page 103.*

In particular, you should be aware that if the engine fails to start, continued use of the starter may result in unburnt fuel damaging the catalytic converter.

1. Check that the handbrake is applied and that the gear lever is in neutral ('P' or 'N' for automatic transmission).
2. Switch off all unnecessary electrical equipment.
3. Turn the starter switch to position 'II' and then on to position 'III' to operate the starter motor. DO NOT press the accelerator pedal while starting, and RELEASE THE KEY as soon as the engine is running.

In temperate climates DO NOT operate the starter for longer than 10 seconds. If the engine fails to start, switch off and wait 10 seconds before re-using the starter.

NOTE: *Continued use of the starter will not only discharge the battery, but may cause damage to the starter motor and the catalytic converter.*

NOTE: *The battery charging and oil pressure warning lights should extinguish as soon as the engine is running.*

In cold weather, or when the battery is in a low state of charge, on manual gearbox vehicles depress the clutch pedal while starting and hold it down until the engine is running. This will reduce the load on the battery.

Cold climates

In very cold climates the oil pressure warning light may take several seconds to extinguish. Similarly, engine cranking times will also increase; at -13°F (-25°C) the starter motor may need to be operated continuously for as long as 30 seconds before the engine will start. For this reason, ensure that all non-essential electrical equipment is switched off.

Block heaters

Only approved block heaters restricted to a maximum of 400 W should be used. Block heaters that exceed this output may damage the emission control components.

Automatic gearbox vehicles

After starting, ensure that the handbrake and foot brake are firmly applied and the accelerator pedal is not depressed while moving the gear selector lever from 'N' or 'P', otherwise, the vehicle may move immediately the selector lever is moved to one of the drive positions (1,2,3,D or R). This is particularly important when the engine is cold, because the engine will be idling at a faster speed than normal.

STARTING - Diesel models

WARNING

Never start or leave the engine running in an unventilated building - exhaust gases are poisonous and contain carbon monoxide, which can cause unconsciousness and may even be fatal.

Before starting the engine and driving, ENSURE you are familiar with the precautions shown under *'CATALYTIC CONVERTER*', page 103.*

In particular, you should be aware that if the engine fails to start, continued use of the starter may result in unburnt fuel damaging the catalytic converter.

1. Check that the handbrake is applied and that the gear lever is in neutral ('P' or 'N' for automatic transmission).
2. Switch off all unnecessary electrical equipment.
3. Insert the starter key and turn the switch to position 'II'. Wait until the glow plug warning light extinguishes.

   NOTE: *The waiting time will vary according to the engine coolant temperature (when the engine is hot, the glow plug warning light will extinguish almost immediately).*
4. Turn the key to position 'III' to operate the starter motor. DO NOT press the accelerator pedal while starting. RELEASE THE KEY as soon as the engine is running.

If the engine stalls or fails to start, you MUST return the starter switch to position 'I' before attempting to restart; the engine will not start by turning the starter switch from position 'II'.

In temperate climates DO NOT operate the starter for longer than 10 seconds. If the engine fails to start, switch off and wait 10 seconds before re-using the starter.

NOTE: *Continued use of the starter will not only discharge the battery, but may cause damage to the starter motor and the catalytic converter.*

NOTE: *The battery charging and oil pressure warning lights should extinguish as soon as the engine is running.*

In cold weather, or when the battery is in a low state of charge, on manual gearbox vehicles depress the clutch pedal while starting and hold it down until the engine is running. This will reduce the load on the battery.

Precautions

- **The diesel engine must not be run above idle speed until the oil pressure warning light extinguishes. This will ensure that the engine and turbo-charger bearings are properly lubricated before being run at speed.**
- **Similarly, ALWAYS allow the engine to idle for 10 seconds before switching off.**

Cold climates

In very cold climates the oil pressure warning light may take several seconds to extinguish. Similarly, engine cranking times will also increase; at -13°F (-25°C) the starter motor may need to be operated continuously for as long as 30 seconds before the engine will start. For this reason, ensure that all non-essential electrical equipment is switched off.

Block heaters

Only approved block heaters restricted to a maximum of 400 W should be used. Block heaters that exceed this output may damage the emission control components.

Automatic gearbox vehicles

After starting, ensure that the handbrake and foot brake are firmly applied and the accelerator pedal is not depressed while moving the gear selector lever from 'N' or 'P', otherwise, the vehicle may move immediately the selector lever is moved to one of the drive positions (1,2,3,D or R). This is particularly important when the engine is cold, because the engine will be idling at a faster speed than normal.

DRIVING

IMPORTANT INFORMATION
Vehicle stability Your vehicle has a higher ground clearance and, hence, a higher centre of gravity than ordinary passenger cars to enable the vehicle to perform in a wide variety of different off-road applications. An advantage of the higher ground clearance is a better view of the road, allowing the driver to more easily anticipate problems. Inexperienced drivers should take additional care, remembering that the Discovery is not designed for cornering at the same speeds as conventional passenger cars, any more than a low slung sports car is designed to perform satisfactorily in off-road conditions. As with other vehicles of this type, failure to operate the Discovery correctly may result in loss of control or even vehicle rollover.
Vehicle height The overall height of your vehicle exceeds that of ordinary passenger cars (for convenience the height is shown on the underside of the sun visor). Always be aware of the height of your vehicle and check the available headroom before driving through low entrances. This is particularly important if the vehicle is fitted with a roof rack or if a sunroof is open.

Instruments and warning lights

Before driving it is important to fully understand the function of the instruments and warning lights (see *'INSTRUMENT PANEL', page 45*).

NOTE: *Red warning lights are of particular importance, illumination indicating that a fault exists. If a red light illuminates, always stop the vehicle and seek qualified assistance before continuing.*

Warming-up

DO NOT warm-up the engine by allowing it to idle at a slow speed.

In the interests of fuel economy, it is advisable to drive the vehicle straight away, remembering that harsh acceleration and labouring the engine before the normal operating temperature has been reached can damage the engine.

Running-in

Proper running-in will have a direct bearing on the reliability and smooth running of your vehicle throughout its life.

In particular, the engine, gearbox, brakes and tyres need time to 'bed-in' and adjust to the demands of everyday motoring. During the first 500 miles (800 km), it is essential to drive with consideration for the running-in process and heed the following advice:

- LIMIT maximum road speed to 70 mph (110 km/h) or 3,000 rev/min. Initially, drive the vehicle on a light throttle and only increase engine speeds gradually once the running-in distance has been completed.
- DO NOT operate at full throttle or allow the engine to labour in any gear.
- AVOID fast acceleration and heavy braking except in emergencies.

FUEL ECONOMY

Fuel consumption is influenced by two major factors:

- How your vehicle is maintained.
- How you drive your vehicle.

To obtain optimum fuel economy, it is essential that your vehicle is maintained in accordance with the manufacturer's service schedule.

Items such as the condition of the air cleaner element, tyre pressures and wheel alignment will have a significant effect on fuel consumption. But, above all, the way in which you drive is most important. The following hints may help you to obtain better value from your motoring:

- Avoid unnecessary, short, start-stop journeys.
- Avoid fast starts by accelerating gently and smoothly from rest.
- Do not drive in the lower gears for longer than necessary.
- Decelerate gently and avoid sudden and heavy braking.
- Anticipate obstructions and adjust your speed accordingly well in advance.
- When stationary in traffic, select neutral to improve fuel economy and air conditioning performance.

AUXILIARY EQUIPMENT

WARNING

DO NOT use auxiliary equipment, such as roller generators, that are driven by one wheel of the vehicle, as they could cause failure of the gearbox differential.

EMISSION CONTROL SYSTEM

WARNING

Exhaust fumes contain poisonous substances which can cause unconsciousness and may even be fatal.

- ***DO NOT inhale exhaust gases.***
- ***DO NOT start or leave the engine running in an enclosed unventilated area, or drive with the taildoor open.***
- ***DO NOT modify the exhaust system from the original design.***
- ***ALWAYS repair exhaust system leaks immediately.***
- ***If you think exhaust fumes are entering the vehicle have the cause determined and corrected immediately.***

Land Rover vehicles are fitted with emission and evaporative control equipment necessary to meet a number of territorial requirements.

In many countries it is against the law for vehicle owners to modify or tamper with emission control equipment, or to sanction the unauthorised replacement or modification of this equipment.In such cases the vehicle owner and the repairer may both be liable for legal penalties.

It is important to remember that all Land Rover dealers are properly equipped to perform repairs and to maintain the emission control system on your Discovery.

CATALYTIC CONVERTER*

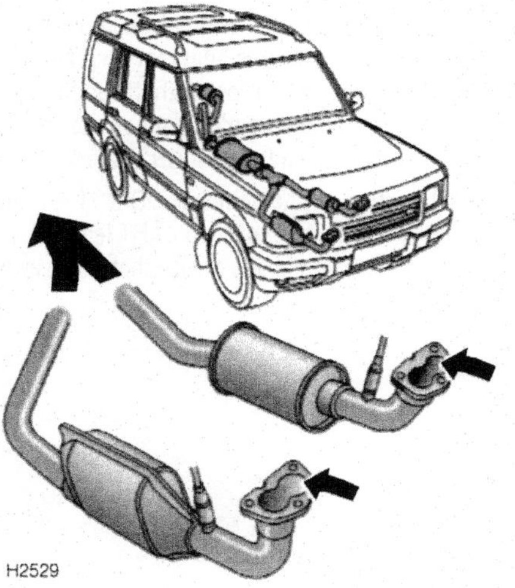
H2529

The exhaust system incorporates a catalytic converter, which converts poisonous exhaust emissions from the engine into environmentally less harmful gases.

WARNING

Catalytic converters can be easily damaged through improper use, particularly if the wrong fuel is used, or if an engine misfire occurs. For this reason it is VERY IMPORTANT that you heed the precautions which follow.

Fuel

ONLY use fuel recommended for your vehicle.

Starting the engine

- DO NOT continue to operate the starter after a few failed attempts (unburnt fuel may be drawn into the exhaust system, thereby poisoning the catalyst), and do not attempt to clear a misfire by pressing the accelerator pedal - seek qualified assistance.
- When starting a COLD engine, DO NOT drive if a misfire is suspected and do not attempt to clear a misfire by pressing the accelerator - seek qualified assistance.
- Do not attempt to push or tow-start the vehicle.

Driving

- If a misfire is suspected, or the vehicle lacks power while driving, provided the engine has reached its normal operating temperature, it may be driven SLOWLY (at risk of catalyst damage) to a Land Rover dealer for assistance.
- NEVER allow the vehicle to run out of fuel (the resultant misfire could damage the catalyst).
- Consult your dealer if your vehicle is burning excessive oil (blue smoke from the exhaust), as this will progressively reduce catalyst efficiency.
- On rough terrain do not allow the underside of the vehicle to be subjected to heavy impacts which could damage the catalytic converter.
- DO NOT overload or excessively 'rev' the engine.
- DO NOT switch off the engine when the vehicle is in motion with a drive gear selected.

WARNING

Exhaust system temperatures can be extremely high - DO NOT park on ground where combustible materials such as dry grass or leaves could come into contact with the exhaust system - in dry weather a fire could result.

Vehicle maintenance

- Any engine misfire, loss of engine performance or engine run-on, could seriously damage the catalytic converter. For this reason, it is vital that unqualified persons do not tamper with the engine, and that regular systematic maintenance is carried out by a Land Rover dealer.
- On petrol engine vehicles, DO NOT run the engine with a spark plug or HT lead removed, or use any device that requires an insert into a spark plug.

Fuel Filling

SAFETY ON THE FORECOURT

WARNING

Petroleum gases are highly inflammable and, in confined spaces, are also extremely explosive.

Always take sensible precautions when refuelling:

- Switch off the engine.
- Do not smoke or use a naked flame or light.
- Do not operate a mobile phone.
- Take care not to spill fuel.
- Do not overfill the tank.

*

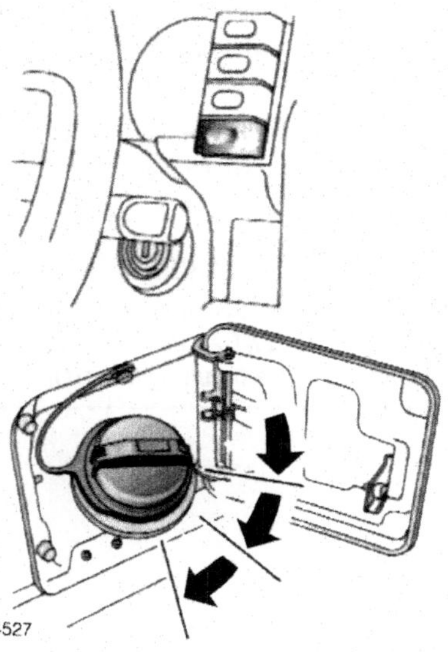

H4527

FUEL FILLER

WARNING

DO NOT fully remove the filler cap until any captive tank pressure has been released (wait until the hissing stops).

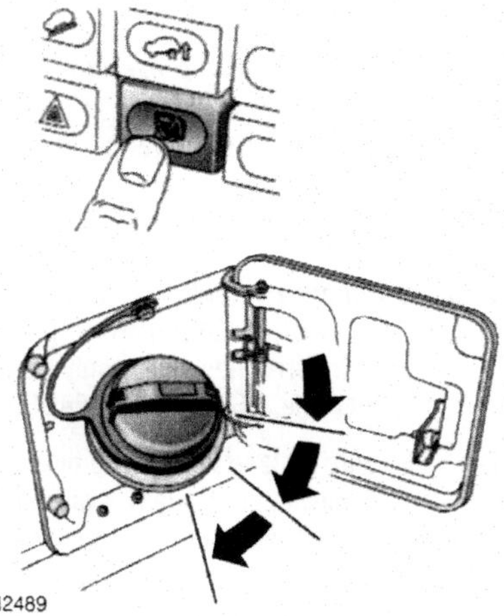

H2489

The fuel filler is located in the rear right-hand wing. With the starter switch turned to position '0' or 'I', press the fascia mounted switch (shown in illustration) to release the filler flap.

The filler cap is designed to allow the fuel tank to vent during the first half turn. Carefully loosen the cap one half turn until resistance is felt, and allow fuel tank pressure to be released. Once the pressure is released (hissing has stopped), it is safe to fully remove the filler cap.

When replacing, tighten the cap clockwise until you hear the fuel cap ratchet click at least three times (see illustration).

TYPE OF FUEL

WARNING

On petrol engine vehicles fitted with a catalytic converter, serious damage to the catalyst will occur if LEADED fuel is used!

Petrol engine vehicles

Vehicles with a catalytic converter:

- *Low compression engines:*
  91 RON UNLEADED to EN228
- *High compression engines:*
  95 RON UNLEADED to EN228

Vehicles without a catalytic converter:

- Use 91 RON UNLEADED petrol wherever possible. In territories where only LEADED fuel is available, USE 95 RON LEADED

The RON value (octane rating) and type of petroleum (unleaded or leaded), available at garage forecourts will vary in different parts of the world. For example, in most European countries 95 RON unleaded fuel is readily available, but in some parts of the world fuel supplies may be limited to leaded or lower octane fuels only. The RON values quoted above are MINIMUM requirements and can be safely exceeded.

During manufacture, engines are tuned to suit the fuel supplies commonly available in the country for which the vehicle is destined. However, if a vehicle is later exported to a different country, or is used to travel between different territories, the owner should be aware that the available fuel supplies may not be compatible with the engine specification. If in doubt, seek advice from the territory concerned.

Using petrol with a lower octane rating, however, can cause persistent, heavy 'engine knock' (a metallic rapping noise). If severe, this can lead to engine damage.

If heavy engine knock is detected when using the recommended octane rated fuel, or if steady engine knocking is present while maintaining a steady speed on level roads, contact your dealer for advice.

NOTE: *An occasional, light, engine knock while accelerating or climbing hills is acceptable.*

Diesel engine vehicles

Use diesel or automotive gas oil (AGO) to EN 590.

The quality of diesel fuel (Derv) can vary in different countries and only clean, good quality fuel should be used. It is important that the sulphur content of diesel fuel does not exceed 0.3%; in Europe all supplies should be within this limit, but in other parts of the world, you should check with your supplier.

In markets where the sulphur content exceeds 0.3%, more frequent engine oil and filter changes will be required.

WARNING

If the fuel tank is accidentally filled with petrol it is ESSENTIAL that you contact your dealer BEFORE attempting to start the engine!

FUEL FILLING

WARNING

DO NOT attempt to fill the tank to its maximum capacity. If the vehicle is to be parked on a slope, in direct sunlight, or high ambient temperature, expansion of the fuel could cause spillage.

Filling station pumps are equipped with automatic cut-off sensing to avoid fuel spillage. Fill the tank SLOWLY until the filler nozzle automatically cuts-off the supply. DO NOT attempt to fill the tank beyond this point or spillage could result due to expansion of the fuel.

Petrol engine vehicles

On petrol engine vehicles designed to operate ONLY on unleaded fuel, the fuel filler neck will accept ONLY a narrow filler nozzle of the type found on pumps that deliver UNLEADED fuel.

On petrol engine vehicles designed to operate on leaded fuel, the fuel filler neck will accept the wider filler nozzles found on pumps that deliver LEADED fuel.

Diesel engine vehicles

The diesel pumps on garage forecourts fill at a maximum of 45 litres (10 gallons) per minute. Use of commercial vehicle diesel pumps with a higher fill rate, may result in premature pump cut-off and fuel spillage.

EMPTY FUEL TANK

Petrol engine vehicles

In the case of petrol engine vehicles equipped with a catalytic converter, running the fuel tank dry could create an engine misfire capable of damaging the catalytic converter. DO NOT RUN THE FUEL TANK DRY!

Diesel engine vehicles

After running the fuel tank dry, refuel the tank with at least 1 gallon (4.5 litres) of diesel fuel, then carry out the following procedure:

1. Turn off the starter switch and wait for 15 seconds.
2. Turn the starter key to position 'II' and wait for 30 seconds.
3. Repeat steps 1 and 2 six times.
4. After the final 30 second period, fully depress the accelerator pedal.
5. Keeping the pedal depressed, start cranking the engine.
6. Continue cranking the engine and as soon as the engine is firing smoothly, ease the accelerator pedal back to approximately halfway through its travel, and release the starter key. The engine should now be running.
7. If the engine fails to start, repeat the process.

IMPORTANT INFORMATION

The engine must NOT be cranked for more than 20 seconds in any one period.
If the above procedure is carried out on a vehicle that has NOT run out of fuel, it will result in the engine flooding with fuel and failing to start.

FUEL CUT-OFF SWITCH

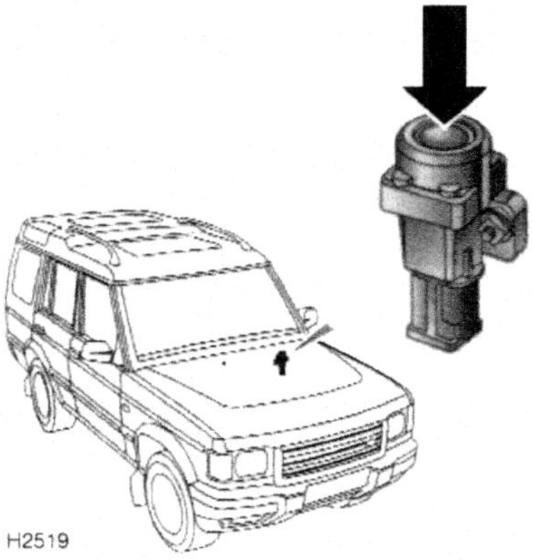

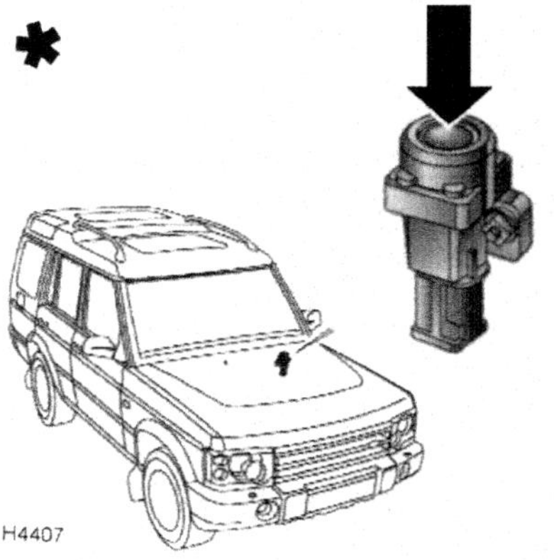

The fuel cut-off switch is a safety device which, in the event of a collision or sudden impact, automatically cuts off the fuel supply to the engine.

The switch is located on the engine compartment bulkhead. After an impact, the switch must be reset by pressing the rubber top (arrowed in illustration) before the engine can be restarted.

WARNING

ALWAYS check for fuel leaks before resetting the switch!

GEAR LEVER

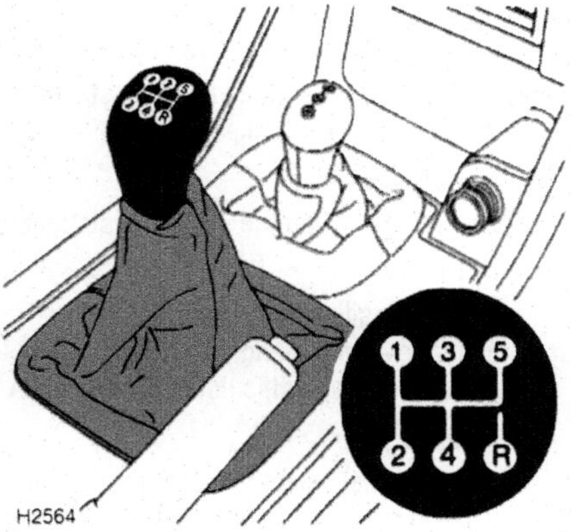

Manual transmission vehicles feature a five speed main gearbox and a two-speed (LOW & HIGH) transfer box. By using the main gearbox in conjunction with the transfer gears, ten forward and two reverse speeds are available.

The gear positions for the main gearbox are shown on the gear lever knob. Note that when the gearbox is in neutral, the gear lever is spring-loaded to lie naturally between third and fourth gear positions.

WARNING

Do not select reverse gear unless the vehicle is stationary.

DO NOT attempt to start the engine with the vehicle in gear. The engine must ONLY be started with the main gear lever in neutral and the handbrake applied.

Precautions while driving

- DO NOT rest your hand on the gear lever while driving - pressure from your hand may cause premature wear to the gear selector mechanism.
- DO NOT use the clutch pedal as a foot rest. To prevent unnecessary wear, always keep the left foot well clear of the clutch pedal except when changing gear.
- DO NOT hold the vehicle stationary on a hill by slipping the clutch. This will wear out the clutch. Always use the handbrake.

GEAR SELECTOR

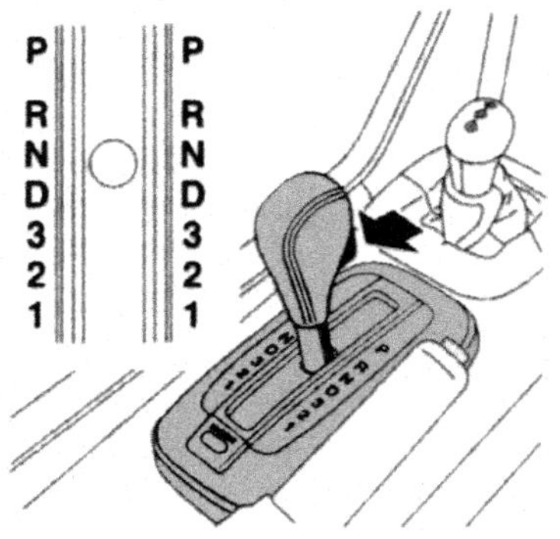

H2565

The Automatic transmission features a four speed main gearbox with a torque converter and a two speed transfer box. Using the main gearbox in conjunction with the transfer gearing produces eight forward and two reverse speeds.

Main gearbox selector lever

A spring loaded catch restricts movement of the lever, thereby preventing inadvertent gear selection. Press and hold the trigger mounted in the handle of the selector lever (arrowed in illustration) to release the catch whilst moving the lever to the required position.

NOTE: *Gear selection between 'D' and '3' in high and low range may be made without operating the trigger.*

Selector lever positions

- **'P' Park**

  In this position the transmission is locked to prevent the vehicle from rolling away.

  Select ONLY when the vehicle is stationary and with the handbrake applied.

- **'R' Reverse**

  Select ONLY when the vehicle is stationary.

- **'N' Neutral**

  Use this position when the vehicle is stationary and the engine is to idle for a short period (at traffic lights for example).

- **'D' Drive**

  In high range, select for all normal driving on good road surfaces; fully automatic gear changing occurs on all four forward gears according to vehicle speed and accelerator position.

- **'3' (1st, 2nd and 3rd gears)**

  Automatic gear changing is limited to first, second and third gears only. In high range, use this position in congested traffic conditions and for town driving.

- **'2' (1st and 2nd gears)**

  Automatic gear changing is limited to first and second ratios only. In high range, use when driving up steep gradients and for negotiating very narrow, twisting, roads. This position also provides moderate engine braking for descending slopes.

- **'1' (1st gear only)**

  Use on very severe gradients, particularly when towing, and when maximum engine braking is required.

WARNING

Always leave the vehicle with the gear selector in 'P' (Park) position when parked.

Automatic Transmission

Starting and driving

Drivers unfamiliar with the performance characteristics of an automatic gearbox should thoroughly familiarise themselves with the following instructions before driving.

- Before starting the engine, ensure that both foot brake and handbrake are applied.
- After starting the engine, KEEP BOTH BRAKES APPLIED before and whilst moving the selector lever to the required drive position.
- Keep the brakes applied until you are ready to move - remember, once a drive position is selected, an 'automatic' will tend to creep forward (or backward) without throttle application, as soon as the brakes are released.
- Never 'rev' the engine while selecting a forward or reverse drive gear, or while the vehicle is stationary with a drive gear selected - remember, an 'automatic' will move immediately the accelerator pedal is pressed.

Gear change speeds

With 'D' selected, the road speeds at which gear changes take place will vary according to the position of the accelerator: minimum acceleration will result in gear changes at low road speed, while larger throttle openings will cause the gearbox to delay gear changes until faster road speeds have been reached (thereby increasing acceleration).

With practice, gear changes can be made to occur at a wide range of road speeds depending on accelerator pedal pressure.

On long inclines the gearbox will sometimes change back and forth between gears. This occurs because the transmission does not include a ratio that is precisely right for the particular incline and vehicle loading circumstances. However, excessive gear changing results in a loss of momentum and is wasteful of fuel. It can be prevented by selecting the '3' or '2' positions which limit the gearbox to lower ratios.

'Kick-down'

To provide rapid acceleration for overtaking, push the accelerator pedal to the full extent of its travel in a single quick movement (this is known as 'kick-down'). Up to a certain speed, this will cause an immediate downshift into the lowest appropriate gear, followed by rapid acceleration. Once the pedal is relaxed, normal gear change speeds will resume (dependent upon road speed and accelerator pedal position).

MODE SWITCH

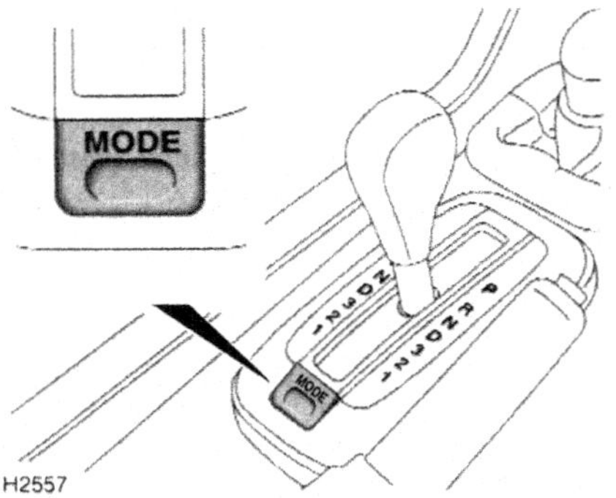

H2557

In High range press the mode switch to select 'Sport' mode (the 'S' information light on the instrument panel will illuminate).

In Low range press the mode switch to select 'Manual' mode (the 'M' manual information light will illuminate).

Press the switch a second time to return the gearbox to normal operation.

'Sport' mode
With 'Sport' mode selected, the gearbox is more responsive to accelerator pedal movement - downshifts occur earlier and upshifts are delayed to make optimum use of the engine's power while accelerating. Select 'Sport' when increased acceleration is required, or when negotiating long inclines or twisting roads. Note that driving in 'Sport' mode will increase fuel consumption.

'Manual' mode
In Low range, with 'Manual' mode selected, the automatic transmission functions as a manual gearbox requiring the driver to move the selector lever manually to change gear ('D' = 4th gear). Manual mode will provide maximum vehicle control and engine braking - ideal for use in severe off-road conditions. Note that 'kick-down' is disabled and that automatic downshifts will only occur to prevent the engine from stalling.

NOTE: *Switching off the engine or using the transfer gearbox will automatically cancel 'Sport' or 'Manual' mode.*

TRANSFER GEARBOX

The second gearbox (known as the transfer box) is used to select either the high or low range of gears.

High range ('H')
The high range of gears should be used for all normal road driving and also for off-road driving across dry, level terrain.

Low range ('L')
Use low range gears ONLY in situations where low speed manoeuvring is necessary, such as reversing a trailer or negotiating a boulder strewn river bed; also use low range for more extreme off-road conditions where progress in high range cannot be maintained. DO NOT attempt to use LOW range gears for normal road driving.

USING THE TRANSFER GEARBOX

There are two ways of operating the transfer gearbox lever; the 'normal' method - recommended for inexperienced drivers - and the 'advanced' method for experienced drivers.

Normal method
Manual gearbox vehicles:
With the vehicle stationary and the engine running, depress the clutch and then move the lever fully forward (or backwards) in TWO distinct but positive moves - 'high to neutral'.... 'neutral to low' (or vice versa).

If there is resistance to the gear engaging, do not force the lever. Instead, with the main lever in gear, release the clutch momentarily and then try again.

Automatic transmission vehicles:
With the vehicle stationary and the engine running, apply both foot brake and handbrake and then move the automatic gearbox selector to the 'N' (neutral) position before moving the transfer lever fully forward or backwards to the required position.

If there is resistance to the gear engaging, do not force the lever. Instead, with the engine running, apply the foot brake and handbrake, momentarily engage 'D' (drive) on the main gearbox, then return it to the 'N' position and try again.

Advanced method (Manual gearbox vehicles)

Changing from high to low on the move:

With the vehicle slowing to a stop and travelling NO FASTER THAN 5 mph (8 km/h), depress the clutch and push the transfer lever into neutral. Just before the road wheels stop turning (and with the clutch still depressed) push the lever fully forward into 'L' (low).

NOTE: *Use positive and confident moves, but do not rush the gear change.*

Changing from low to high on the move:

Changing from 'L' (low) to 'H' (high) can be achieved without stopping the vehicle, as follows:

1. Apply slight backward pressure to the transfer gear lever in preparation for changing.
2. Then, in three simultaneous moves, depress the clutch, release the accelerator and pull the transfer lever into neutral.
3. Release the clutch pedal for approximately 3 seconds before depressing it again and moving the transfer lever firmly into the high position.
4. Finally, select a suitable main gear, release the clutch and continue driving in the normal way.

NOTE: *After a little practice, this operation can be carried out smoothly and quickly by using firm, positive moves.*

On automatic models, reduce (or increase) the speed of the vehicle to 5 mph (8 km/h) and release the accelerator. Select 'N' and move the transfer lever quickly to the required 'H' or 'L' position. Finally, reselect 'D' with the main gear selector and continue driving as normal.

TRANSFER GEARBOX

Manual and automatic vehicles

The second gearbox (known as the transfer box) is used to select either the high or low range of gears. It also has a neutral position between high and low.

High range ('H')

High range should be used for all normal road driving and also for off-road driving across dry, level terrain.

Low range ('L')

Low range should be used ONLY in situations where low speed manoeuvering is necessary, such as reversing a trailer or negotiating a boulder-strewn river bed. Also use low range for more extreme off-road conditions where progress in high range cannot be maintained. DO NOT attempt to use LOW range gears for normal road driving.

Transfer box Neutral ('N')

With the Transfer box in neutral, drive cannot be transmitted to the road wheels, regardless of the position of the main gear lever.

Use transfer box neutral when being towed.

USING THE TRANSFER GEARBOX

There are two ways of operating the transfer gearbox lever:

1. 'Statically', i.e shifting whilst the vehicle is stationary.
2. 'Shift on the move', this is the recommended method, which after a little practice, can be carried out smoothly and quickly.

'Static' method

Manual vehicles:

With the vehicle stationary and the engine running, depress the clutch and then move the lever fully forward (or backwards) in TWO distinct but positive moves - 'high to neutral'.... 'neutral to low' (or vice versa).

If there is resistance to the gear engaging, (from the neutral position to either high or low), do not force the lever. Instead:

1. Still with the clutch depressed, (and the transfer box in neutral), select 2nd gear in main gearbox.
2. Release the clutch momentarily, depress the clutch and then try engagement again.
3. Select appropriate main gearbox gear to pull away.

Automatic vehicles:
With the vehicle stationary and the engine running, apply the foot brake and then move the automatic gearbox selector to the 'N' (neutral) position.Then move the transfer lever fully forward or backwards to the required position. If there is a resistance to the gear disengaging, do not force the lever. Instead, move the automatic gearbox selector to the 'R' (reverse) position for 2 seconds and then return to the 'N' (neutral) position and then try range change again.
If there is resistance to the gear engaging, (from the neutral position to the either high or low), do not force the lever. Instead:

1. Apply handbrake.
2. With the automatic gearbox still in 'N' (neutral), momentarily rev the engine whilst applying pressure to the transfer box lever to engage gear.
3. Select appropriate main gearbox gear to pull away.

'Shift on the move' method
Manual vehicles:
Changing from high to low on the move:
With the vehicle slowing to a stop and travelling NO FASTER THAN 5 mph (8 km/h), depress the clutch and push the transfer lever into neutral. Just before the road wheels stop turning (and with the clutch still depressed) push the lever fully forward into 'L' (low).

NOTE: *Use positive and confident moves, but do not rush the gear change.*

Changing from low to high on the move:
Changing from 'L' (low) to 'H' (high) can be achieved without stopping the vehicle, as follows:

1. Apply slight backward pressure to the transfer gear lever in preparation for changing.
2. Then, in three simultaneous moves, depress the clutch, release the accelerator and pull the transfer lever into neutral.
3. Release the clutch pedal for approximately 3 seconds before depressing it again and moving the transfer lever firmly into the high position.
4. Finally, select a suitable main gear, release the clutch and continue driving in the normal way.

NOTE: *After a little practice, this operation can be carried out smoothly and quickly by using firm, positive moves.*

Automatic vehicles:
With the vehicle driving forwards, reduce (or increase) the speed of the vehicle to to 5 mph (8 km/h), then:

1. Release the accelerator and select auto gearbox 'N'.
2. As the vehicle reaches walking pace, move the transfer lever to the required 'H' or 'L' position. (Use positive and confident moves, but do not rush the gear change).
3. Finally, reselect appropriate gear with the main gear selector and continue driving as normal.

THE DIFFERENTIAL LOCK*

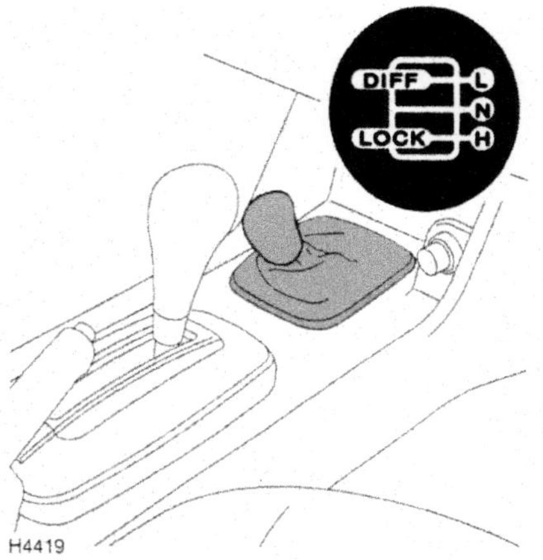

Unlike most other four-wheel-drive vehicles, all Land Rover products have permanent four-wheel drive.

Discovery is enhanced by the inclusion of an optional lockable differential (diff lock) between the front and rear drive shafts. With the differential locked, the drive shafts to front and rear axles are, in effect, joined together, causing both to rotate at the same speed.

This is a normal feature with all four-wheel-drive vehicles and enhances traction on difficult off-road surfaces. However, with the differential unlocked, the different running requirements of the two axles can be accommodated, thereby enabling Discovery to operate permanently in four-wheel drive for both normal AND off-road use.

WARNING

DO NOT engage the diff lock if one or more wheels are slipping - this could damage the transmission. If wheels are slipping, ease off the accelerator before engaging the diff lock.

Selecting diff lock

The diff lock can be engaged or disengaged either with the vehicle stationary, or when driving at any speed. However, with the vehicle in motion, it is ESSENTIAL to be travelling on firm ground, in a straight line, and without wheel slip.

To lock the differential

Move the transfer gear lever to the left - from either 'H' (high) or 'L' (low) gearbox (the warning light on the instrument panel will illuminate). If the vehicle is fitted with a manual gearbox, fully depress and then release the clutch as you select the diff lock, just as you would when changing gear normally.

To unlock the differential

Move the transfer gear lever to the right - to either 'H' (high) or 'L' (low) gearbox as required; when the diff lock disengages, the warning light will extinguish.

When to use the diff lock

As a general rule, the differential should be locked only in order to drive on loose or slippery off-road surfaces. ALWAYS unlock the differential for normal road driving or as soon as a surface giving good grip is reached whether high or low gears are selected.

WARNING

DO NOT drive the vehicle at speeds in excess of 40 mph (60 km/h) with the differential locked.Driving with the differential locked at speeds above 40 mph (60 km/h) may, under certain situations affect the brake performance under ABS conditions.

✱ Transfer Gearbox

NOTE: *A valuable introduction to off-road driving, which includes many useful references to the transfer gearbox and diff lock is included in the handbook section 'Off-road Driving'.*

WARNING

If the vehicle is driven on normal road surfaces with the differential locked, the steering will feel stiff, excessive tyre wear will occur and the transmission will be 'wound up' putting excessive strain on the transmission.

CRUISE CONTROL*

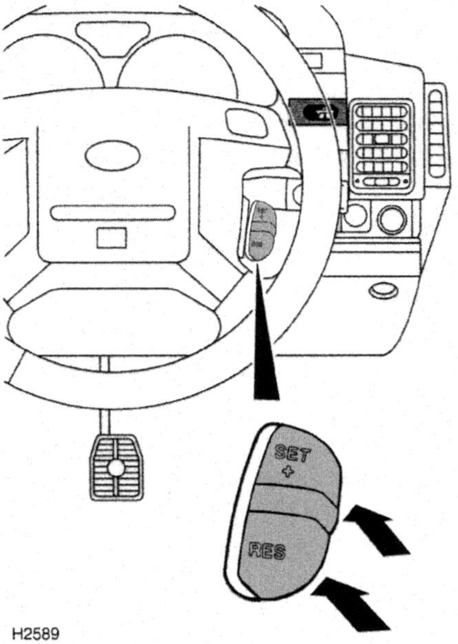

H2589

Cruise control enables the driver to maintain a constant road speed without using the accelerator pedal. This is particularly useful for motorway cruising or for any journey where a constant speed can be maintained for a lengthy period.

The cruise control system has three switches; a master switch on the right hand side of the instrument panel and two control switches marked 'SET +' and 'RES' mounted on the steering wheel.

WARNING

On petrol engine vehicles, DO NOT rest your foot under the accelerator pedal while cruise control is engaged - your foot could be trapped.

IMPORTANT INFORMATION

Always observe the following precautions:

- DO NOT use cruise control when using low range or reverse gears.
- DO NOT use cruise control on winding or slippery road surfaces, or in traffic conditions where a constant speed cannot easily be maintained.
- Use of 'sport' mode on automatic gearbox vehicles is not recommended when cruise control is selected.
- ALWAYS switch off the master switch when you no longer intend to use cruise control.

To operate

1. Press the master switch (the switch indicator light illuminates whenever the switch is pressed to the 'on' position).
2. Accelerate until the desired cruising speed is reached. This must be above the system's operational minimum speed of 28 mph (45 km/h).
3. Press the 'SET +' switch to set the vehicle speed in the system's memory. Cruise control will now maintain that road speed without the need for operation of the accelerator pedal.

With cruise control operating, speed can be increased for periods of up to 30 seconds, by normal use of the accelerator e.g. for overtaking. When the accelerator is released, road speed will return to the selected cruising speed.

NOTE: *If the 30 second period is exceeded, cruise control will automatically disengage. Press the 'RES' switch to re-engage.*

To reduce the cruising speed:
Press the 'RES' switch to slow the vehicle, until the required speed has been reached. Then press the 'SET +' switch to establish the new cruising speed (remember that cruise control will not operate at speeds below 28 mph (45 km/h).

To increase the set cruising speed:
Press and hold the 'SET +' switch - the vehicle will accelerate automatically. Release the switch as soon as the desired speed has been reached.

Alternatively, the set speed can be increased incrementally by 'tapping' the 'SET +' switch. Each press of the switch will increase the speed by 1 mph (1.5 km/h approx).

Disengaging cruise control
On manual gearbox vehicles, the cruise control will automatically disengage if the brake or clutch pedals are pressed. On automatic gearbox vehicles, cruise control will disengage when the gear selector is moved into neutral, or when the brake pedal is pressed. Cruise control can also be disengaged by pressing the 'RES' switch.

To re-engage cruise control at the previously set speed, press the 'RES' switch.

NOTE: *The speed held in the cruise control memory will be cancelled when either the cruise control master switch or the starter switch is turned off.*

FOOT BRAKE

For your safety, the hydraulic braking system operates through dual circuits. If one circuit should fail, the other will continue to function. However, in the event of brake failure where only one circuit is operational, the vehicle should only be driven at slow speed to the nearest qualified dealer. In these circumstances, exercise extreme caution and be aware that increased brake pedal travel, greater pedal pressure, and longer stopping distances will be experienced.

Servo assistance

The braking system is servo assisted, but ONLY when the engine is running. Without this assistance greater braking effort is necessary to safely control the vehicle, resulting in longer stopping distances. Always observe the following precautions:

- NEVER allow the vehicle to freewheel with the engine turned off.
- ALWAYS take particular care when being towed with the engine turned off.
- If the engine should stop for any reason while the vehicle is in motion, bring the vehicle to a halt as quickly as traffic conditions safely allow, and DO NOT pump the brake pedal as the braking system may lose any remaining assistance available.

Electronic brake force distribution

In addition, your vehicle is equipped with Electronic Brake Force Distribution (EBD), which balances the distribution of braking forces between front and rear axles, in order to maintain maximum braking efficiency under all load conditions.

For example; under light loads EBD applies less effort to the rear brakes to maintain vehicle stability, conversely reducing front braking effort when the vehicle is towing or is heavily laden.

Brake pads

Brake pads require a period of bedding in. For the first 500 miles (800 km), you should avoid situations where heavy braking is required.

Remember! regular servicing is vital to ensure that the brake pads are examined for wear and changed periodically to ensure long term safety and optimum performance.

WARNING

DO NOT rest your foot on the brake pedal while travelling as this may overheat the brakes, reduce their efficiency and cause excessive wear.

NEVER move a vehicle without the engine running because braking assistance will not be available. The pedal brakes will still function, but more pressure will be required to operate them.

If the brake warning light should illuminate while the vehicle is in motion, bring the vehicle to a halt as quickly as traffic conditions and safety permit and seek qualified assistance before continuing.
DO NOT pump the brake pedal - the braking system may lose any remaining servo assistance available.

Wet conditions

Driving through water or even very heavy rain may adversely affect braking efficiency. Always dry the braking surfaces by intermittent light application of the brakes, first ensuring that you are at a safe distance from other road users.

HANDBRAKE

Unlike most other vehicles, the handbrake operates on the rear propeller shaft, and NOT on the road wheels. This may result in slight movement of the vehicle after the handbrake is applied.

To engage the handbrake, pull the lever up fully.

To release, pull the lever up slightly, depress the button and lower the lever.

Always apply the handbrake fully whenever you park.

When parking on a slope, do not rely on the handbrake alone to hold the vehicle. On manual gearbox models, the vehicle should be parked in a low forward gear when facing uphill and in reverse gear when facing downhill. For extra security on steep slopes, move the transfer lever into low range.

On automatic gearbox models, particularly when low range is selected, ensure the parking pawl of the gearbox has fully engaged by carefully releasing the foot brake and allowing the vehicle to 'rock' into 'P' (park).

WARNING

DO NOT apply the handbrake while the vehicle is in motion as this could result in loss of vehicle control and damage to the transmission.

DO NOT rely on the handbrake to operate effectively if the vehicle has been subjected to immersion in mud and water (see 'Off-road driving' section).

ANTI-LOCK BRAKES

WARNING

ABS cannot overcome the physical limitations of stopping the vehicle in too short a distance, cornering at too high a speed, or the danger of aquaplaning, i.e. where a layer of water prevents adequate contact between the tyres and the road surface.

The fact that a vehicle is fitted with ABS must never tempt the driver into taking risks that could affect his/her safety or that of other road users. In all cases, it remains the driver's responsibility to drive within normal safety margins, having due consideration for prevailing weather and traffic conditions.

The driver should always take account of the surface to be travelled over and the fact that brake pedal reactions will be different to those experienced on a non-ABS vehicle.

The purpose of the anti-lock braking system (ABS) is to allow efficient braking without wheel locking - thereby allowing the driver to retain steering control of the vehicle.

Under normal braking conditions, (where sufficient road surface friction exists to reliably bring the vehicle to a halt without the wheels locking), ABS will not be activated. However, should the braking force exceed the available adhesion between the tyres and the road surface, then ABS will automatically come into operation. This will be recognisable by a rapid pulsation felt through the brake pedal.

In normal road use, in an emergency situation full braking effort should always be applied even when the road surface is slippery. The anti-lock braking system constantly monitors the speed of each wheel and varies braking pressure to each, according to the amount of traction available, thereby ensuring that the wheels do not lock.

No matter how hard you brake, you should be able to continue steering the vehicle as NORMAL.

- DO NOT pump the brake pedal at any time; this will interrupt operation of the system and may increase braking distance.
- DO NOT place non-approved floor mats or any other obstruction under the brake pedal. This restricts pedal travel and therefore impairs braking efficiency.

Warning light

The anti-lock braking system incorporates a monitoring system, which checks that all the electrical components are in working order, as soon as the starter switch is turned on and also at frequent intervals during your journey.

The warning light on the instrument panel is an important part of this system. The light should illuminate for approximately 3 seconds when the starter switch is turned to position 'II' and then extinguish.

If the light illuminates while driving, or remains illuminated for more than 3 seconds after the starter switch is turned on, a fault has been detected by the self monitoring system and full ABS control may not be available - consult your dealer at the earliest opportunity.

The normal braking system remains fully operational and is not affected by partial or full loss of the ABS. However, braking distances may increase.

Off-road driving

While anti-lock braking is designed to operate equally effectively in 'off-road' driving conditions, on certain surfaces total reliance on the system may be unwise - remember, in normal circumstances, anti-lock braking operates only AFTER the driver has already lost control. It cannot reliably compensate for driver error or inexperience on difficult off-road surfaces.

Note the following:

- On soft or deep surfaces such as powdery snow, sand or gravel, and on extremely rough ground, the braking distance required by the anti-lock braking system may be greater than for normal braking, even though improved steering would be experienced. This is because the natural action of locked wheels on soft surfaces is to build up a wedge of surface material in front which assists the wheels to stop.
- If the vehicle is stopped on a very steep slope where little traction is available, it may slide with the wheels locked because there is no wheel rotation to signal movement to the ABS. To counteract this, briefly release the brakes to permit some wheel movement, then re-apply the brakes to allow ABS to gain control.
- Before driving off-road read and thoroughly understand the *'Off-road driving'* section of this handbook.

ELECTRONIC TRACTION CONTROL

The purpose of electronic traction control is to aid traction when one or more wheels are spinning while others have good grip, e.g. if one wheel is on ice and others are on tarmac. The system works by applying the brake to a spinning wheel in order to transfer torque to the remaining wheels.

NOTE: *Traction control can operate up to speeds of 62 mph (100 km/h).*

Warning light

The instrument panel has a traction control warning (TC) which illuminates for a minimum of 2 seconds whenever the system is active and also illuminates as a bulb check (for approximately 3 seconds) when the starter switch is turned to position 'II'.

If there is a fault with the system, the warning light will illuminate continuously and remain illuminated when the vehicle is stopped, in which case you should contact your dealer at the earliest opportunity.

NOTE: *Faults with the ETC system will invariably cause the Hill Descent Control warning light to illuminate too. In most cases the ABS and brake system lights will also illuminate.*

HILL DESCENT CONTROL

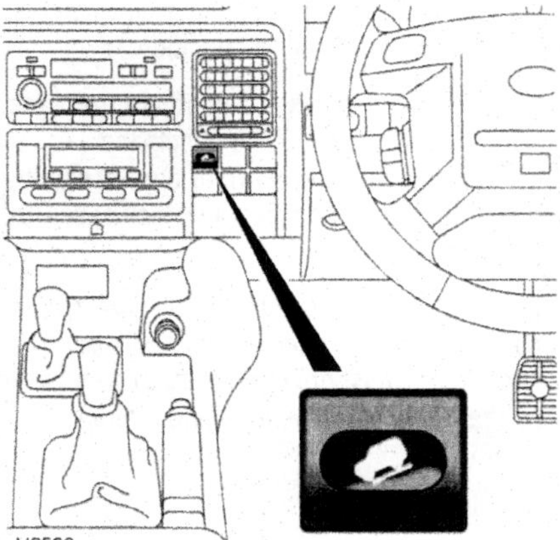
H2566

Hill Descent Control (HDC) operates in conjunction with the anti-lock braking system to provide greater control in off-road situations particularly when descending severe gradients.

To select HDC

HDC can be selected with the vehicle in any gear, but will only operate when low range gears are engaged with the vehicle travelling at less than 31 mph (50 km/h), and the clutch is engaged (manual gearbox vehicles).

Press the switch (illustrated above) to select HDC.

If low range gears are engaged, the HDC information light (GREEN) on the instrument panel will illuminate (if low range gears have NOT been selected, the light will flash).

To deselect HDC, press the switch a second time (the information light will extinguish and a single warning sound will chime).

Hill descent control in action

During a descent, if engine braking is insufficient to control the vehicle speed, HDC (if selected) automatically operates the brakes to slow the vehicle and maintain a speed relative to the selected gear and the accelerator pedal position.

When driving off-road, HDC can be permanently selected, to ensure that control is maintained whenever low range gears are engaged. ABS and traction control are still fully operational and will assist if the need arises.

NOTE: *With HDC selected, gear changes can be carried out in the normal way.*

If the brake pedal is depressed when HDC is active, HDC is overridden and the brakes will perform as normal (a pulsation might be felt through the brake pedal). If the brake pedal is then released, HDC will recommence operating if necessary.

If the clutch is depressed for longer than 3 seconds while HDC is operating, the HDC information light will flash. If, after 60 seconds the clutch is still depressed, the information light extinguishes and the HDC 'failure' warning light flashes as the system gradually fades out (see *'HDC fade-out', page 122*).

In extreme circumstances, the HDC system may cause brake temperatures to exceed their pre-set limits. If this occurs, the HDC 'failure' warning light (AMBER) will start to flash and the warning chime will sound continuously. During this time HDC will function as normal.

To avoid further cause for brake temperatures to rise, engage an appropriate low gear for steep descents and avoid descending hills at higher than the minimum descent speed. If the 'failure' warning light continues to flash, the HDC system will gradually fade out (see *'HDC fade-out', page 122*).

Hill Descent Control

HDC fade-out

HDC fade-out gradually decreases the HDC brake intervention with the effect that the rate of hill descent will increase. If this occurs the HDC information light will flash and the warning chime will sound for the period that HDC takes to fade. HDC will be disabled completely once the descent is complete.

If required (e.g. the angle of the descent levels out significantly), fade-out may be achieved deliberately by either:

- deselecting HDC while the system is operating.
- depressing the clutch for longer than 60 seconds.

If a fault with the HDC system is detected, or if the braking system reaches a pre-set temperature due to extreme conditions, HDC will automatically fade out.

Warning lights

HDC information light - GREEN
The light illuminates briefly as a bulb and system check when the starter switch is turned to position 'II' and also when HDC is selected.

If HDC is selected when the operating gears (LOW range) are engaged, the light will illuminate continuously.

If HDC has been selected but the system's operating criteria are not met (i.e. clutch pedal depressed, gearbox still in high range or vehicle speed too high), the information light will flash and the warning chime will sound continuously.

If the light flashes while HDC is active, normal functionality may cease and HDC 'fade out' may be induced.

HDC 'failure' light - AMBER
The light illuminates briefly as a bulb and system check when the starter switch is turned to position 'II'.

If the light illuminates at any other time, either a fault has occurred which affects the functionality of the system, or over-use of the system has been detected, in which case HDC may 'fade out'.

NOTE: *System faults which cause the 'failure' light to illuminate after the initial system checks, or whilst driving, will be accompanied by the warning chime sounding 3 times.*

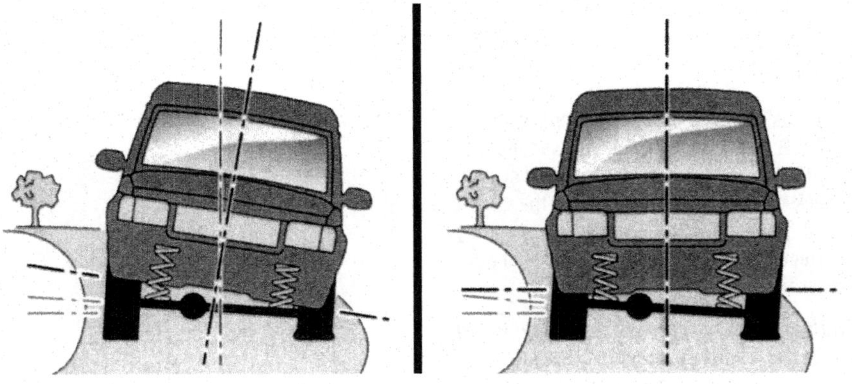

H2605

ACTIVE CORNERING ENHANCEMENT*

WARNING

If the warning light illuminates RED a system fault has occurred that may result in serious damage to vehicle components. Stop the vehicle and switch off the engine as soon as safety permits. Seek qualified assistance immediately.

Active Cornering Enhancement (ACE) is a patented feature unique to Land Rover. The system is designed to eliminate vehicle body roll at low cornering speeds and reduce body roll at higher cornering speeds, while maintaining a soft, car-like, suspension for straight line travelling. On uneven surfaces and rough tracks, the ACE system will adjust the suspension according to the vehicle speed and roughness of the surface to provide improved passenger comfort.

At very low speeds the roll bars are effectively decoupled, giving significant benefits in off-road axle articulation and improved traction.

The system is entirely automatic in operation and cannot be influenced by the driver in any way. However, the functionality of the ACE warning light in the instrument panel is very important and drivers should be aware of the following:

Warning light

The warning light illuminates RED when the starter switch is turned on (to position 'II'). After two seconds, the RED illumination changes to AMBER and, after a further two seconds, the light extinguishes. This process is a system check that takes place every time the vehicle is used. Provided the ACE system is operating correctly, illumination will not occur at any other time.

If illumination occurs while driving, a fault with the system is indicated, as follows:

- ***If the light shows RED*** *(a flashing red light, which changes to constant illumination after two minutes, and is accompanied by a warning chime):*
  This indicates a system fault that may result in serious damage to vehicle components and reduced ACE performance. You must stop the vehicle as soon as safety permits and switch off the engine. DO NOT CONTINUE DRIVING! Seek qualified assistance immediately.
- ***If the light shows AMBER*** *(constant illumination):*
  This indicates a system fault that will result in reduced ACE performance, but will not leave the vehicle in a dangerous condition. You may continue driving, but reduce speed, take additional care, and consult a Land Rover dealer at the earliest opportunity.

SELF-LEVELLING SUSPENSION*

When the engine is running, the self-levelling suspension system (SLS) operates automatically on the rear of the vehicle to maintain a level or efficient vehicle height regardless of vehicle load.

AUTOMATIC OPERATION

If the height of the vehicle is reduced by additional loading (passengers occupying the occasional rear seats or the attachment of a trailer, for example), the SLS system automatically increases air pressure to the springs to compensate for the additional weight or changed attitude of the vehicle. Similarly, if loads are removed and the vehicle height increases in consequence, the system will reduce air pressure to bring the vehicle back to a level attitude.

Extended mode

Off-road, if the vehicle becomes grounded and traction control is induced, the SLS system automatically pumps more air to the rear springs to raise the body clear of the obstruction, thereby enabling the vehicle to be freed. This is known as 'Extended mode' and will cause the off-road warning light to flash. Once forward motion is regained, the suspension height will automatically return to its previous setting and the warning light will extinguish.

MANUAL OPERATION

The SLS system can also be manually controlled to either:

- Raise the rear of the vehicle by 40 mm (approx.) to increase ground clearance and improve the departure angle for off-road driving. Note that this function operates ONLY below a speed of 18 mph (30 km/h) - above this speed, the vehicle will automatically return to its standard ride height.
- Lower the vehicle in order to ease loading, or to enable various heights of trailer hitch to be connected more easily. The SLS system will assume automatic control - adjusting the height of the vehicle 10 seconds after a road speed of 3 mph (5 km/h) is reached, or immediately once a road speed of 7 mph (12 km/h) has been achieved.

WARNING

DO NOT operate the off-road switch while driving on the road, or when the suspension has been manually lowered below standard ride height - any sudden or unexpected change to the vehicle's height or attitude could cause an inexperienced driver to lose control, or disturb the load/weight distribution within the vehicle.

DO NOT select off-road height while towing.

Self-levelling Suspension

To manually raise the suspension for off-road driving

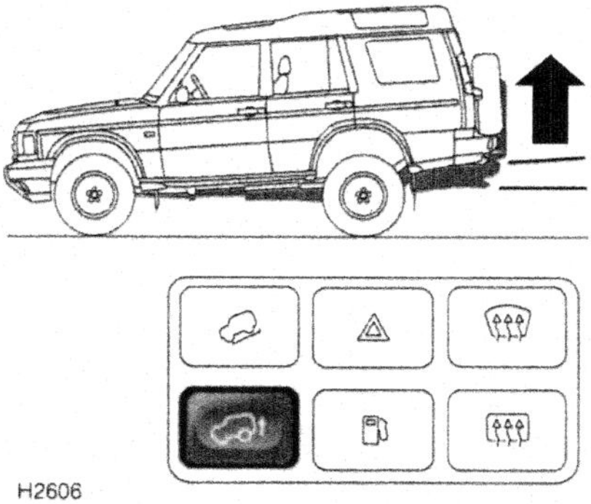

H2606

With the engine running and all doors fully closed, press the fascia-mounted off-road mode switch (see illustration). A single warning chime will sound, the off-road warning light on the instrument panel will commence flashing and the rear of the vehicle will start to rise. Once the pre-set off-road height has been reached, the warning light will stop flashing and illuminate constantly instead. Constant illumination will remain while the vehicle is operating at off-road height.

To return the vehicle to standard ride height, press the off-road mode switch a second time. Note that a single chime will sound and the warning light will flash while the rear suspension is lowered.

NOTE: *If axle displacement is excessive, selection of the off-road height setting may be prohibited. In this case three warning chimes will sound.*

NOTE: *If changes to or from off-road height are prohibited (e.g. door open) the chime will sound three times.*

To manually lower the suspension

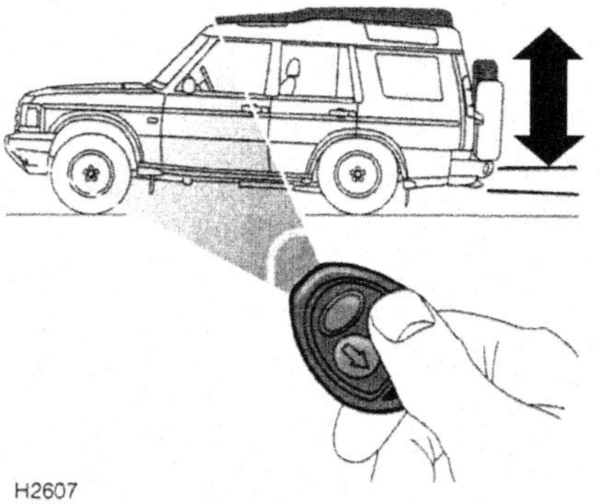

H2607

To lower the suspension you will need a remote suspension control (handset) - see illustration.

With the vehicle stationary at standard ride height, and the starter switch turned to position 'II', press and hold the 'DOWN' button to lower the vehicle. Release the button when the desired height has been reached. The SLS warning light on the instrument panel will flash and a warning chime will sound continually while the vehicle is lowering.

To return the vehicle to its standard ride height, press and hold the 'UP' button on the handset. Again the warning light flashes (and chime sounds) while the vehicle is rising. All suspension movement and warning light activity ceases once the vehicle has returned to standard ride height.

NOTE: *The SLS system will not operate while a door is open.*

NOTE: *At high altitude the system will take significantly longer to raise the vehicle.*

Self-levelling Suspension

NOTE: *If this feature is subjected to excessive use, the system will automatically disable to prevent components from overheating. The system has a cumulative total of three minutes operation at any one time. If this is exceeded the system will close down (partial operation will return after a few minutes).*

Remote SLS handset

The remote SLS handset is available as an accessory from a Land Rover dealer.

Battery replacement is similar to the equivalent process for the handset key (see *'REMOTE HANDSET BATTERY', page 20.* Battery specification is identical.

IMPORTANT INFORMATION
Note that the handset will operate effectively from inside the vehicle. It is therefore important to keep it out of reach of children at all times, and especially while towing. When operating the handset from inside the passenger compartment for the purpose of lowering the vehicle to attach a trailer, ensure that the underside of the vehicle has been checked for obstructions before lowering, and that a responsible adult has been posted outside the vehicle to supervise the lowering process.

WARNING LIGHTS

Off-road - AMBER

Illuminates briefly as a bulb and system check when the starter switch is turned to position 'II' and then extinguishes.

If the off-road switch is pressed:
The light flashes while the rear of the vehicle is either; rising to off-road height, or returning to standard ride height. The light then illuminates constantly while the suspension remains at off-road height.

In addition, the light will flash while Extended mode is induced.

Self-levelling suspension - AMBER

Illuminates briefly as a bulb and system check when the starter switch is turned to position 'II' and then extinguishes.

If the remote handset is operated:
The light flashes continually while the rear of the vehicle is being lowered, or raised.

If the light illuminates constantly:
A fault with the suspension is indicated. Seek qualified assistance as soon as possible.

While it is possible to continue driving the vehicle in this condition, there is a considerable risk of causing further damage to the suspension. Preferably, the vehicle should be brought to a halt as soon as conditions allow. Further travel should be limited to reaching the nearest Land Rover dealer, or driving to a place of safety while awaiting recovery. In any event, speed must be restricted to a rate that will guarantee a smooth, and totally bump-free, ride at all times, ideally traversing only smooth, metalled roads.

USING THE PARKING AID SYSTEM

WARNING

The parking aid is not infallible; it is for guidance only! The sensors may not be able to detect certain types of obstruction (narrow posts or small narrow objects, small objects close to the ground and some objects with dark, non-reflective surfaces, for example).

H4525

The parking system assists the driver when manoeuvring the vehicle into a parking space, or anywhere that there are obstacles that need to be avoided, warning the driver accordingly.

The vehicle is fitted with four ultrasonic sensors on its rear bumper.

The range of the two outer sensors is approximately 2ft (0.6 m); the two inner sensors have a range of approximately 6 ft 6 in. (2 m).

WARNING

Keep the sensors free from dirt, ice and snow. If deposits build up on the surface of the sensors, their performance may be impaired. When washing the vehicle, avoid aiming high pressure jets directly at the sensors from close range.

Activating Parking Aid

The Parking Aid is automatically activated whenever reverse gear ('R') is engaged. When the starter switch is turned on, the indicator light in the switch illuminates and a short tone sounds after one second as confirmation.

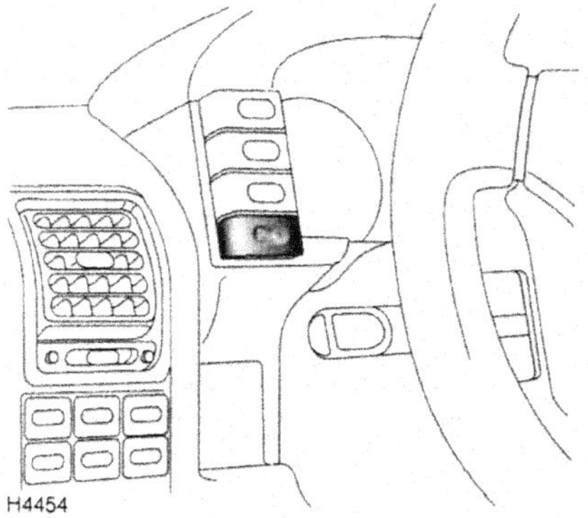

H4454

Parking Aid can also be manually selected by pressing the switch on the left-hand set of binnacle switches (the indicator light in the switch illuminates and a short tone sounds as confirmation). A second press of the switch de-activates the system.

If a long, high pitched tone sounds and the switch indicator light flashes when Parking Aid is activated, a fault in the system has been detected - contact your dealer for assistance.

Parking Aid in operation

The distance from an obstruction is identified by an intermittent tone sounding. As the vehicle moves closer to an obstruction, the frequency of the tone increases proportionally.

When the distance between the sensor and the obstruction is less than approximately 1 ft (0,4 m), the tone becomes continuous.

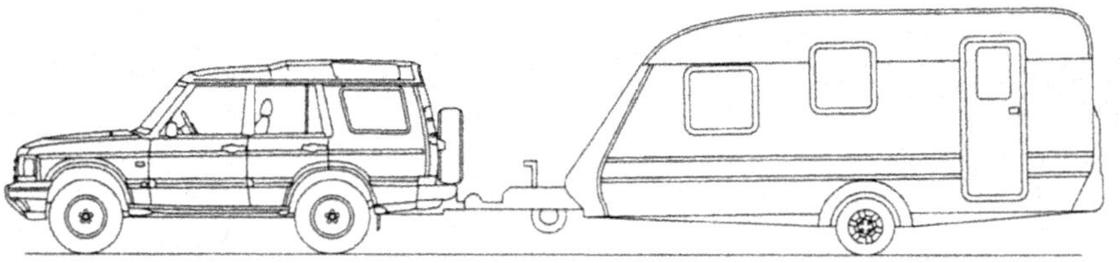

H3533

TOWING

The torque ranges of Land Rover engines allow maximum-weight loads to be pulled smoothly from standstill, and reduce gear changing on hills or rough terrain. A smooth start will be achieved with trailers over 4400 lb (2000 kg) by moving off in low range then changing to high range while on the move.

The suspension is designed to cope with a heavy trailer load without upsetting the balance or feel of the vehicle.

WARNING

It is recommended that you fit only towing accessories approved by Land Rover.

In the interest of safety, the gross vehicle weight, maximum rear axle weight, maximum trailer weight and tow hitch load (nose weight) must not be exceeded.

DO NOT use lashing eyes or vehicle recovery towing eyes to tow a trailer or caravan.

It is the driver's responsibility to ensure that the towing vehicle and trailer/caravan are loaded and balanced so that the combination is stable when in motion. When preparing your vehicle for towing, pay attention to any instructions provided by the trailer/caravan manufacturer as well as to the information that follows.

Balancing the combination

To ensure optimum stability, it is essential that the trailer adopts a level aspect. In other words, the trailer must be level with the ground, with the towing hitch and trailer drawbar set at the same height (note the illustration at the top of the page). This is particularly important when towing twin axle trailers!

- The trailer should be level with the ground when loaded.
- The height of the drawbar hitch point should be set so that the trailer is level when connected to the loaded vehicle (in the case of vehicles equipped with self-levelling suspension, the engine must be running, the doors closed and the suspension at standard ride height).

Points to remember:

- When calculating the laden weight of the trailer, remember to include the weight of the trailer PLUS the load.
- The recommended trailer nose weight plus the combined weight of the vehicle's load carrying area and rear seat passengers must never exceed the specified maximum rear axle load (see *'TOWING WEIGHTS', page 217*).
- Where the load can be divided between trailer and tow vehicle, loading more weight into the vehicle will generally improve the stability of the combination. However, ensure that the gross vehicle and maximum rear axle weights are not exceeded and that the combination remains level.
- Towing regulations vary from country to country. Always ensure national regulations governing towing weights and speed limits are observed (refer to the relevant national motoring organisation for information). The vehicle's maximum permissible towed weight refers to its design limitations and NOT to any specific territorial restriction (see *'TOWING WEIGHTS', page 217*).

NOTE: *The maximum speed when towing is 100 kph (62 mph).*

Automatic gearbox models

To avoid overheating the gearbox, it is not advisable to tow heavy trailer loads at speeds of less than 20 mph (32 km/h) using the main gearbox in high range. Use the transfer gearbox to select low range instead.

NOTE: *Above 1,000 feet (300 metres) the effects of altitude can adversely affect engine performance and also cause overheating.*

Vehicle weights

When loading a vehicle to its maximum (gross vehicle weight), take account of the unladen vehicle weight and load distribution to ensure that axle loadings do not exceed the permitted maximum values. It is your responsibility to limit the vehicle load in such a way that neither the maximum axle loads nor the gross vehicle weight are exceeded.

Trailer socket

When the engine is running, power output from the trailer socket must NOT exceed 5 amps.

ESSENTIAL TOWING CHECKS	
Tyre pressures:	Increase rear pressures of towing vehicle by at least 3 lbf/in (0.2 bar) up to maximum of 46 lbf/in (3.2 bar). Ensure trailer/caravan tyres are at recommended pressures.
Loading:	Keep trailer loads securely anchored, evenly distributed and as low as possible with heavy loads over the axle. Towing vehicle maximum axle weights and gross vehicle weight must not be exceeded.
Nose weight:	Must be minimum of 7% of gross caravan/trailer weight up to maximum of 551 lb (250 kg) - see vehicle/trailer/tow hitch chart in 'Technical Data'.
Hitch height:	Must be set so that caravan/trailer is level when connected to the tow vehicle with engine running.

LUGGAGE ANCHOR POINTS

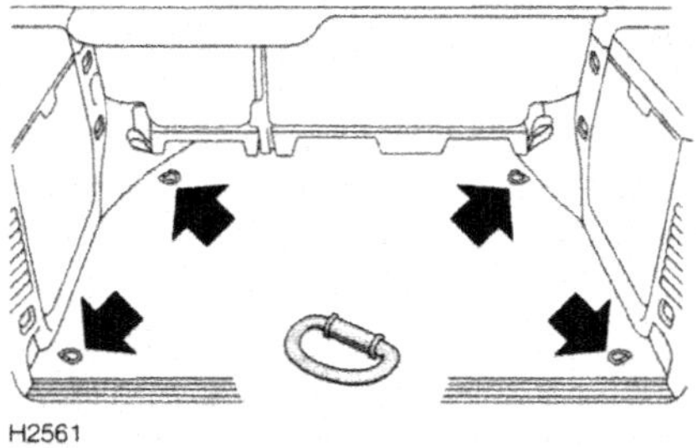
H2561

Four fixing points are provided in the rear luggage compartment floor to assist in safely securing large items of luggage.

WARNING

DO NOT carry unsecured equipment, tools or luggage which could move and cause personal injury in the event of an accident or emergency manoeuvre either on or off-road.

STORAGE BINS

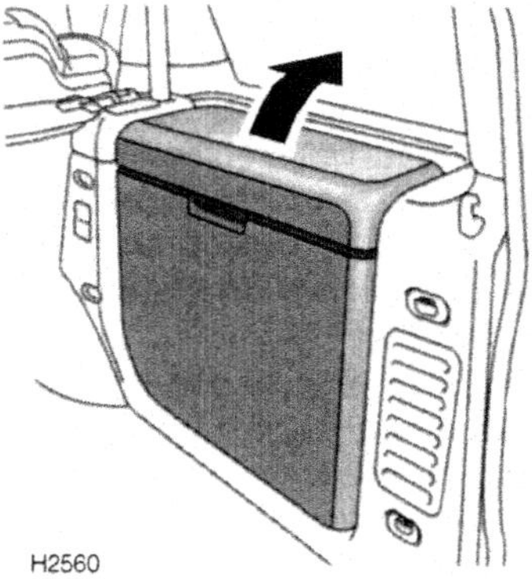
H2560

Some vehicles are equipped with storage bins on each side of the loadspace. Raise the lid to open.

ROOF RACKS

The roof rack system comprises two side rails permanently fixed to the roof of the vehicle and cross bars available as an accessory from a Land Rover dealer.

IMPORTANT INFORMATION
Always observe the following precautions: • The **MAXIMUM** load for approved roof rack systems is 110 lb (50 kg) for normal road use and 66 lb (30 kg) off-road. • A loaded roof rack can reduce the stability of the vehicle, particularly when cornering and encountering cross winds. • All loads should be evenly distributed, and secured within the periphery of the roof rack system. • Only fit roof racks that have been designed for your vehicle. If in doubt, consult your dealer. • Driving off-road with a loaded roof rack is not recommended. If it is necessary to stow luggage on the roof rack while driving off-road, all loads must be removed before traversing side slopes.

Off-road Driving

BEFORE YOU DRIVE

Before venturing off-road, it is **absolutely essential** that inexperienced driver's become fully familiar with the vehicle's controls, in particular the transfer gearbox, and also study the off-road driving techniques described on this and the following pages.

WARNING

Off-road driving can be hazardous!

- ***DO NOT take unnecessary risks and be prepared for emergencies at all times.***
- ***Familiarise yourself with the recommended driving techniques in order to minimise risks to yourself, your vehicle AND your passengers.***

IMPORTANT INFORMATION
• Always wear a seat belt for personal protection in all off-road driving situations. • DO NOT drive if the fuel level is low - undulating ground and steep inclines could cause fuel starvation to the engine and consequent damage to the catalytic converter. • As a precaution against accidental loss, remove the towing eye cover from the front spoiler before driving off-road (see *'TOWING EYES', page 186*).

BASIC OFF-ROAD TECHNIQUES

These basic driving techniques are an introduction to the art of off-road driving and do not necessarily provide the information needed to successfully cope with every single off-road situation.

We strongly recommend that owners who intend to drive off-road frequently, should seek as much additional information and practical experience as possible.

Before driving off-road it is important that you check the condition of the wheels and tyres and that the tyre pressures are correct. Worn or incorrectly inflated tyres will adversely affect the performance, stability and safety of the vehicle.

Gear selection - manual gearbox

Correct gear selection is possibly the single most important factor for safe and successful off-road driving. While only experience will tell you which is the correct gear for any section of ground, the following basic rules apply:

- NEVER change gear or operate the clutch while negotiating difficult terrain - the drag on the wheels may cause the vehicle to stop when the clutch is depressed and restarting may be difficult.
- Generally, and especially where slippery or soft ground conditions prevail, the higher the gear you select the better.
- When descending very steep slopes always select first gear in LOW range and Hill Descent Control (HDC).

Inexperienced drivers are advised to stop the vehicle (on firm ground) and carefully consider which gear will be most appropriate for each manoeuvre before continuing.

Slipping the clutch
Use of excessive clutch slip to prevent the engine stalling will result in premature clutch wear. Always select a gear low enough to enable the vehicle to proceed without needing to slip the clutch.

DO NOT drive with your foot resting on the clutch pedal; driving across uneven terrain could cause you to inadvertently depress the clutch, resulting in loss of control of the vehicle.

Gear selection - automatic gearbox
On automatic models, with the main selector lever set at 'D', the gearbox automatically provides the correct gear for the appropriate gear range selected (HIGH or LOW). Remember that position '1' will hold the gearbox in first gear to give maximum engine braking when required.

HIGH range gears should be used whenever possible - only change to LOW range when ground conditions become very difficult.

✱

The diff lock* should be engaged whenever there is a risk of losing wheel grip, and disengaged as soon as firm, level, non-slippery ground is reached. (See *'THE DIFFERENTIAL LOCK*', page* 114c).

'Manual' mode
Press the mode switch whilst the automatic gearbox is in Low range to select 'Manual' mode; this enables the transmission to function as a manual gearbox locking the gearbox into whichever gear position has been selected ('D' = 4th gear), providing maximum vehicle control and engine braking - ideal for use in severe off-road conditions.

NOTE: *Changing from Low to High range will automatically cancel 'Manual' mode.*

Braking
As far as possible, vehicle speed should be controlled through correct gear selection and the use of Hill Descent Control (HDC). Application of the brake pedal should be kept to a minimum. In fact, if the correct gear and HDC have been selected, braking will be largely unnecessary.

If the brake pedal is depressed when HDC is active, HDC is overridden and the brakes will perform as normal. If the brake pedal is then released, HDC will recommence operating, if necessary,

Use of engine for braking
Before descending steep slopes, stop the vehicle at least its length before the descent, engage LOW range and then select first or second gear ('1' or '2' for automatic transmission) depending on the severity of the incline.

While descending the slope it should be remembered that the engine will provide sufficient braking effort to control the rate of descent, and that the brakes should not be applied.

Accelerating
Use the accelerator with care - any sudden surge of power may induce wheel spin and, therefore, invoke unnecessary operation of traction control, or in extreme conditions could lead to loss of control of the vehicle.

Steering

H2543

WARNING

DO NOT hold the steering wheel with your thumbs inside the rim - a sudden 'Kick' of the wheel as the vehicle negotiates a rut or boulder could seriously injure them. ALWAYS grip the wheel on the outside of the rim (as shown) when traversing uneven ground.

Survey the ground before driving

Before negotiating difficult terrain, it is wise to carry out a preliminary survey on foot. This will minimise the risk of your vehicle getting into difficulty through a previously unnoticed hazard.

Ground clearance

Don't forget to allow for ground clearance beneath the chassis, axles and under the front and rear bumpers. Note that the axle differentials are situated BELOW the chassis and are positioned slightly to the right of the centre of the vehicle. Note also that there are other parts of the vehicle which may come into contact with the ground - take care not to ground the vehicle.

Ground clearance is particularly important at the bottom of steep slopes, or where wheel ruts are unusually deep and where sudden changes in the slope of the ground are experienced.

On soft ground the axle differentials will clear their own path in all but the most difficult conditions. However, on frozen, rocky or hard ground, hard contact between the differentials and the ground will generally result in the vehicle coming to a sudden stop.

ALWAYS attempt to avoid obstacles that may foul the chassis or axle differentials.

Self-levelling suspension

On vehicles equipped with self-levelling suspension, the rear suspension can be raised to increase departure angles and ground clearance at the rear of the vehicle (see *'SELF-LEVELLING SUSPENSION*', page 125*).

Loss of traction

If the vehicle is immobilised due to loss of wheel grip, the following hints could be of value:

- Avoid prolonged wheel spin; this will only make matters worse.
- Remove obstacles rather than forcing the vehicle to cross them.
- Clear clogged tyre treads.
- Reverse as far as possible, then attempt an increased speed approach - additional momentum may overcome the obstacle.
- Brushwood, sacking or any similar material placed in front of the tyres may improve tyre grip.

CD Autochanger

Playing CDs while negotiating arduous off-road terrain is not recommended. Severe jolting of the vehicle may disturb the operation of the autochanger, causing the disc to 'jump' or 'skip'.

AFTER DRIVING OFF-ROAD

IMPORTANT INFORMATION
Before rejoining the public highway, or driving at speeds above 25 mph (40 km/h), consideration should be given to the following: ✱ De-select differential lock if required. • Wheels and tyres must be cleaned of mud and inspected for damage. • If wheels and tyres are not cleaned properly, damage to the wheels, tyres, braking system and suspension components could occur. • Brake discs and callipers should be examined and any stones or grit that may affect braking efficiency removed.

SERVICING REQUIREMENTS

Vehicles operated in arduous conditions, particularly on dusty, muddy or wet terrain, and vehicles undergoing frequent or deep wading conditions will require more frequent servicing. See *'OWNER MAINTENANCE', page 148* and contact a Land Rover dealer for advice.

After wading in salt water or driving on sandy beaches, use a hose to wash the underbody components and any exposed body panels with fresh water. This will help to protect the vehicle's cosmetic appearance.

DRIVING ON SOFT SURFACES & DRY SAND

The ideal technique for driving on soft surfaces (dry sand for example) requires the vehicle to be kept moving at all times - soft sand causes excessive drag on the wheels resulting in a rapid loss of motion once driving momentum is lost. For this reason, gear changing (particularly on manual gearbox vehicles) should be avoided.

✱ Engage the diff lock*.

- Select the highest suitable gear and REMAIN in that gear until a firm surface is reached. It is generally advisable to use LOW range gears, as they will enable you to accelerate through worsening conditions without the risk of being unable to restart.

✱ Disengage the diff lock*.

Stopping the vehicle on soft ground, in sand or on an incline

If you do stop the vehicle, remember:

Starting on an incline or in soft ground or sand may be difficult. Always park on a firm level area, or with the vehicle facing downhill.

To avoid wheel spin, select second or third gear, ('D' for automatic gearbox), and use the MINIMUM throttle necessary to get the vehicle moving.

If forward motion is lost, avoid excessive use of the throttle - this will cause wheel spin and tend to dig the vehicle into the sand. Clear sand from around the tyres and ensure that the chassis and axles are not bearing on the sand before again attempting to move.

If the wheels have sunk, use an air bag lifting device or high lift jack to raise the vehicle, and then build up sand under the wheels so that the vehicle is again on level ground. If a restart is still not possible, place sand mats or ladders beneath the wheels.

DRIVING ON SLIPPERY SURFACES (ice, snow, mud, wet grass)

✱ Engage the diff lock*.

- Select the highest gear possible.
- Drive away using the MINIMUM throttle possible.
- Drive slowly at all times, keeping braking to a minimum and avoiding violent movements of the steering wheel.

✱ Disengage the diff lock* as soon as firm ground is reached.

DRIVING ON ROUGH TRACKS

Although rough tracks can sometimes be negotiated in normal drive, it is advisable to engage diff lock* if excessive suspension movement is likely to induce wheel spin. On very rough tracks, engage LOW range to enable a steady, low speed to be maintained without constant use of the brake and clutch pedals.

WARNING

DO NOT drive the vehicle at speeds in excess of 40 mph (60 km/h) with the differential locked.Driving with the differential locked at speeds above 40 mph (60 km/h) may, under certain situations affect the brake performance under ABS conditions.

CLIMBING STEEP SLOPES

ALWAYS follow the fall line of the slope - travelling diagonally could encourage the vehicle to slide broadside down the slope.

Steep climbs will usually require the LOW gear range. If the surface is loose or slippery, use sufficient speed in the highest practical gear to take advantage of your vehicle's momentum. However, too high a speed over a bumpy surface may result in a wheel lifting, causing the vehicle to lose traction. In this case try a slower approach. Traction can also be improved by easing off the accelerator just before loss of forward motion.

If the vehicle is unable to complete a climb, do not attempt to turn it around while on the slope. Instead, adopt the following procedure to reverse downhill to the foot of the slope.

1. Hold the vehicle stationary using both foot and hand brakes.
2. Restart the engine if necessary.
3. Engage reverse gear LOW range ('R' for automatic transmission).
4. Select hill descent control (HDC).
5. Release the handbrake. Then release the foot brake and clutch (where applicable) simultaneously, and allow the vehicle to reverse down the slope using engine braking and HDC to control the rate of descent.
6. Unless it is necessary to stop the vehicle to negotiate obstructions, DO NOT apply the brake or clutch pedal during the descent - even a light application may cause the front wheels to lock, rendering the steering ineffective.
7. If the vehicle begins to slide, accelerate slightly to allow the tyres to regain grip.

When the vehicle is back on level ground or where traction can be regained, a faster approach will probably enable the hill to be climbed. However, DO NOT take unnecessary risks, if the hill is too difficult to climb, find an alternative route.

WARNING

DO NOT attempt to reverse down a slope without the engine running, or HDC and the braking effect of the gearbox will be lost.

DESCENDING STEEP SLOPES

H2521

WARNING

Failure to follow these instructions may cause the vehicle to roll over.

- Stop the vehicle at least a vehicle length before the start of the slope and engage first gear ('1', for automatic transmission) LOW range and hill descent control.
- Unless it is necessary to stop the vehicle in order to negotiate obstructions, **DO NOT** touch the brake or clutch pedals during the descent - the engine and HDC will limit the speed, keeping the vehicle under perfect control provided the front wheels are rotating. If the vehicle begins to slide, the limits of adhesion have been reached, and it may be impossible to maintain the minimum speed relative to the gear selected. In this case, HDC may automatically accelerate the vehicle sufficient to maintain directional stability. DO NOT use the accelerator or the brakes or attempt to change gear. HDC will automatically slow the vehicle down again as soon as possible.
- Once level ground is reached, select a suitable gear for the next stage of your journey.

TRAVERSING A SLOPE

H2531

WARNING

Failure to follow these instructions may cause the vehicle to roll over.

Before crossing a slope ALWAYS observe the following precautions:

- Check that the ground is firm and not slippery.
- Check that the wheels on the downhill side of the vehicle are not likely to drop into depressions in the ground and that the 'uphill' wheels will not run over rocks, tree roots, or similar obstacles that could suddenly increase the angle of tilt.
- Ensure that passenger weight is evenly distributed, that all roof rack luggage is removed and that all other luggage is properly secured and stowed as low as possible. Always remember; any sudden movement of the load could cause the vehicle to overturn.
- Rear seat passengers should sit on the uphill side of the vehicle or, in extreme conditions, should vacate the vehicle until the sloping ground has been safely negotiated.

NEGOTIATING A 'V' SHAPED GULLY

Observe extreme caution! Steering up either of the gully walls could cause the side of the vehicle to be trapped against the opposite gully wall.

DRIVING IN EXISTING WHEEL TRACKS

As far as possible allow the vehicle to steer itself along the bottom of the ruts. However, always keep a light hold of the steering wheel to prevent it from spinning free.

Particularly in wet conditions, if the steering wheel is allowed to spin free, the vehicle may appear to be driving straight ahead in the ruts, but in actual fact (due to the lack of traction caused by the wet ground) is unknowingly on full right or left lock. Then, when level ground is reached, or if a dry patch of ground is encountered, the wheels will find traction and cause the vehicle to suddenly veer to left or right.

CROSSING A RIDGE

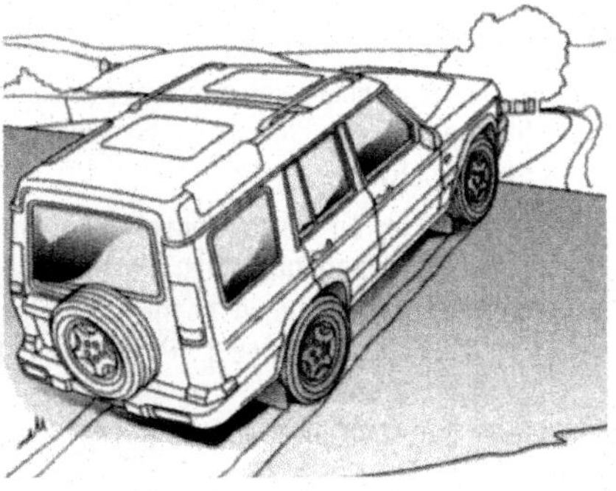

H2532

Approach at right angles so that both front wheels cross the ridge together - an angled approach could cause traction to be lost through diagonally opposite wheels lifting from the ground at the same time.

*

CROSSING A DITCH

H4435

CROSSING A DITCH

H2530

Cross ditches at an angle so that three wheels always maintain contact with the ground. If a ditch is approached head on, both front wheels will drop into the ditch together, possibly resulting in the chassis and front bumper being trapped on opposite sides of the ditch. On vehicles equipped with self-levelling suspension, and if the severity of terrain makes this inevitable, manually operating the self-levelling suspension to increase clearance between the ground and the rear of the vehicle may help.

With the diff lock* engaged, cross ditches at an angle so that three wheels always maintain contact with the ground. If a ditch is approached head on, both front wheels will drop into the ditch together, possibly resulting in the chassis and front bumper being trapped on opposite sides of the ditch. On vehicles equipped with self-levelling suspension, and if the severity of terrain makes this inevitable, manually operating the self-levelling suspension to increase clearance between the ground and the rear of the vehicle may help.

WADING

WARNING

The maximum advisable wading depth is 20 inches (0,5 m).

Severe electrical damage may occur if the vehicle remains stationary for any length of time when the water level is above the door sills.

If the water is likely to exceed 20 inches (0,5 m), the following precautions should be observed:

- Fix a plastic sheet in front of the radiator grille to prevent water from soaking the engine and mud from blocking the radiator.
- Remove the CD autochanger*.
- Ensure that the silt bed beneath the water is free of obstacles and firm enough to support the vehicle's weight and provide sufficient traction.
- Ensure that the engine air intake is clear of the water level.
- ✱ Engage the diff lock*.
- Select a low gear and maintain sufficient throttle to prevent the engine from stalling. This is particularly important if the exhaust pipe is under water.
- Drive slowly into the water and accelerate to a speed which causes a bow wave to form; then maintain that speed.

At all times, keep all the doors fully closed.

After wading

- ✱ Disengage the diff lock* as soon as firm ground is reached.
- Drive the vehicle a short distance and apply the foot brake to check that the brakes are fully effective.
- DO NOT rely on the handbrake to hold the vehicle stationary until the transmission has thoroughly dried out; in the meantime, leave the vehicle parked in gear ('P' for automatic gearbox vehicles).
- Remove any protective covering from in front of the radiator grille.
- If the water was particularly muddy, remove any blockages (mud and leaves) from the radiator to reduce the risk of overheating.
- If deep water is regularly negotiated, check all oils for signs of water contamination - contaminated oil can be identified through its 'milky' appearance. In addition, check the air filter element for water ingress and replace if wet - consult a Land Rover dealer if necessary.
- If salt water is frequently negotiated, thoroughly wash the underbody components and exposed body panels with fresh water.

NOTE: *Vehicles required to undergo frequent or deep wading conditions will require more frequent servicing. Contact a Land Rover dealer for advice.*

Owner Maintenance

Owner Maintenance

ROUTINE MAINTENANCE

Regular systematic maintenance is the key to ensuring the continued reliability and efficiency of your vehicle.

Maintenance is the owner's responsibility and you must ensure that owner maintenance operations, oil services, inspections and brake fluid and coolant changes are carried out when required and according to the manufacturer's recommendations.

The routine maintenance requirements for your vehicle are shown in the Service Portfolio book. Most of this necessary workshop maintenance requires specialised knowledge and equipment, and should preferably be entrusted to a Land Rover dealer.

Service Portfolio

The Service Portfolio book includes a Service Record section, which enables a record to be kept of all the oil services and inspections that are carried out on the vehicle. This section of the book also provides a facility for the dealer to record brake fluid and camshaft drive belt changes, as well as the fitting of replacement airbag modules.

Ensure your dealer signs and stamps the book after each oil service and inspection.

Brake fluid/component replacement

Brake fluid must be completely renewed every 24,000 miles (40,000 km) or 24 months, whichever is the sooner.

At 72,000 mile (120,000 km) intervals or every 6 years, whichever is the sooner, all hydraulic brake fluid, seals and flexible hoses should be renewed. All working surfaces of the calliper cylinders should be examined and the components renewed where necessary. Under arduous operating conditions, these intervals may need to be reduced. Please consult your Land Rover dealer.

Coolant replacement

The engine coolant (anti-freeze and water solution) needs to be replaced every 36,000 miles (60,000 km) or 36 months, whichever is the sooner. Your dealer will replace the coolant at the scheduled oil service.

OWNER MAINTENANCE

In addition to the routine services and inspections referred to previously, a number of simple checks must be carried out more frequently. You can carry out these checks yourself and advice is given on the pages that follow.

Any significant or sudden drop in fluid levels, or uneven tyre wear, should be reported to a dealer without delay.

Daily checks

- Operation of lights, horn, direction indicators, wipers, washers and warning lights.
- Operation of seat belts and brakes.
- Look for fluid deposits underneath the vehicle that might indicate a leak.

Weekly checks

- Engine oil level.

  NOTE: *The engine oil level should be checked more frequently if the vehicle is driven for prolonged periods at high speeds.*
- Coolant level.
- Brake fluid level.
- Power steering fluid level.
- Screen washer fluid level.
- Tyre pressures and condition.
- Operate air conditioning*.
- Active cornering enhancement fluid level.

All fluid specifications and capacities are shown in *'LUBRICANTS AND FLUIDS', page 207.*

IMPORTANT INFORMATION
Special operation conditions When a vehicle is operated in extremely arduous conditions or a dusty, wet or muddy terrain, more frequent attention must be paid to servicing requirements. For example: if your vehicle experiences deep wading conditions, even DAILY servicing could be necessary to ensure the continued safe and reliable operation of the vehicle. Contact a Land Rover dealer for advice.

SAFETY IN THE GARAGE

WARNING

Cooling fans may continue to operate after the engine is switched off. When the engine is hot, the cooling fans may also COMMENCE operating after the engine is switched off and continue operating for up to 10 minutes. Keep clear of all fans while working in the engine compartment.

If you need to carry out maintenance, observe the following safety precautions at all times:

- ***Keep your hands and clothing away from drive belts and pulleys.***
- ***If the vehicle has been driven recently, DO NOT TOUCH exhaust and cooling system components until the engine has cooled.***
- ***DO NOT TOUCH electrical leads or components while the engine is running, or with the starter switch turned on.***
- ***NEVER leave the engine running in an unventilated area - exhaust gases are poisonous and extremely dangerous.***
- ***DO NOT work beneath the vehicle with the wheel changing jack as the only means of support.***
- ***Ensure sparks and naked lights are kept away from the engine compartment.***
- ***Wear protective clothing, including, where practicable, gloves made from an impervious material.***
- ***Remove metal wrist bands and jewellery before working in the engine compartment.***
- ***DO NOT allow tools or metal parts of the vehicle to make contact with the battery leads or terminals.***

WARNING

Under no circumstances should any part of the fuel system be dismantled or replaced by anyone other than a suitably qualified motor vehicle technician. Failure to comply with this instruction may result in fuel spillage with a consequent serious risk of fire.

Poisonous fluids

Fluids used in motor vehicles are poisonous and should not be consumed or brought into contact with open wounds. These include; battery acid, anti-freeze, brake and power steering fluid, petrol, diesel, engine oil and windscreen washer additives.

For your own safety, ALWAYS read and obey all instructions printed on labels and containers.

Used engine oil

Prolonged contact with engine oil may cause serious skin disorders, including dermatitis and cancer of the skin. ALWAYS wash thoroughly after contact.

It is illegal to pollute drains, water courses or soil. Use authorised waste disposal sites to dispose of used oil and toxic chemicals.

EMISSION CONTROL

Your vehicle is fitted with various items of emission and evaporative control equipment designed to meet specific territorial requirements. You should be aware that unauthorised replacement, modification or tampering with this equipment by an owner or repair shop may be unlawful and subject to legal penalties.

In addition, engine settings must not be tampered with. These have been established to ensure that your vehicle complies with stringent exhaust emission regulations. Incorrect engine settings may adversely affect exhaust emissions, engine performance and fuel consumption, as well as causing high temperatures, which will result in damage to the catalytic converter and the vehicle.

ROAD TESTING DYNAMOMETERS ('rolling roads')

Because your vehicle is equipped with anti-lock brakes and permanent four-wheel drive, it is essential that any dynamometer testing is carried out ONLY by a qualified person familiar with the dynamometer testing and safety procedures practiced by Land Rover dealers. Contact your Land Rover dealer for further information.

BONNET OPENING

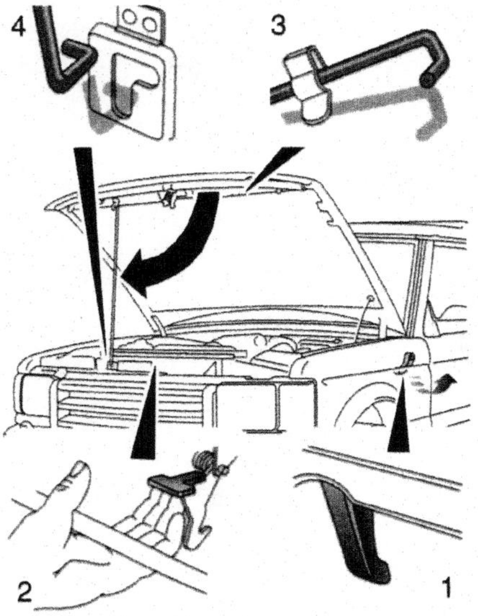

H2525

1. From inside the vehicle on the left hand side, pull the bonnet release handle (see illustration).
2. Lift the bonnet safety catch lever and raise the bonnet.
3. Release the bonnet support stay from the underside of the bonnet.
4. Fit the support stay into the slotted hole in the bonnet locking platform.

Closing the bonnet

WARNING

DO NOT drive with the bonnet retained by the safety catch alone.

Replace the support stay in its retaining clip, then lower the bonnet, allowing it to drop for the last 12 inches (30 cm) approx.

After closing the bonnet, check that the lock is fully engaged by attempting to lift the front edge of the bonnet. This should be free from all movement.

DIESEL ENGINE

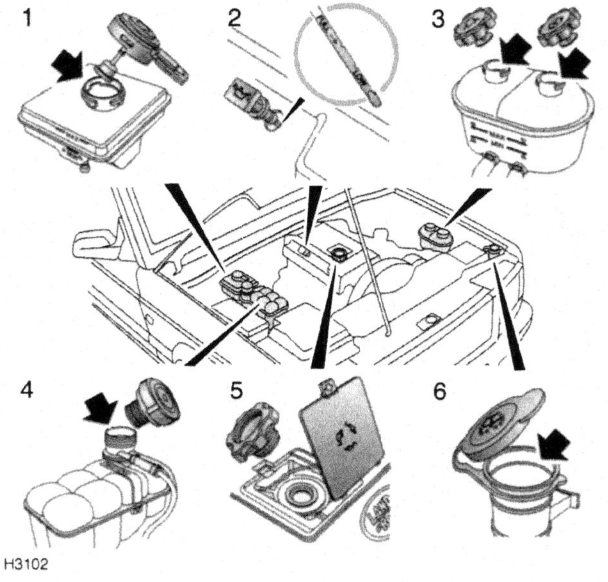

1. Brake fluid reservoir.
2. Engine oil dipstick.
3. Power steering and active cornering enhancement*.
4. Cooling system reservoir.
5. Engine oil filler cap.
6. Washer reservoir.

WARNING

While working in the engine compartment, ALWAYS observe the safety precautions listed under 'Safety in the garage' on a previous page.

*

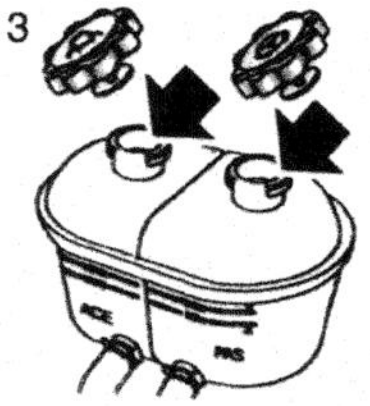

PETROL ENGINE

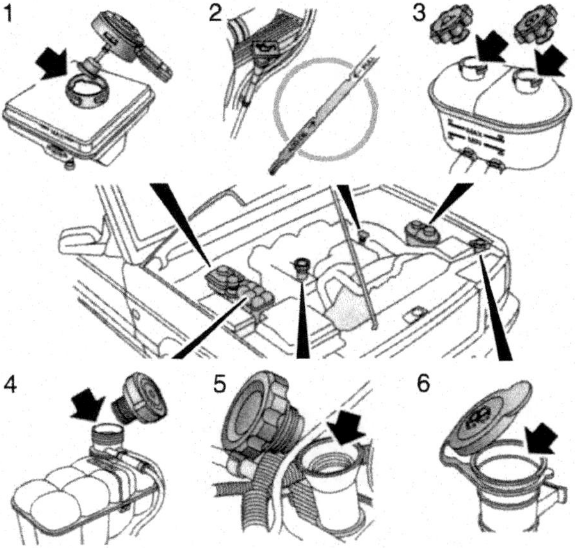

H3103

1. Brake fluid reservoir.
2. Engine oil dipstick.
3. Power steering and active cornering enhancement*.
4. Cooling system reservoir.
5. Engine oil filler cap.
6. Washer reservoir.

WARNING

While working in the engine compartment, ALWAYS observe the safety precautions listed under 'Safety in the garage' on a previous page.

*

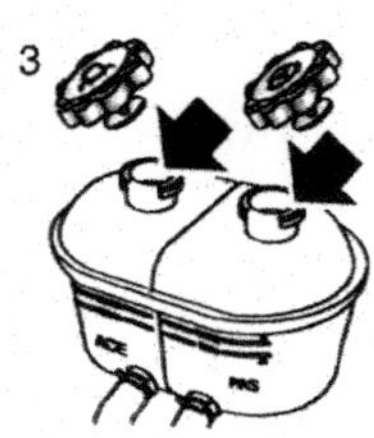

CHECK & TOP-UP

Check the oil level at least every 250 miles (400 km) when the engine is COLD and with the vehicle resting on level ground.

NOTE: *If it is necessary to check the oil level when the engine is hot, switch off the engine and let the vehicle stand for five minutes to allow the oil to drain back into the sump. DO NOT start the engine.*

As a general guide, if the level on the dipstick:

- is nearer to the upper mark than the lower, add no oil.
- is nearer to the lower mark than the upper, add half a litre of oil.
- is below the lower mark, add one litre of oil and re-check the level after a further five minutes.

Oil specification

It is essential to use an oil suitable for the climatic conditions in which the vehicle is to be operated. Precise specifications are shown in *'LUBRICANTS AND FLUIDS', page 207*. If in doubt, contact your Land Rover dealer.

Diesel engine vehicles

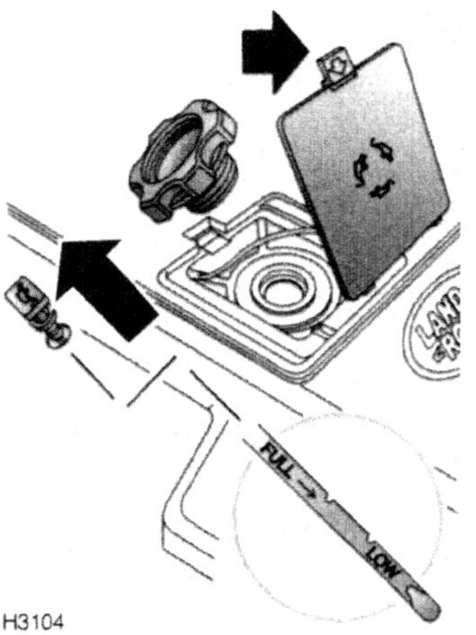

H3104

1. Withdraw the dipstick and wipe the blade clean.
2. Fully re-insert the dipstick and withdraw again to check the level, which should NEVER be allowed to fall below the lower mark on the dipstick.
3. Lift the release tab (arrowed) and remove the access flap.
4. To top-up, unscrew the oil filler cap and add oil to maintain the level between the UPPER and LOWER marks on the dipstick.

   DO NOT OVERFILL!

Petrol engine vehicles

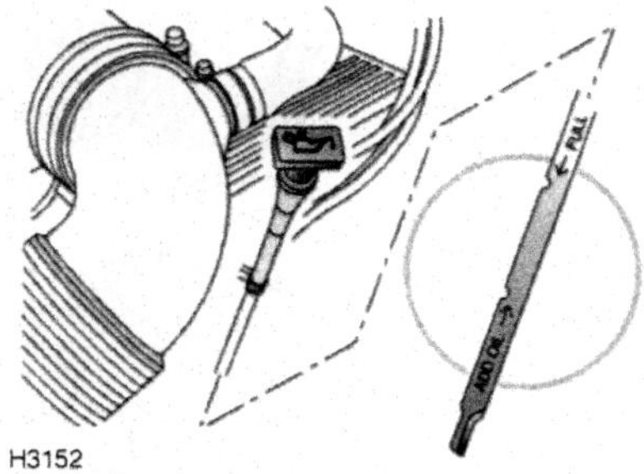

H3152

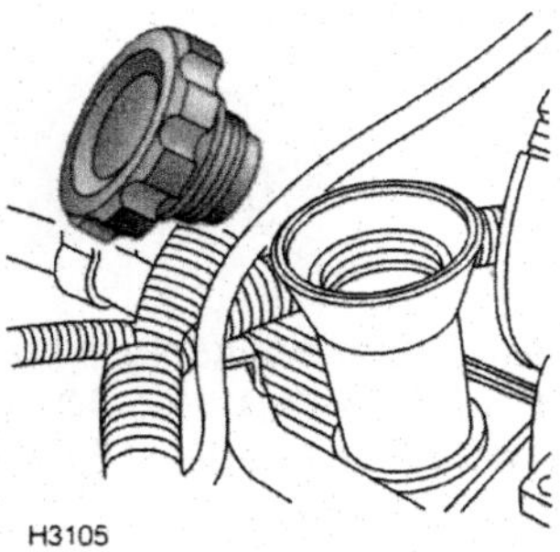
H3105

1. Withdraw the dipstick and wipe the blade clean.
2. Fully re-insert the dipstick and withdraw again to check the level, which should NEVER be allowed to fall below the lower mark on the dipstick.
3. To top-up, unscrew the oil filler cap and add oil to maintain the level between the UPPER and LOWER marks on the dipstick.

   DO NOT OVERFILL!

COOLANT CHECK AND TOP-UP

WARNING

NEVER remove the filler cap when the engine is hot -escaping steam or scalding water could cause serious personal injury.

Unscrew the filler cap slowly, allowing the pressure to escape before removing completely.

NEVER run the engine without coolant.

Anti-freeze will damage painted surfaces; soak up any spillage with an absorbent cloth immediately and wash the area with a mixture of car shampoo and water.

NEVER top-up with salt water. When travelling in territories where the water supply contains salt, always ensure you carry a supply of fresh (rain or distilled) water.

Avoid spilling anti-freeze onto a hot engine - a fire may result.

The coolant level in the expansion tank should be checked at least weekly (more frequently in high mileage or arduous operating conditions). Always check the level WHEN THE SYSTEM IS COLD.

If it is necessary to remove the filler cap before the system has fully cooled, loosen the cap slowly, allowing the air pressure to escape gradually.

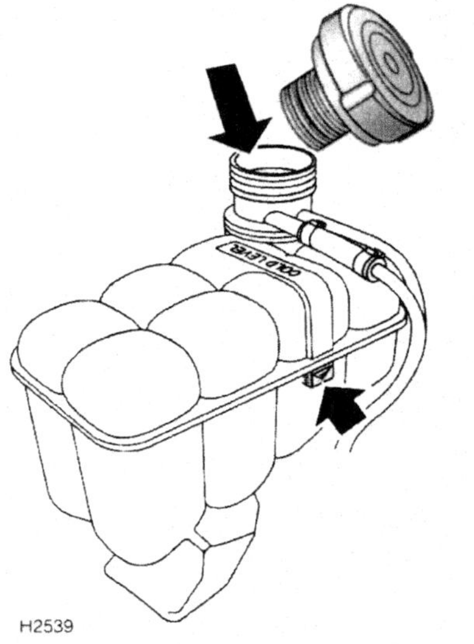

H2539

Top-up with a 50% mixture of anti-freeze and water so that the surface of the coolant is level with the indicator on the side of the tank (arrowed in illustration).

Ensure the cap is tightened fully after top-up is completed.

If the level has fallen appreciably, suspect leakage or overheating and arrange for your dealer to examine the vehicle. **DO NOT OVERFILL!**

ANTI-FREEZE

WARNING

Anti-freeze is poisonous and can be fatal if swallowed - keep containers sealed and out of the reach of children. If accidental consumption is suspected, seek medical attention immediately.

Prevent anti-freeze coming in contact with the skin or eyes. If this occurs, rinse immediately with plenty of water.

Anti-freeze contains important corrosion inhibitors. The anti-freeze content of the coolant must be maintained at 50% ± 5% all year round (not just in cold conditions). To ensure that the anti-corrosion properties of the coolant are retained, the anti-freeze content should be checked once a year and completely renewed every 36,000 miles (60,000 km) or 36 months, whichever is the sooner. Failure to do so may cause corrosion of the radiator and engine components.

The specific gravity of a 50% anti-freeze solution at 20°C (68°F) is 1.075 and protects against frost down to -36°C (-33°F).

Coolant specification
Use ONLY a 50% mix of water and Havoline Extended Life Coolant (XLC) or any ethylene glycol based anti-freeze (containing no methanol) with only Organic Acid Technology (OAT) corrosion inhibitors.

In an emergency - and only if this type of anti-freeze is unavailable - top-up the cooling system with clean water, but be aware of the resultant reduction in frost protection. DO NOT top-up or refill with conventional anti-freeze formulations. If in doubt consult a Land Rover dealer.

BRAKE FLUID

WARNING

Brake fluid is highly toxic - keep containers sealed and out of the reach of children. If accidental consumption of fluid is suspected, seek medical attention immediately.

If brake fluid should come into contact with the skin or eyes, rinse immediately with plenty of water.

Take care not to spill fluid onto a hot engine - a fire may result.

DO NOT drive the vehicle with the fluid level below the 'MIN' mark.

Brake fluid will damage painted surfaces; soak up any spillage with an absorbent cloth immediately and wash the area with a mixture of car shampoo and water.

Check

The fluid level may fall slightly during normal use as a result of brake pad wear but should not be allowed to fall below the 'MIN' mark. Any substantial drop in fluid indicates a leak in the system, in which case the vehicle must NOT be driven and you should contact your dealer.

WARNING

Contact your dealer immediately if brake pedal travel is unusually long or if there is any appreciable drop in brake fluid level.

With the vehicle on level ground, check the fluid level at least every week (more frequently in high mileage or arduous operating conditions). Check the level visually through the side of the transparent reservoir without removing the filler cap.

Top-up

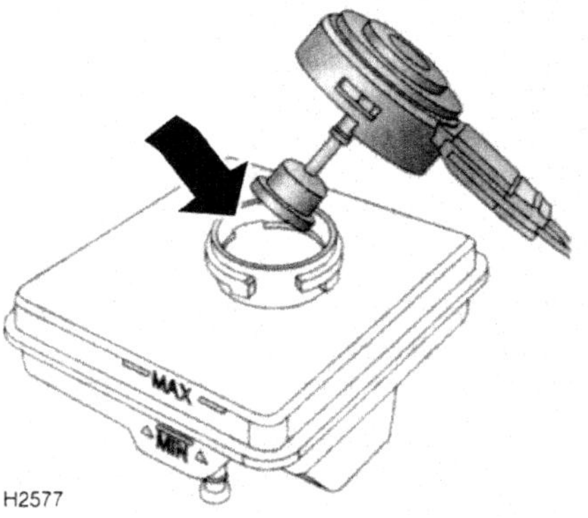

H2577

Wipe the filler cap clean before removing to prevent dirt from entering the reservoir. Unscrew the cap (1/8 turn) and top-up the reservoir to the 'MAX' mark using Shell Donax YB brake fluid conforming to DOT 4 specification.

Use only new fluid from an airtight container (old fluid from opened containers or fluid previously bled from the system will have absorbed moisture, which will adversely affect performance, and must NOT be used). **DO NOT OVERFILL!**

Brake fluid must be completely renewed every 24,000 miles (40,000 km) or 24 months, whichever is the sooner.

NOTE: *The brake fluid reservoir also supplies fluid to operate the hydraulic clutch.*

POWER STEERING FLUID

WARNING

Power steering fluid is highly toxic - keep containers sealed and out of reach of children. If accidental consumption of fluid is suspected, seek medical attention immediately.

If power steering fluid should come into contact with the skin or eyes, rinse immediately with plenty of water.

Do not spill power steering fluid onto a hot engine - a fire may result.

Power steering fluid will damage painted surfaces: Soak up any spillage with an absorbent cloth immediately and wash the area with a mixture of car shampoo and water.

Emergency operation

Any large or sudden drop in the fluid level must be investigated by a qualified dealer.

If it can be established that fluid loss is slow, then the reservoir may be topped-up to the upper level mark to enable the vehicle to be driven to the nearest qualified dealer for examination.

If the fluid level has dropped below the lower level mark, top-up the reservoir before starting the engine, or damage to the steering pump could result.

Check and Top-up

Check and top-up the fluid level ONLY with the engine switched off and the system cold, and ensure that the steering wheel is not turned after stopping the engine.

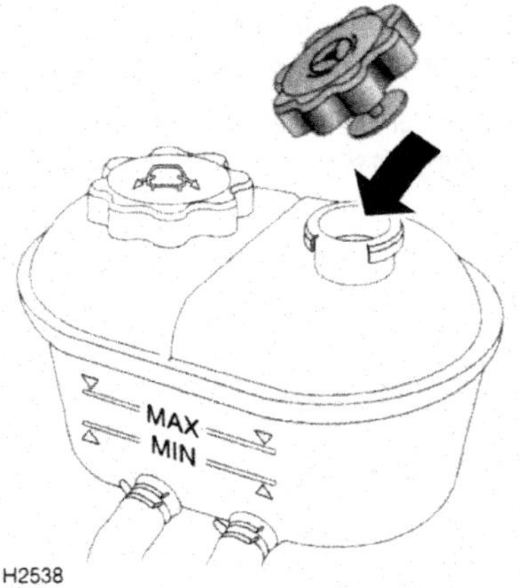

H2538

Check the fluid level against the level marks on the side of the reservoir. If more fluid is needed, first wipe the filler cap clean to prevent dirt from entering the reservoir, then twist the cap a quarter turn anti-clockwise and pull to remove. Top up the reservoir until the fluid reaches the upper level mark. **DO NOT OVERFILL!**

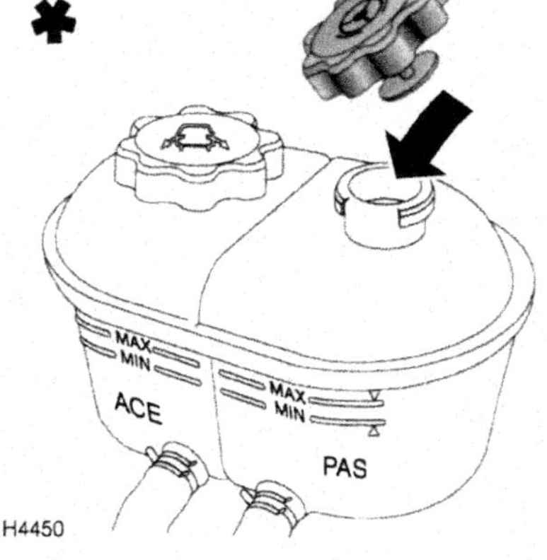

H4450

ACTIVE CORNERING ENHANCEMENT FLUID

WARNING

Fluid is highly toxic - keep containers sealed and out of reach of children. If accidental consumption of fluid is suspected, seek medical attention immediately.

If fluid should come into contact with the skin or eyes, rinse immediately with plenty of water.

Do not spill fluid onto a hot engine - a fire may result.

Fluid will damage painted surfaces: Soak up any spillage with an absorbent cloth immediately and wash the area with a mixture of car shampoo and water.

*

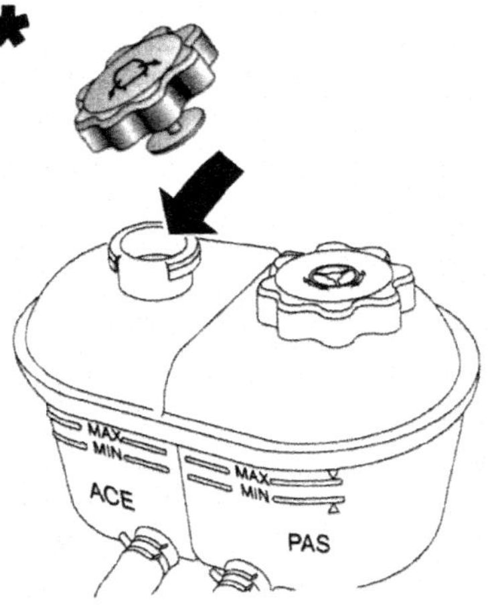

Check and Top-up

Check the fluid level against the level marks on the side of the reservoir. If more fluid is needed, first wipe the filler cap clean to prevent dirt from entering the reservoir, then twist the cap a quarter turn anti-clockwise and pull to remove. Top up the reservoir until the fluid reaches the upper level mark. **DO NOT OVERFILL!**

Any large or sudden drop in the fluid level must be investigated by a qualified dealer.

NOTE: *While the power steering and active cornering enhancement systems share the same fluid specification and reservoir, both systems are entirely independent of each other. The reservoir is divided into two compartments and each system has its own filler cap.*

WINDSCREEN WASHER TOP-UP

H2541

The windscreen washer reservoir supplies both front and rear screen washer jets and headlight washer jets*.

Check the reservoir level at least every week and top-up with a mixture of water and Land Rover Parts STC 8249 Screenwash. Preferably mix the recommended quantities of water and screenwash in a separate container before topping-up, and always follow the instructions on the container. Note that an approved screenwash is necessary to prevent freezing in very cold weather.

Operate the washer switches periodically to check that the nozzles are clear and properly directed.

WARNING

DO NOT use an anti-freeze or vinegar/water solution in the washer reservoir - anti-freeze will damage painted surfaces, while vinegar can damage the windscreen washer pump.

Some screenwash products are inflammable, particularly if high or undiluted concentrations are exposed to sparking. DO NOT allow screenwash to come into contact with naked flames or sources of ignition.

Body panels may suffer discolouration as a result of screenwash spillage. Take care to avoid spillage, particularly if an undiluted or high concentration is being used. If spillage occurs, wash the affected area immediately with water.

WASHER JETS

The windscreen washer jets are set during manufacture and should not need adjusting. However, if adjustment is ever necessary, insert a needle into the jet orifice and lever gently to position each jet so that the spray is directed towards the centre of the windscreen.

The rear screen jets located in the wiper arm are not adjustable.

Should any jet become obstructed, insert a needle or thin strand of wire into the orifice to clear the blockage.

HEADLIGHT WASHERS*

The spray jets are set during manufacture and should not need to be adjusted.

NOTE: *Ensure an approved screen washer solvent is used in the windscreen washer reservoir to prevent freezing.*

WIPER BLADE REPLACEMENT

Front wiper blades

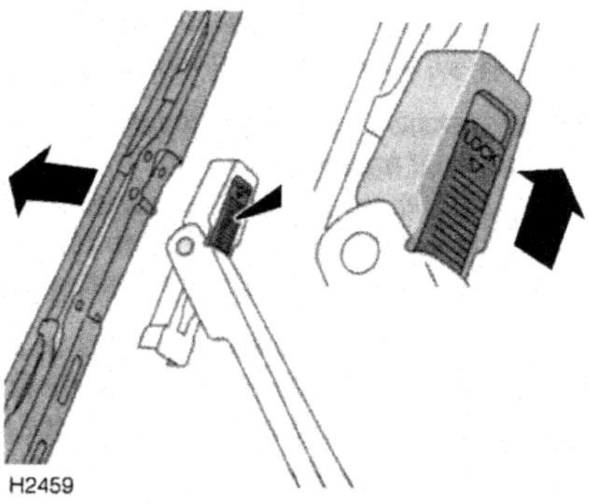

H2459

Lift the wiper arm away from the windscreen. Disconnect the blade by pushing the locking tab (see inset in illustration) to the unlock position.

Fitting a replacement blade is a reversal of this process. Check that the blade is securely locked before returning the wiper assembly to the windscreen.

Only fit replacement wiper blades that are identical to the original specification.

Grease, silicone and petrol based products impair the blade's wiping capability. Wash the wiper blades in warm soapy water and periodically check their condition.

If signs of hardness or cracking in the rubber are found, or if the wipers leave streaks or unwiped areas on the windscreen during use, then the wiper blades should be replaced.

Clean the windscreen regularly with an approved glass cleaner and ensure the screen is thoroughly cleaned before fitting replacement wiper blades.

Rear wiper blade

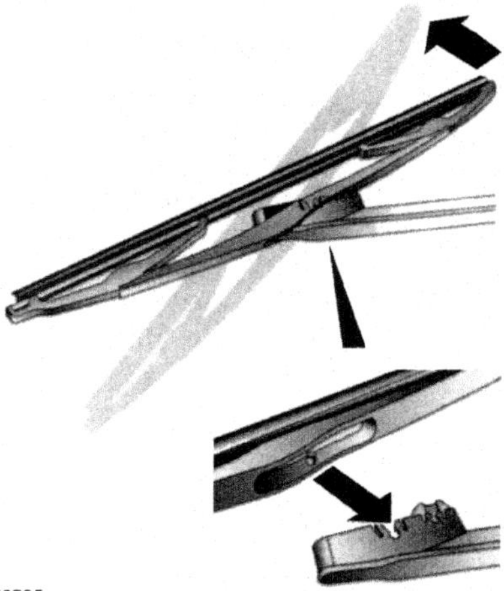

H2595

With the spare wheel removed from the taildoor, lift the wiper arm away from the rear screen. Pivot the blade assembly away from the arm (as arrowed), levering against resistance, until the two retaining lugs detach from their slots at the end of the arm. Carefully replace the arm to its stowed position.

To replace, position the wiper arm into the aperture in the middle of the blade assembly, line up the retaining lugs with the corresponding slots in the wiper arm and push firmly into position until the blade clips into place.

BATTERY SAFETY

WARNING

Batteries contain acid, which is both corrosive and poisonous. If spillage occurs:

- ***On clothing or the skin - remove any contaminated clothing immediately, flush the skin with large amounts of water, and seek medical attention urgently.***
- ***In the eyes - flush with clean water immediately for at least 15 minutes. Seek medical attention urgently.***

Swallowing battery acid can be fatal unless IMMEDIATE action is taken - seek medical attention urgently.

During normal operation batteries emit explosive hydrogen gas - ensure sparks and naked lights are kept away from the engine compartment.

For your safety, remove all metal wrist bands and jewellery before working in the engine compartment and NEVER allow the battery terminals or vehicle leads to make contact with tools or metal parts of the vehicle.

BATTERY MAINTENANCE

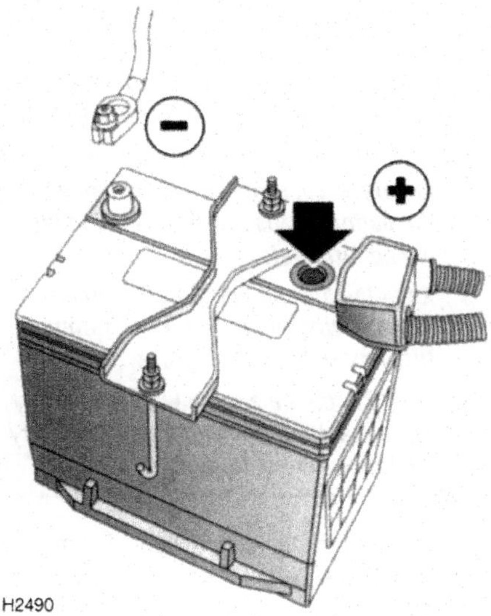

H2490

The battery is designed to be maintenance free, so topping-up is unnecessary. On the top of the battery there is a battery condition indicator (arrowed in illustration). Examine the indicator periodically to check the battery's condition. When the indicator shows:

- GREEN - the battery is in a good state of charge.
- DARK (turning to black) - the battery needs charging.
- CLEAR (or light yellow) - the battery must be replaced. Do not charge the battery or jump start the vehicle in this condition.

NOTE: *When checking the battery condition indicator, if necessary, clean the battery top to ensure a clear view.*

If the indicator shows clear or yellow, tap the indicator with the handle of a screwdriver to disperse any air bubbles. If the colour is unchanged, the battery must be replaced.

Battery removal and replacement

WARNING

- ***ALWAYS remove the starter key before disconnecting the battery. Failure to do this may cause a failure of the airbag SRS.***
- ***Do not reverse the polarity of the battery - the electrical system may be damaged if the battery leads are connected to the wrong terminals.***
- ***Keep the battery upright at all times - damage will be caused if the battery is tilted more than 45 degrees.***
- ***DO NOT run the engine with the battery disconnected, or disconnect the battery while the engine is running.***

Before disconnecting the battery, disarm the alarm, and ensure that the starter switch and all electrical equipment is turned off.

To remove: disconnect the negative ('-') cable first and then the positive ('+') cable. When reconnecting, connect the positive cable first and then the negative cable. Do not allow the battery terminals to make contact with metal parts of the vehicle.

To release the battery from the vehicle, undo the nuts securing the battery clamping plate and remove the clamping plate.

When replacing, ensure the battery is fitted the right way round (terminal posts towards the rear of the vehicle) and that the clamping plate is secure. Tighten the clamping plate nuts until the clamping plate is free from movement, but do not overtighten.

Replacement batteries

Only fit a replacement battery of the same type and specification as the original - other batteries may vary in size or have different terminal positions which could cause a fire hazard when connected to the vehicle's electrical system.

Battery disposal

Used batteries should be recycled. However, batteries are hazardous - you should seek advice about disposal from a Land Rover dealer or your local authority.

Battery charging

Batteries generate explosive gases, contain corrosive acid and produce levels of electric current sufficient to cause serious injury. While charging always heed the following precautions:

- Before charging, disconnect and remove the battery from the vehicle - charging the battery with the cables connected may damage the vehicle's electrical system.
- Make sure the battery charger leads are securely clamped to the battery terminals BEFORE switching on the battery charger. Do not move the leads once the charger is switched on.
- While charging, shield your eyes or avoid leaning over the battery and keep the area around the top of the battery well ventilated.
- Do not allow naked lights near the battery (batteries generate inflammable hydrogen during and after charging).
- The battery will be charged sufficiently once the battery condition indicator shows GREEN. When charging is finished, switch off the battery charger BEFORE disconnecting the leads from the battery terminals.

  NOTE: *Be aware that a battery will take longer to charge in a cold environment.*

After charging, leave the battery for an hour BEFORE reconnection to the vehicle - this will allow time for explosive gases to disperse, thereby minimising the risk of fire or explosion.

WARNING

DO NOT charge the battery if it is connected to the vehicle - this may seriously damage the electrical system.

DO NOT attempt to charge the battery if the battery condition indicator is clear or light yellow.

DO NOT charge the battery if it is suspected of being frozen.

CARING FOR YOUR TYRES

WARNING

DEFECTIVE TYRES ARE DANGEROUS! Do not drive if any tyre is damaged, is excessively worn, or is inflated to an incorrect pressure.

Always drive with consideration for the condition of the tyres, and regularly inspect the tread and side walls for any sign of distortion (bulges), cuts or wear.

The most common causes of tyre failure are:

- Bumping against kerbs
- Driving over deep potholes in the road
- Driving with under or over-inflated tyres

NOTE: *If possible, protect tyres from contamination by oil, grease, fuel and other automotive fluids.*

Tyre pressures

Correctly inflated tyres will ensure that you enjoy the best combination of tyre life, ride comfort, fuel economy and road handling.

Under-inflated tyres wear more rapidly, can seriously affect the vehicle's road handling characteristics and fuel consumption, as well as increasing the risk of tyre failure. Over-inflated tyres give a harsher ride, wear unevenly and are more prone to damage.

Tyre pressures should be checked at least once a week with normal road use, but should be checked DAILY if the vehicle is used off-road.

Check the pressures (including the spare wheel) when the tyres are cold - be aware that it only takes a mile (1.6 km) of driving to warm up the tyres sufficiently to affect the tyre pressures.

Air pressure naturally increases in warm tyres; if it is necessary to check the tyres when they are warm (after the vehicle has been driven for a while), you should expect the pressures to have increased between 4 and 6 lbf/in^2. In this circumstance, NEVER let air out of the tyres in order to match the recommended pressures.

WARNING

If the vehicle has been parked in strong sunlight or used in high ambient temperatures, DO NOT reduce tyre pressures; instead, move the vehicle into the shade and allow the tyres to cool before checking.

The recommended pressures for cold tyres are shown in *'WHEELS & TYRES', page 213.*

Tyre wear

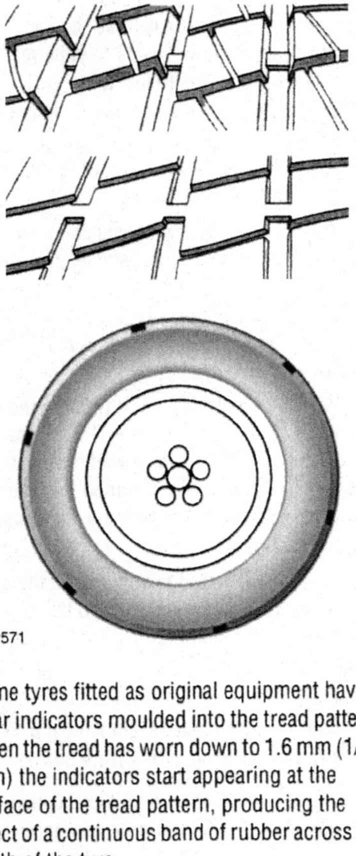

H2571

Some tyres fitted as original equipment have wear indicators moulded into the tread pattern. When the tread has worn down to 1.6 mm (1/16 inch) the indicators start appearing at the surface of the tread pattern, producing the effect of a continuous band of rubber across the width of the tyre.

A tyre MUST be replaced as soon as an indicator band becomes visible or the tread depth reaches the minimum permitted by legislation.

Tread depth must be checked regularly (at every maintenance service, or more frequently). Always replace a tyre before the tread reaches a remaining depth of 1.6 mm. DO NOT drive with tyres worn to this limit, the safety of the vehicle and occupants will be adversely affected.

NOTE: *After off-road use, check to make sure there are no lumps or bulges in the tyres or exposure of the ply or cord structure.*

Valves

Keep the valve caps screwed down firmly - they prevent dirt from entering the valve. Check the valve for leaks (listen for a tell-tale hissing) when you check the tyre pressure.

Punctured tyres

Your vehicle is fitted with tubeless tyres, which may not leak if penetrated by a sharp object, provided the object remains in the tyre. If you are aware of this occurring, reduce speed immediately and drive with caution until the spare wheel can be fitted.

A puncture of this kind will eventually cause the tyre to lose pressure, which is why regular (and frequent) checking of tyre pressures is important. Punctured or damaged tyres must be permanently repaired or replaced as soon as possible - if in doubt, seek expert advice. DO NOT DRIVE WITH A PUNCTURED TYRE!

Replacement tyres

Wheel rims and tyres are matched to suit the handling characteristics of the vehicle. For safety, ALWAYS check that replacement tyres comply with the original specification (see *'WHEELS & TYRES', page 213*) and that the load and speed ratings shown on the side wall are the same as that of the original equipment. Contact your Land Rover dealer for further information or assistance.

WARNING

ALWAYS use the same make and type of radial-ply tyres front and rear. DO NOT use cross-ply tyres, or interchange tyres from front to rear.

Your vehicle is fitted with road wheels that will NOT accept inner tubes. DO NOT fit a tubed tyre.

DO NOT replace wheels with any type other than genuine Land Rover parts. Wheels and tyres are designed for both off-road and on-road use and have a very important influence on vehicle handling. Alternative wheels which do not meet original equipment specifications should not be fitted.

Always have replacement wheels and tyres balanced before use.

SNOW CHAINS

Snow chains are designed for use on metalled roads in extreme conditions only, and are not recommended for off-road use. If it is necessary to fit snow chains to your vehicle, ALWAYS observe the following:

- ***Front wheels:*** Snow chains must not be fitted to the front wheels unless the vehicle is equipped with 215/75 R16 Pirelli Scorpion S/T 107T tyres.
- ***Rear wheels:*** Snow chains can be fitted to the rear wheels of any vehicle, provided the wheels and tyres conform to one of the original equipment specifications listed in the handbook (see *'WHEELS & TYRES', page 213*).
- Whether chains are to be fitted to the front wheels only, or to all four wheels, then ONLY Land Rover approved chains should be used - these are designed for your vehicle and will eliminate any risk of damage to other components.
- Always adhere to the snow chain fitting and retensioning instructions and the speed limitations recommended for varying road conditions. NEVER exceed 30 mph (50 km/h).
- Avoid tyre damage by removing the chains a soon as the road is free from snow.

For further information about approved snow chains, consult your Land Rover dealer.

WARNING

DO NOT fit unapproved snow chains to the front wheels - this could damage brake components.

WASHING YOUR VEHICLE

H2575

WARNING

Some high pressure cleaning systems are sufficiently powerful to penetrate door and window seals and damage rubbing strips and locking mechanisms. Never aim the water jet directly at heater air intakes, body and sunroof seals, or at any components that might easily be damaged.

WARNING

Read individual product warnings before using any car cleaning or washing products.

Wash your vehicle frequently using a sponge and generous quantities of cold or lukewarm water containing a car shampoo. Rinse and dry off with a chamois leather.

- Do not use hot water!
- Do not use detergent soap products or washing-up liquid!
- In hot weather, do not wash the vehicle in direct sunlight.

Underbody maintenance

Corrosive materials used for snow and ice removal and dust control can collect on underbody parts. If these materials are not removed, accelerated rusting can occur. Use a hose to regularly flush the underbody with plain water, taking particular care to thoroughly clean those areas where mud and other debris can easily collect.

Similarly, after off-road driving or wading in muddy or salt water conditions, use a hose to wash underbody components and other exposed parts of the vehicle.

When using a hose, do not direct the jet into the heater air intake ducts, or through the wheel trim apertures onto the brake components, or at the door, window or sunroof seals, where water pressure could penetrate the seals.

Steam cleaning

Before steam cleaning the engine compartment, cover the power steering reservoir to prevent contamination of fluid. After steam cleaning carefully re-wax the metallic components, especially the steering column, engine coolant pipes, hose clips and the ignition coil clamp, to prevent corrosion.

Removing tar spots

Use white spirit to remove tar spots and stubborn grease stains from paintwork. Then wash immediately with soapy water to remove all traces of spirit.

Body protection

After washing, inspect the paintwork for damage. Any stone chips, fractures or deep scratches in the bodywork should be repaired promptly. Bare metal will corrode quickly and can develop into major repair expense. Some exterior panels of your vehicle are made of aluminium which will not corrode in the same manner as steel. However, any damage should still receive prompt attention. Minor chips and scratches can be repaired with touch-up materials available from your dealer. Larger areas of damage need to be corrected to professional standards immediately.

Polishing

Occasionally treat the paint surface with an approved polish containing the following properties:

- Very mild abrasives to remove surface contamination without removing or damaging the paint.
- Filling compounds that will fill scratches and reduce their visibility.
- Wax to provide a protective coating between the paint and the elements.

NOTE: *DO NOT apply car polish to the bumper mouldings - polish will become ingrained in the textured finished.*

Glass and mirrors

Clean the rear window with a soft cloth to avoid damaging the heating elements. DO NOT scrape the glass or use an abrasive cleaning fluid.

Mirror glass is particularly susceptible to damage. Wash with soapy water. DO NOT use abrasive cleaning compounds or metal scrapers to remove ice.

CLEANING THE INTERIOR

WARNING

Read individual product warnings before using any car cleaning or washing products.

RECOMMENDED CARE PRODUCTS (Available in the UK)	
De icer	STC 717
Alloy wheel cleaner	STC 718
Glass cleaner	STC 719
Black bumper cleaner	STC 721
Shampoo	STC 722
Wax polish	STC 723
Screen wash	STC 8249

Plastic materials

Clean plastic-faced or cloth covered surfaces with diluted upholstery cleaner and wipe with a clean cloth.

NOTE: *DO NOT polish fascia components - for safety, these should remain non-reflective.*

Leather

Leather seats, steering wheel and trim features should be cleaned with a damp cloth moistened with undiluted upholstery cleaner. Leave for five minutes, and then repeat the operation using a clean cloth and water - but avoid flooding the area! Dry and polish the leather with a dry, lint-free cloth.

DO NOT use petrol, detergents, furniture creams or polishes!

Carpet and fabrics

Clean with diluted nylon upholstery cleaner - test on a concealed area first.

Instrument pack, clock and radio

Clean with a dry cloth only! DO NOT use cleaning fluids or sprays.

Seat belts

Extend the belts, then use warm water and a non-detergent soap to clean. Allow the belts to dry naturally, and do not retract them or use the vehicle until they are completely dry.

Airbag module covers

To prevent airbag SRS damage, the steering wheel centre pad and area of the fascia panel containing the passenger airbag should ONLY be cleaned sparingly with a damp cloth and upholstery cleaner.

DO NOT allow these areas to be flooded with liquid, and DO NOT use petrol, detergent, furniture cream or polishes.

VEHICLE IDENTIFICATION NUMBER (VIN)

If you need to communicate with a Land Rover dealer, you may be asked to quote the Vehicle Identification Number (VIN).

The VIN (and recommended maximum vehicle weights) is stamped on a plate riveted to the top of the radiator grille panel in the engine compartment (this should match the VIN recorded in the Service Portfolio book).

In addition, as a deterrent to car thieves and to assist the police, the VIN is stamped on a plate which is visible through the lowest part of the left side of the windscreen and also on the vehicle's chassis.

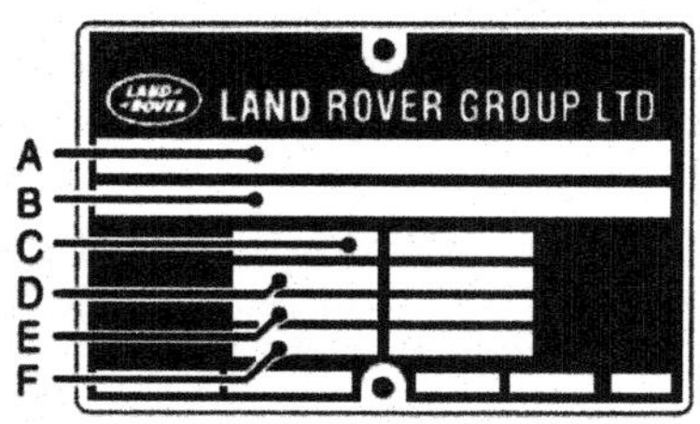

H3551

A. Type approval (where required)
B. Vehicle Identification Number (VIN)
C. Gross vehicle weight (where required)
D. Gross train weight (where required)
E. Maximum front axle load (where required)
F. Maximum rear axle load (where required)

PARTS AND ACCESSORIES

WARNING

The fitting of non-approved parts and accessories, or the carrying out of non-approved alterations or conversions, may be dangerous and could affect the safety of the vehicle and occupants, and also invalidate the terms and conditions of the vehicle warranty.

Your vehicle has been designed, built and tested to cope with a variety of off-road driving conditions, some of which can place the severest possible demands on control systems and components. As such, fitting replacement parts and accessories that have been developed and tested to the same stringent standards as the original components will safeguard the continued reliability, safety and performance of your vehicle.

To augment the vehicle's already impressive performance, a comprehensive range of Land Rover-approved spare parts and accessories is available, enabling the vehicle to fulfil a wide variety of roles, and enhancing and protecting the vehicle in the many tasks to which it can be applied.

Land Rover parts are the only parts built to original equipment specifications AND approved by Land Rover designers; this means that every single part and accessory has been rigorously tested by the same engineering team that designed and built the vehicle and can therefore be guaranteed for twelve months with unlimited mileage.

A full list and description of all accessories is available from your Land Rover dealer.

Electrical equipment

WARNING

It is extremely hazardous to fit or replace parts or accessories whose installation requires the dismantling of or addition to either the electrical or fuel systems.

If an airbag SRS is fitted ALWAYS consult a Land Rover dealer before fitting any accessory.

Fitting inferior quality parts or accessories, may be dangerous and could invalidate the vehicle warranty.

It is recommended that you always consult a Land Rover dealer for advice regarding the approval, suitability, installation and use of any parts or accessories before fitting.

AFTER SALES SERVICE

The After Sales Parts service is of paramount importance, both in the UK and across the world. In the UK there are over 100 authorised Land Rover dealers, all computer linked for rapid ordering of parts and accessories.

In addition, with franchised representation in over 100 countries worldwide, Land Rover are able to support your vehicle wherever you go.

Only Land Rover dealers are able to provide the full range of recommended parts and accessories that meet our rigorous standards of safety, durability and performance.

Travelling abroad

In certain countries, it is illegal to fit parts which have not been made to the vehicle manufacturers' specification.

Owners should ensure that any parts or accessories fitted to the vehicle while travelling abroad will also conform to the legal requirements of their own country when they return home.

Emergency Information

TOOL KIT

Jack

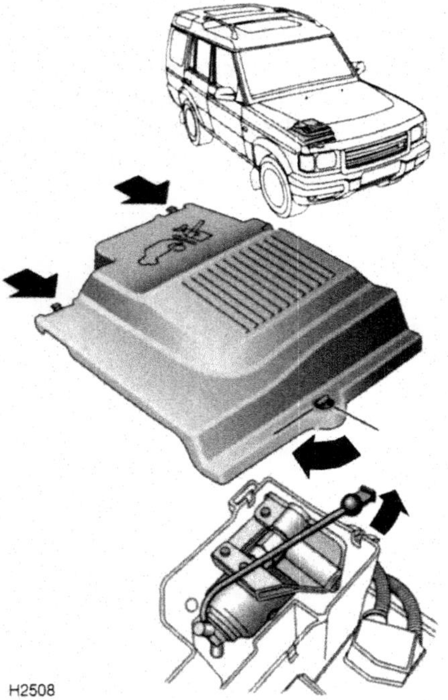

H2508

The jack is stowed in the front of the engine compartment next to the battery. To access the jack, remove the battery cover.

WARNING

Due to its stowage position in the engine compartment the jack may be hot if the engine has been running.

Tools

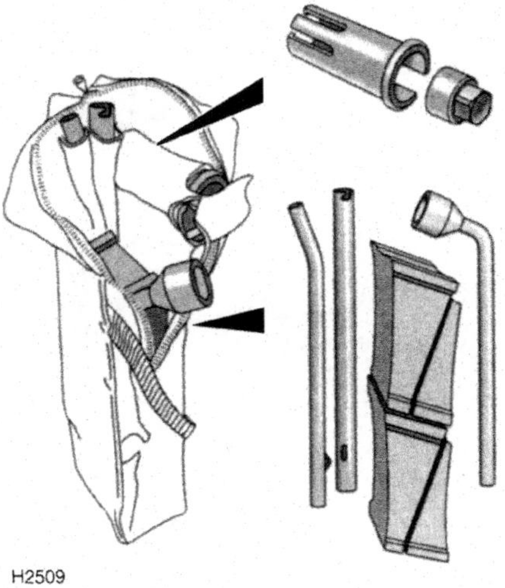

H2509

The jack handle and other tools are stowed in a tool bag in the taildoor storage pocket.

Care of the jack

Examine the jack occasionally, clean and grease the moving parts, particularly the ram.

To avoid contamination, the jack should always be returned to its fully closed position.

WARNING

After wheel changing, always secure tools, chocks, jack and spare wheel in their correct storage positions.

SPARE WHEEL

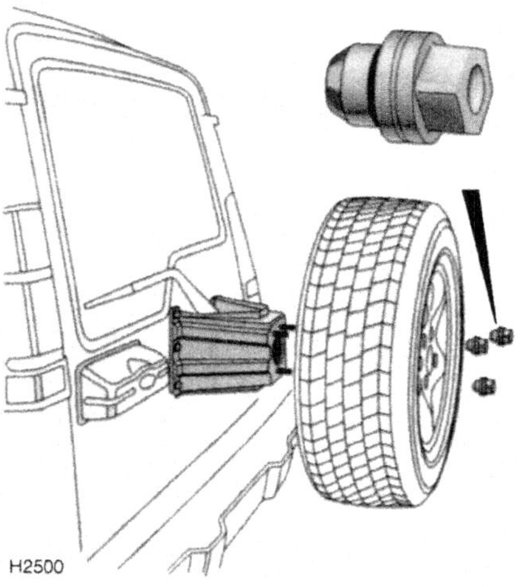

H2500

Vehicles fitted with a steel spare wheel are supplied with a cover, which fits over the wheel. Use the wheel nut wrench supplied in the tool kit to remove the nuts securing the cover.

Similarly, use the wheel nut wrench to remove the nuts securing the spare wheel to the carrier and then lift off the wheel.

NOTE: *In some markets, vehicles fitted with alloy wheels have a locking wheel nut fitted to each wheel, including the spare (see 'LOCKING WHEEL NUTS', page 179). In other markets, vehicles fitted with alloy wheels have a single locking wheel nut fitted to the spare wheel only.*

Locking wheel nuts are not specified for steel wheels.

WARNING

- ***DO NOT use the spare wheel securing nuts in place of the road wheel nuts, or use the road wheel nuts to secure the spare wheel - the nuts are not inter-changeable.***
- ***The wheels are extremely heavy. Take care when lifting and particularly when removing the spare wheel from its mounting position on the tail door.***

LOCKING WHEEL NUTS

Vehicles fitted with alloy wheels may be equipped with a locking wheel nut on each wheel (including the spare). The locking wheel nut covers are visually very similar to standard wheel nuts but can be identified by a concave indent on the surface. The locking wheel nut and cover can only be removed using the special tools provided, as follows:

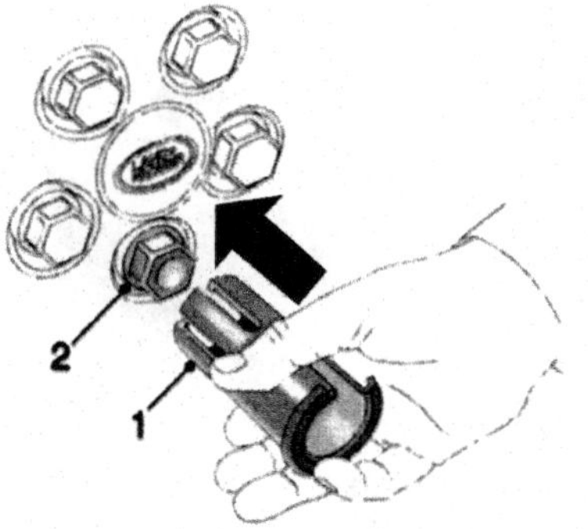

H2511

Push the extractor tool (1) firmly over the stainless steel nut cover (2).

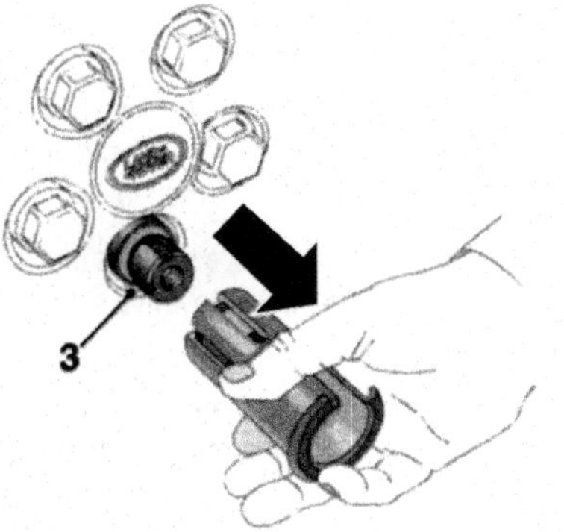

H2512

Pull the extractor tool **squarely** away from the wheel to remove the nut cover and reveal the locking wheel nut (3).

NOTE: *If the extractor tool has been inadvertently pushed onto a standard wheel nut, it can be removed ONLY by first undoing and removing the nut; slide the wheel nut wrench down the centre of the extractor and onto the wheel nut.*

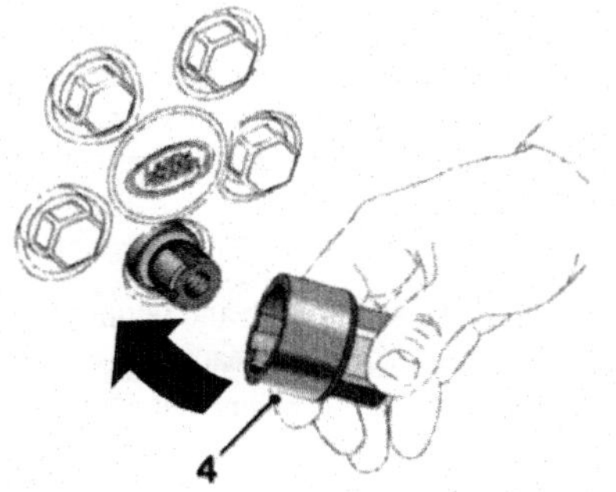

H2513

Fit the metal key socket (4) securely over the locking wheel nut.

Fit the wheel nut wrench onto the key socket and unscrew the nut in the normal way.

NOTE: *A code letter is stamped on the face of the key socket. Ensure the code letter is entered in the space provided on your Security Information card - you will need to quote this number if replacement components are required. Keep the card in a safe place away from the vehicle.*

CHANGING THE WHEEL

If possible, choose a safe place to stop away from the main thoroughfare. Always ask your passengers to get out of the vehicle and wait in a safe area away from other traffic.

NOTE: *Switch on the hazard warning lights to alert other road users.*

Before changing a wheel, ensure the front wheels are in the straight ahead position, apply the handbrake and engage 1st gear in the main gearbox (select 'P' for automatic transmission) and select 'L' in the transfer box.

Turn off the starter switch and remove the key. Observe the following precautions:

- Ensure the jack is positioned on firm, level ground; NEVER on soft ground, or over metal gratings or manhole covers. DO NOT place additional material between the jack and the ground, this may jeopardise the safety of the jacking operation.
- Place chocks at the front and rear of the wheel diagonally opposite the one to be removed.
- NEVER raise the vehicle with passengers inside, or with a caravan or trailer connected!

WARNING

Before raising the vehicle, it is ESSENTIAL to chock the road wheels in two places; the handbrake acts on the transmission, not on the rear wheels, and therefore may not hold the vehicle when raised.

Using the wheel chocks

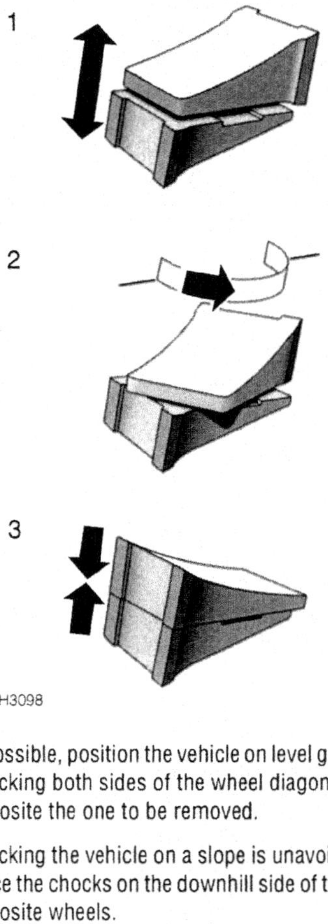

If possible, position the vehicle on level ground, chocking both sides of the wheel diagonally opposite the one to be removed.

If jacking the vehicle on a slope is unavoidable, place the chocks on the downhill side of the two opposite wheels.

The wheel chocks are stowed with the jack handle and wheel nut spanner in the tool bag.

Assemble the wheel chocks as follows:

1. Pull the two halves of the chock apart.
2. Twist one half of the chock 180°.
3. Push the two halves back together.

Operating the jack

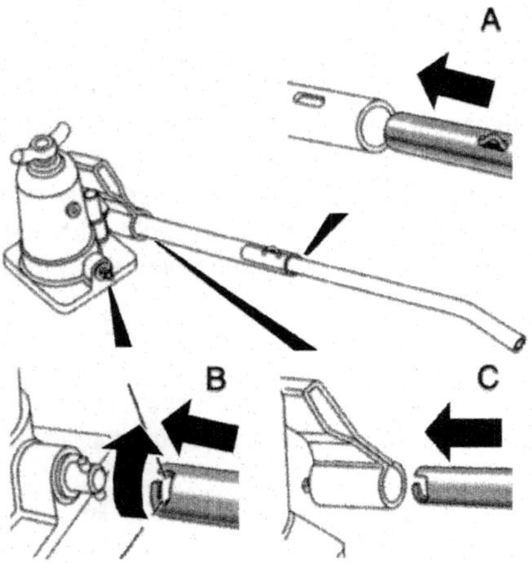

H2510

Slot the two parts of the jack lever together, ensuring that the spring clip protrudes from the engagement slot where the two parts join (see inset 'A'). Close the jack release valve by using the notched end of the jack lever to turn the valve fully clockwise (see inset 'B'). Insert the lever into the socket as shown (inset 'C') and twist the lever to lock it into the socket.

Pump the lever up and down to raise the jack.

To lower the jack, detach the lever (twist and pull) and then slot the notched end over the pegs on the release valve. Slowly turn the release valve anti-clockwise allowing the weight of the vehicle to lower the jack.

DO NOT fully unscrew the release valve.

Positioning the jack

WARNING

NEVER work beneath the vehicle with the jack as the only means of support. The jack is designed for wheel changing only!

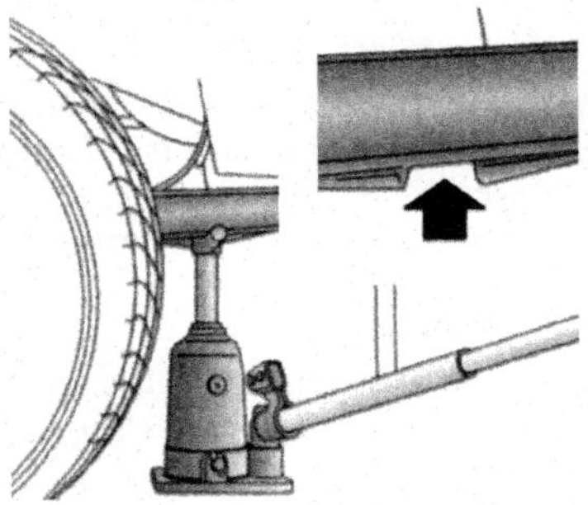

H2516

Front jacking point

H2515

Rear jacking point

Always position the jack from the side of the vehicle, approximately in line with the appropriate jacking point. Ensure the jack is positioned on firm, level ground.

Position the jack so that, when raised the cradle head of the jack engages with the shaped notch on the underside of the front or rear suspension links - either just forward of the rear wheels or just to the rear of the front wheels.

WARNING

ALWAYS use the complete, two-piece, jack lever throughout to minimise any chance of accidental damage or injury.

ONLY jack the vehicle using the jack location points described, or damage to the vehicle could occur.

Changing a wheel

1. Use the wheel nut wrench to slacken the wheel nuts half a turn anti-clockwise.
2. Raise the vehicle until the tyre is clear of the ground.
3. Remove the wheel nuts and place to one side to prevent them from being lost.
4. Remove the road wheel.

   NOTE: *DO NOT damage the surface of the wheel by placing it face down on the road.*
5. On alloy wheels, use an approved anti-seize compound to treat the wheel mounting spigot. This will minimise any tendency for adhesion between the wheel and the spigot.

   Ensure that no compound comes into contact with the brake components or the flat mounting surfaces of the wheel.

   If, due to an emergency situation, this treatment is not practicable; refit the spare wheel for the time being, but remove and treat the wheel at the earliest opportunity.
6. Fit the spare wheel and lightly tighten the wheel nuts, ensuring they are firmly seated. DO NOT fully tighten whilst the tyre is clear of the ground.

WARNING

When fitting a wheel, ensure that the mating faces of the hub and wheel are clean and free from rust or anti-seize compound - any accumulation of dirt or rust could cause the wheel nuts to become loose and result in an accident.

7. Ensure that the space under and around the vehicle is free from obstructions then lower the vehicle and remove the jack and wheel chocks.
8. Fully tighten the wheel nuts in an alternating pattern until all are tightened. DO NOT OVERTIGHTEN by using foot pressure or extension bars on the wheel nut wrench, as this could overstress the wheel studs. Check the wheel nut torque at the earliest opportunity (see *'WHEELS & TYRES', page 213*).
9. Return tools, chocks, jack and spare wheel in their correct storage positions.
10. REMEMBER to change to 'H' (high range) before driving.
11. Finally, check the tyre pressure at the earliest opportunity (see *'WHEELS & TYRES', page 213*).

STARTING AN ENGINE WITH A DISCHARGED BATTERY

Using booster cables (jump leads) from a donor battery, or a battery fitted to a donor vehicle, is the only approved method of starting a vehicle with a discharged battery. Push or tow starting is NOT recommended!

WARNING

During normal use, batteries emit explosive hydrogen gas sufficient to cause severe explosions capable of causing serious injury - keep sparks and naked lights away from the engine compartment.

DO NOT attempt to start the vehicle if the electrolyte in the battery is suspected of being frozen.

Make sure BOTH batteries are of the same voltage (12 volts), and that the booster cables have insulated clamps and are approved for use with 12 volt batteries.

DO NOT disconnect the discharged battery.

DO NOT connect positive (+) terminals to negative (-) terminals, and ensure booster cables are kept away from any moving parts in the engine compartment.

Take care when working near rotating parts of the engine.

USING BOOSTER CABLES

If a donor vehicle is to be used, both vehicles should be parked with their battery locations adjacent to each other. Ensure that the two vehicles do not touch.

Apply the handbrakes and ensure that the transmission of both vehicles is set in neutral ('P' or Park for vehicles with automatic transmission).

Turn off the starter switch and ALL electrical equipment of BOTH vehicles, then follow the connection instructions on the following page.

CONNECTING THE BOOSTER CABLES

Diesel engine vehicles

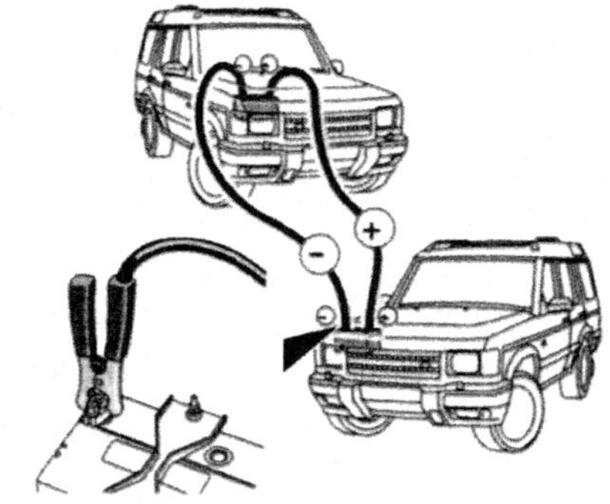

H2570

Always adopt the following procedure, ensuring the cables are connected in the order shown below:

1. Connect one end of the RED booster cable to the positive (+) terminal of the donor battery.
2. Connect the other end of the RED booster cable to the positive (+) terminal of the discharged battery.
3. Connect one end of the BLACK booster cable to the negative (-) terminal of the DISCHARGED battery.
4. Connect the other end of the BLACK booster cable to the negative (-) terminal of the donor battery.

WARNING

For safety reasons:

- ***ALWAYS connect the BLACK cable to the donor battery LAST.***
- ***ENSURE that each connection is securely made and that there is no risk of the clips accidentally slipping or being pulled from the battery terminals - this could cause sparking, which could lead to explosion or fire.***

Check that the cables are clear of any moving parts of both engines, then start the engine of the donor vehicle and allow it to idle for a few minutes.

Now start the vehicle with the discharged battery. Once both engines are running normally, allow them to idle for two minutes before switching off the donor vehicle engine.

DO NOT switch on any electrical circuits on the previously disabled vehicle until AFTER the booster cables have been removed.

Disconnecting the booster cables must be an EXACT reversal of the procedure used to connect them, i.e. disconnect the BLACK cable from the negative (-) terminal on the donor vehicle FIRST.

*

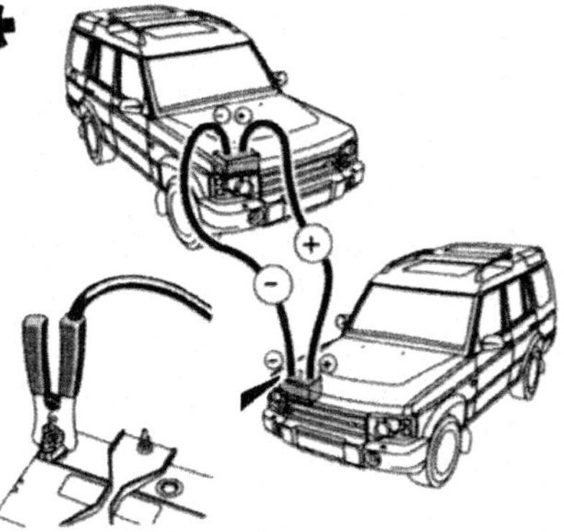

H4429

Petrol engine vehicles

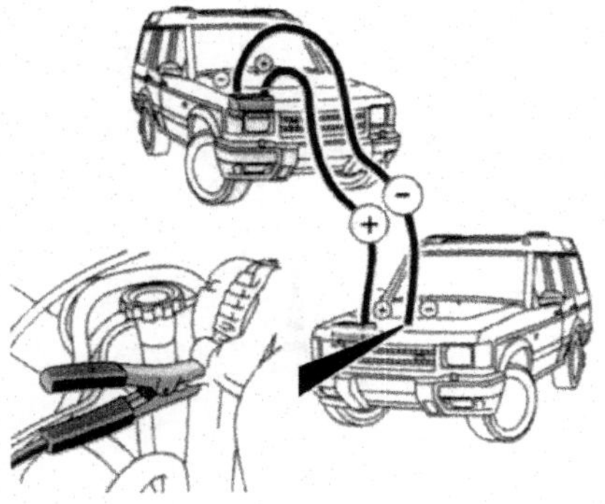

H2569

Always adopt the following procedure:

Connect the RED booster cable between the positive (+) terminal of the donor battery and the positive (+) terminal of the discharged battery.

Connect the BLACK booster cable from the negative (-) terminal of the donor battery to a good earth point (e.g. an engine mounting or other unpainted surface) away from the battery and away from fuel and brake lines on the disabled vehicle (lug on alternator casting shown in illustration).

*

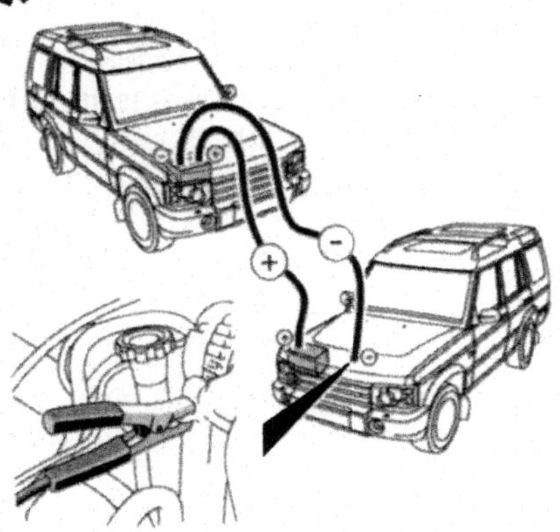

H4430

WARNING

For safety reasons:

- ***DO NOT connect the BLACK cable to the negative terminal of the discharged battery - if in doubt, seek qualified assistance.***
- ***ENSURE that each connection is securely made and that there is no risk of the clips accidentally slipping or being pulled from the battery terminals - this could cause sparking, which could lead to fire or explosion.***

Check that the cables are clear of any moving parts of both engines, then start the engine of the donor vehicle and allow it to idle for a few minutes.

Now start the vehicle with the discharged battery. Once both engines are running normally, allow them to idle for two minutes before switching off the engine of the donor vehicle.

DO NOT switch on any electrical circuits on the previously disabled vehicle until AFTER the booster cables have been removed.

Disconnecting the booster cables must be an EXACT reversal of the procedure used to connect them, i.e. disconnect the BLACK cable from the earth point on the disabled vehicle FIRST.

TOWING EYES

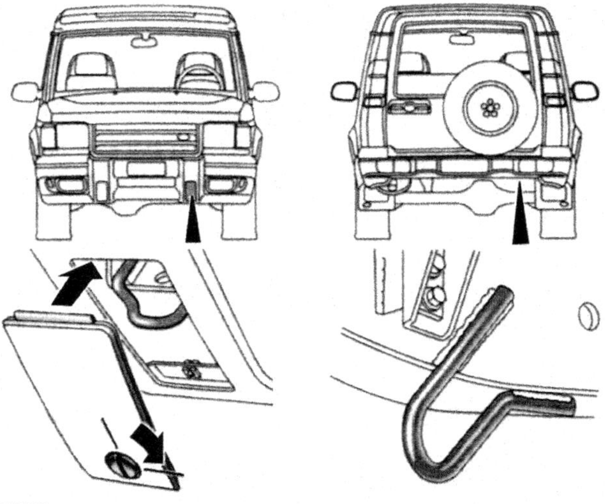

H2487

WARNING

The towing eyes at the front and rear of the vehicle are designed for on-road vehicle recovery purposes only and must NOT be used to tow a trailer or caravan.

*

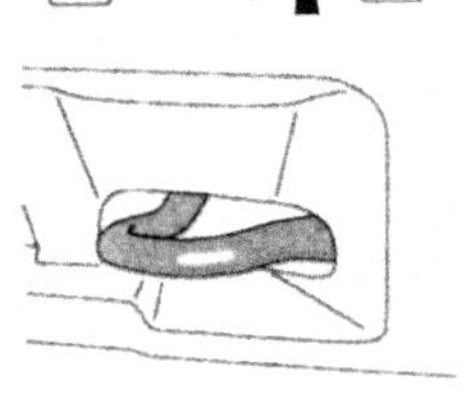

H4431

Front

A single towing eye, set behind a removable panel in the front spoiler is provided at the front of the vehicle for on-road recovery. DO NOT use the front lashing rings for towing purposes.

Before driving off-road, remove the panel from the spoiler as a precaution against accidental loss.

Rear

A pair of towing eyes are provided at the rear of the vehicle. These can be used as lashing rings and for towing your vehicle.

TOWING ON 4 WHEELS

Most vehicle recovery specialists will load Discovery onto a trailer. However, if it is necessary to recover the vehicle by towing with all four wheels on the ground, or to similarly tow the vehicle for recreational purposes, observe the following procedure:

1. Apply the handbrake.
2. Set the main gearbox in 'P' (Park) for automatic transmission vehicles and neutral for manual vehicles.
3. Set the transfer box in neutral.
4. Turn the starter switch to position 'II', so that the brake lights and direction indicators can be operated.
5. Secure the towing attachment to the front towing eye of the distressed vehicle.
6. Release the handbrake.

NOTE: *If, due to an accident or electrical fault, it is not considered safe to turn the starter switch, the battery should first be disconnected. Brake lights and indicators will not operate. (See item 4 above).*

WARNING

DO NOT attempt to tow the vehicle unless the starter switch is turned to position 'II'. If the vehicle is towed with the starter switch in position 'I', an inconsistency in the recorded vehicle mileage will occur. This must then be rectified by a Land Rover dealer.

DO NOT remove the key or turn the starter switch to position '0' while the vehicle is in motion; the starter switch must be at position 'II'.

Without the engine running, the brake servo and power steering pump cannot provide assistance; greater effort will therefore be required to operate the brake pedal and turn the steering wheel. Longer stopping distances will also be experienced.

CAUTION: Leaving the starter switch in position 'II' for extended periods will put a draw on the battery, which can lead to voltage drop and ultimately to a discharged battery.

TRANSPORTER OR TRAILER LASHING

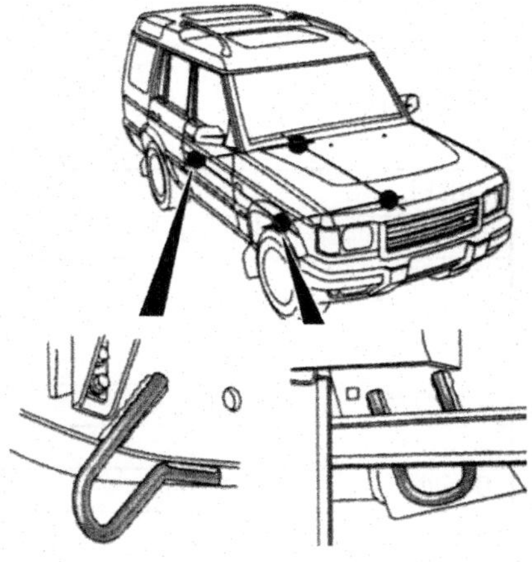

H2486

Pairs of lashing rings are fixed to the underside of the vehicle - at the front (to the rear of the front wheels) and at the rear (backward of the rear wheels). DO NOT secure lashing hooks or trailer fixings to any other part of the vehicle.

NOTE: *The front rings are for lashing only and must NOT be used for towing. The rear lashing rings are designed for both towing and lashing.*

FUSES

Fuses are simple circuit devices which protect electrical equipment against the effects of excess current.

A 'blown' fuse is indicated when the electrical equipment it protects becomes inoperative.

Fuses are colour coded to help identify their amperage, as follows:

Fuse colours

VIOLET	3 amp
TAN	5 amp
BROWN	7.5 amp
RED	10 amp
BLUE	15 amp
YELLOW	20 amp
WHITE	25 amp
GREEN	30 amp
ORANGE	40 amp

MAIN FUSE BOX

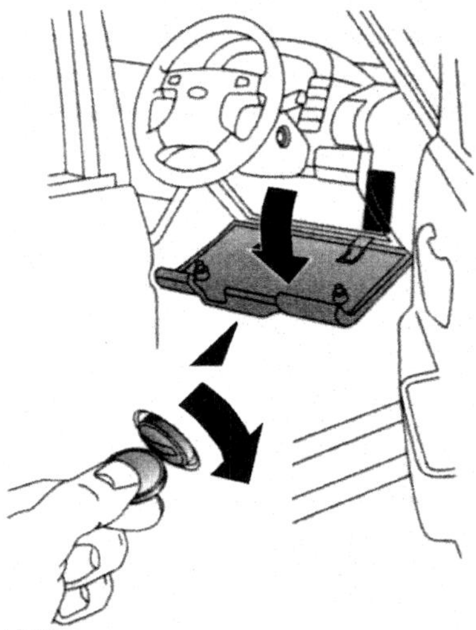

The main fuse box is fitted below and to one side of the steering column; to access the fuses, remove the cover by releasing the fixing screws using a coin or small screwdriver to twist the turnbuckle screw through 90 degrees.

Checking or renewing a fuse

Always turn the starter switch to position '0' and switch off the affected electrical circuit before removing a fuse.

WARNING

Fit only replacement fuses of the same rating and type. Always rectify the cause of the failure before replacing a fuse. Seek qualified assistance if necessary.

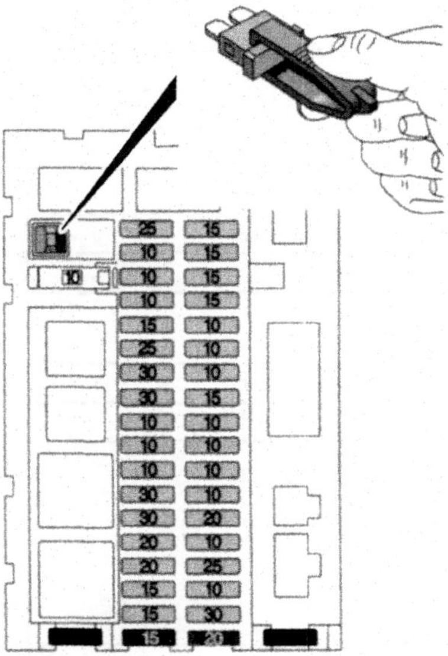

H2495

Press the fuse removal tweezers onto the head of the suspect fuse (as shown) and pull to remove. A break in the wire inside the fuse indicates that the fuse has 'blown' and must be replaced.

Always replace a fuse with another of the same value, however, if the replacement fuse blows immediately the circuit MUST be checked by a qualified dealer.

NOTE: *There are a number of spare fuses included within the fuse box (see fuse box label).*

A label in the fuse box cover shows the circuits protected, the fuse values and their locations. They are also listed on the following page.

Fuse specification

Fuse number	Rating (amps)	Circuit protected
1	25	Central door locking
2	10	Fuel flap release
3	10	Headlight main beam - LH
4	10	Fog guard lights - rear
5	15	Daylight running lights*
6	25	Air conditioning blower - rear
7	30	Heater blower - front
8	30	Heated rear window Heated mirrors
9	10	Headlight dipped beam - LH
10	10	Headlight dipped beam - RH
11	10	Side & tail lights - LH Number plate light Headlight levelling motors Interior illumination Trailer socket Sunroof
12	30	Sunroof
13	30	Electric windows - rear
14	20	Ignition coils (Petrol models)
15	20	Cigar lighter Interior lights Seat heaters Vanity mirror illumination
16	15	Clock Radio
17	15	Radio amplifier Speakers
18	15	Wiper motor - rear
19	15	Wiper motor - front Screen washer - front
20	15	Interior lights Clock/radio memory Engine remobilisation Compact disc player*
21	15	Transfer box Alarm audible warning

Fuses

Fuse number	Rating (amps)	Circuit protected
22	10	Headlight main beam - RH
23	10	Starter motor
24	10	Alternator Auto transmission
25	15	Brake lights Reverse lights
26	10	Auxiliary circuits relays
27	10	Instruments Hill descent control
28	10	Self levelling suspension Anti-lock braking
29	10	Active cornering enhancement (ACE)
30	20	Cruise control Electric mirrors Screen washer - rear
31	10	Air conditioning blower - front
32	25	Accessory socket
33	10	Side & tail lights - RH Headlight levelling switch Radio Trailer socket Interior illumination
34	30	Electric windows - front
35	10	**Airbag SRS - DO NOT REMOVE**

Fuse specification

Fuse number	Rating (amps)	Circuit protected
1	25	Central door locking
2	10	Fuel flap release
3	10	Instrument pack & switch illumination
4	10	Fog guard lights - rear
5	10	Headlight main beam - LH
6	25	Air conditioning blower - rear
7	30	Heater blower - front
8	30	Heated rear window Heated mirrors
9	10	Headlight dipped beam - LH
10	10	Headlight dipped beam - RH
11	10	Side & tail lights - LH Number plate light Headlight levelling motors Switch illumination Trailer socket Sunroof
12	30	Sunroof
13	30	Electric windows - rear
14	20	Ignition coils (Petrol models)
15	20	Cigar lighter Interior lights Seat heaters Vanity mirror illumination
16	15	Clock Radio
		Parking aid system Rear headphones
17	15	Radio amplifier
		Speakers
18	15	Wiper motor - rear
19	15	Wiper motor - front Screen washer - front

✱ Fuses

Fuse number	Rating (amps)	Circuit protected
20	15	Interior lights Clock/radio memory Engine remobilisation Compact disc player* Key i/lock Diagnostics
21	15	Transfer box Alarm audible warning Shift i-lock
22	10	Headlight main beam - RH
23	10	Starter motor
24	10	Alternator Auto transmission Engine management
25	15	Brake lights Reverse lights
26	10	Auxiliary circuits relays
27	10	Instruments Hill descent control
28	10	Self levelling suspension Anti-lock braking
29	10	Active cornering enhancement (ACE)
30	20	Cruise control Electric mirrors Screen washer - rear Diesel ECU
31	10	Air conditioning blower - front Power-fold mirrors
32	25	Accessory socket
33	10	Side & tail lights - RH Headlight levelling switch Radio Trailer socket Switch illumination
34	30	Electric windows - front
35	10	**Airbag SRS - DO NOT REMOVE**

ENGINE COMPARTMENT FUSE BOX

WARNING

Batteries emit explosive hydrogen gas; ensure that sparks, flames and other ignition sources are kept away from the engine compartment.

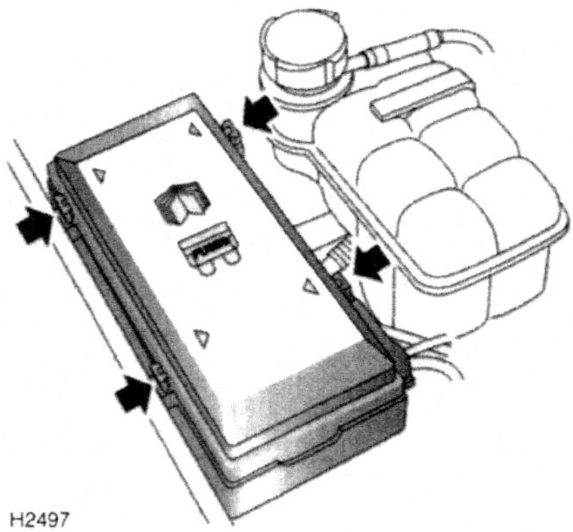

H2497

A second fuse box is located on the right side of the engine compartment adjacent to the coolant reservoir.

Press all four latches in the direction of the arrows shown on the illustration to release the fuse box cover.

Information on the underside of the cover identifies the fuses and their ratings. This information is also listed on the following page.

When replacing, the cover, locate the four latches, then push firmly downwards until the latches can be heard to 'snap' closed.

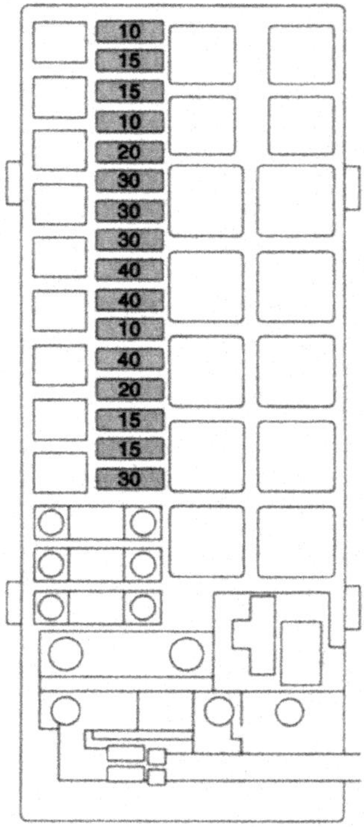

H2498

Owners are advised against removing or replacing the relays (identified as R1-R14) and fusible links (FL1-FL13). Failure of any of these items should be investigated by a qualified technician.

Fuse specification

Fuse number	Rating (amps)	Circuit protected
1	30	Fuel injectors (Petrol models) Engine control module (Diesel models)
2	15	Engine management system
3	15	Front fog lights
4	20	Headlight washers
5	40	Cooling fans
6	10	Air conditioning
7	40	Heated front screen - LH
8	40	Heated front screen - RH
9	30	Trailer lights
10	30	Fuel pump
11	30	ABS valve
12	20	Automatic gearbox
13	10	Body Control Unit (BCU)
14	15	Direction indicators Hazard lights
15	15	Active cornering enhancement (ACE)
16	10	Horn

UNDERSEAT FUSES

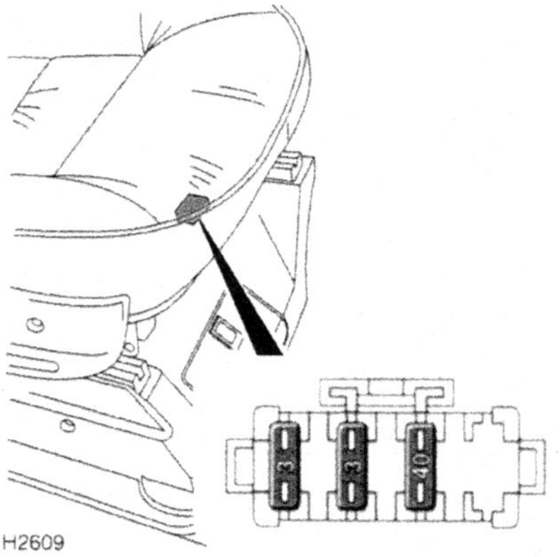

H2609

Two identical small fuse blocks are situated one beneath each front seat.

Fuse specification

Fuse number	Rating (amps)	Circuit protected
1	40	Seat electrics
2	3	Lumbar support - pump
3	3	Lumbar support - solenoid

REPLACING BULBS

Check the operation of all exterior lights before you drive the vehicle.

IMPORTANT INFORMATION
Before replacing a bulb, always switch off the starter switch and appropriate lighting switch to prevent any possibility of a short circuit. Only replace bulbs with the same type and specification.

Replacement bulbs

Bulb	Watts
Headlights dipped/main beam	60/55
Front side lights	5
Front side marker lights	5
Direction indicators	21
Front fog lights	55
Side repeater lights	5
Reverse lights	21
Rear fog guard lights	21
Tail lights	5
Stop lights	21
High mounted stop light	21
Number plate light	5
Interior light	5
Interior courtesy lights	10
Glovebox light	5
Vanity mirror light	1.2

NOTE: *All bulbs must be rated at 12 volts*

Halogen bulbs

Halogen bulbs are used for dipped/main, supplementary main beam and front fog lights. Take care NOT to touch this type of bulb with your fingers; always use a cloth to handle them. If necessary, clean the bulb with methylated spirits to remove fingerprints.

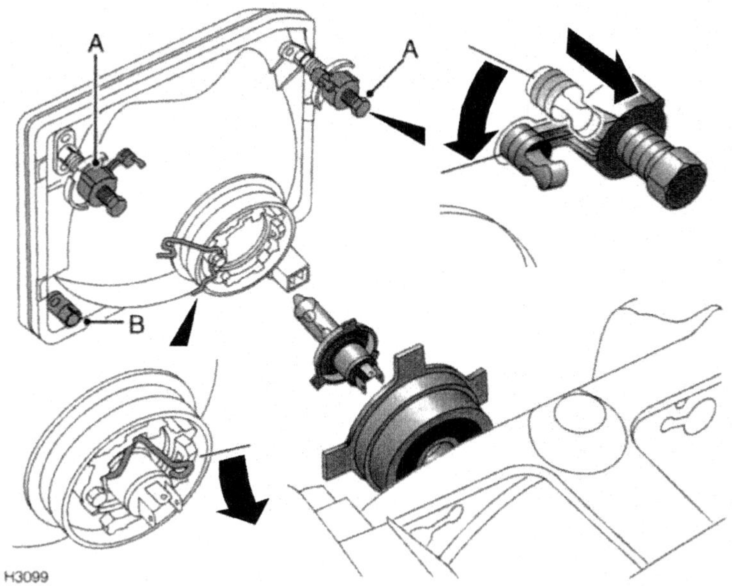

HEADLIGHT AND SIDELIGHT

Light unit removal

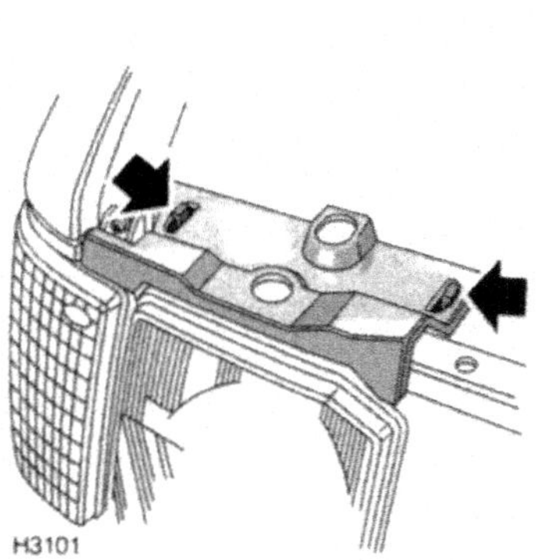

First remove the access panel set into the bonnet locking platform above each headlight.

For round headlight models see pages 203a to 203k.

To replace either the headlight or sidelight bulb, remove the light unit as follows:

Disengage the retaining clips 'A' and rotate them approximately 10 degrees (see inset) until they align with the slots in the headlight mounting panel. The light unit can now be released forward.

NOTE: *Vehicles fitted with headlight levelling (as illustration) have two retaining clips at the top only (the bottom of the light unit is mounted on the headlight height adjustment operating rod 'B'). Remove the lamp by gently pulling it off the ball socket of the operating rod.*

WARNING

DO NOT screw or unscrew the retaining clips more than described - their position affects the alignment of the headlights.

Headlight bulb replacement

Disconnect the electrical multi-plug and remove the rubber cover. Release the spring clip which holds the bulb and withdraw the bulb from the light unit. When replacing the bulb, ensure that the larger tab is pointing towards the top of the headlight.

Replace the spring clip and rubber cover, ensuring the slit in the cover is at the top of the headlight, and pressing the centre firmly to seal around the electrical contacts of the bulb.

***NOTE:** Do not touch the bulb glass with your fingers. If necessary, clean the bulb with methylated spirits.*

Replacing the headlight unit

Replacement is a reversal of the removal procedure. However if headlight levelling is fitted, it is necessary to carefully align the lower fixing position 'B' to the height adjustment operating lever before fitting the retaining clips 'A'.

Once the retaining clips are secure, firmly push the bottom of the headlight unit towards the rear of the vehicle to fully engage the height adjustment operating lever.

Sidelight bulb replacement

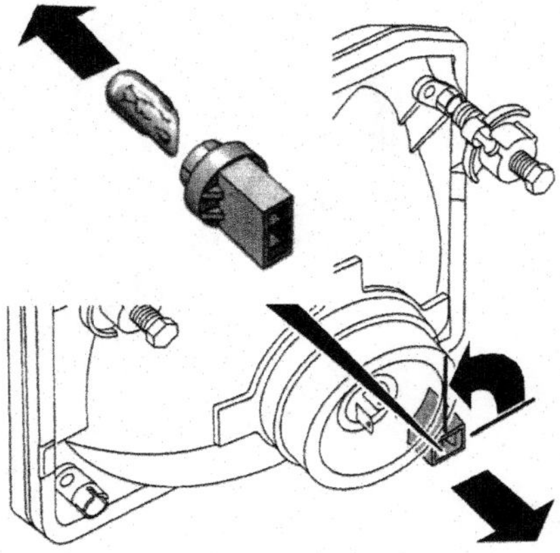

H3100

With the light unit removed (see previous instructions), disconnect the electrical multi-plug and disengage the bulb holder by twisting a quarter turn anti-clockwise. Pull the bulb from the holder to remove.

FRONT DIRECTION INDICATOR AND SIDE MARKER LIGHT

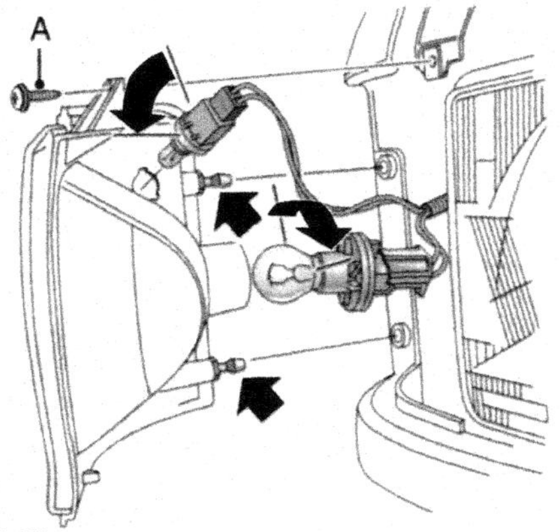

H2504

Remove the retaining screw 'A', then ease the light unit forward to release it from the vehicle.

Both the small side marker light and larger direction indicator bulb holders are released from the light unit by twisting anti-clockwise.

Pull the side marker bulb to remove. Push and twist the direction indicator bulb to remove.

To replace the light unit, insert the two location pins (arrowed) on the outer side of the light unit into the vehicle body, push firmly into position and, finally, replace the retaining screw.

SIDE REPEATER LIGHT

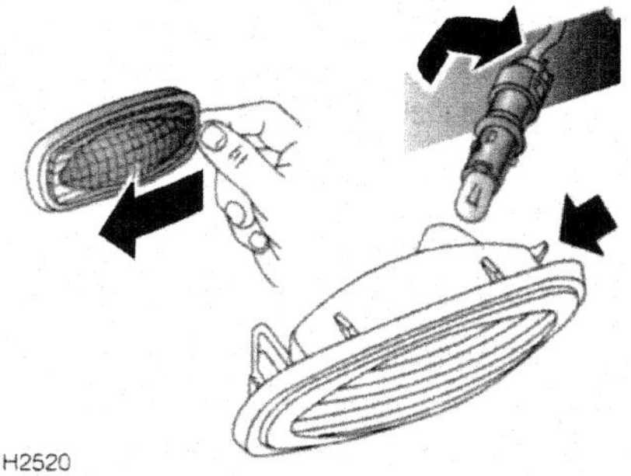
H2520

Push the lens firmly to the left and withdraw the light unit from the wing. Twist to release the bulb holder from the lens unit, then pull the bulb from its socket.

When refitting, ensure that the little tabs (arrowed in illustration) are pointed to the right and are inserted into the aperture before pushing the light unit into position in the wing.

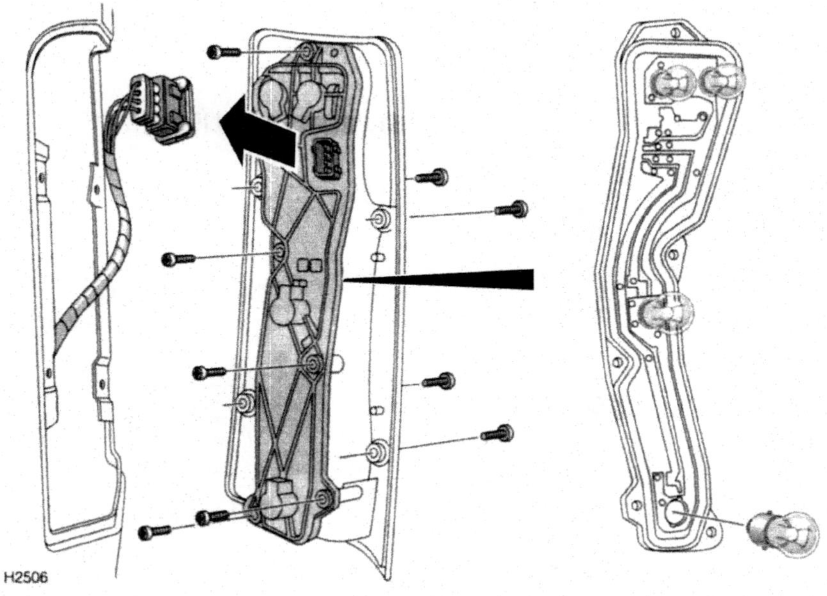

REAR LIGHT CLUSTER
(Tail, stop & reverse lights)

From outside the vehicle remove the four retaining screws to release the light unit from the vehicle, then detach the electrical multi-plug connector, by pressing the metal retaining spring.

To gain access to the bulbs, remove the five screws from the rear of the light unit and detach the bulb holder. Push and twist to release each bulb.

BUMPER MOUNTED LIGHTS
(Fog guard lights & direction indicators)

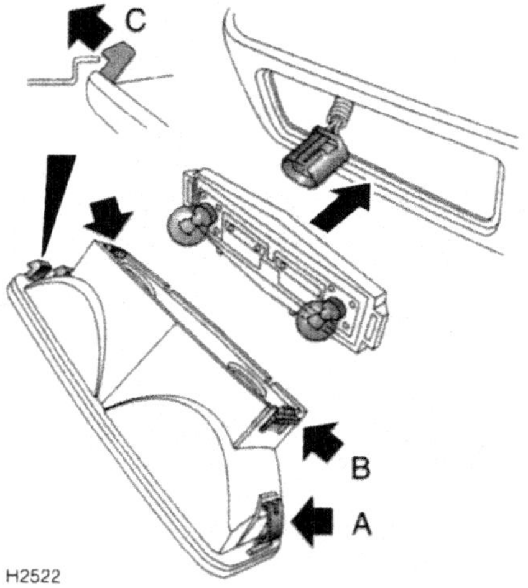

H2522

WARNING

If the engine is warm, the exhaust system may be hot - to prevent personal injury, avoid contact with a hot exhaust system when reaching behind the bumper.

Reach behind the bumper and press the spring clip 'A' to release the light unit.

Squeeze both levers 'B' to release the bulb holder from the lens. Push and twist to release the bulbs.

NOTE: *If necessary, the light unit can first be detached from the electrical harness by releasing the multi-plug from the rear of the bulb holder.*

Before reassembling the light unit, make sure the seal (between holder and lens) is in place.

FRONT FOG LIGHTS

To replace the light unit, first locate the hooks 'C' in the bumper aperture and firmly push the other side of the light against spring pressure until it clicks into place.

NUMBER PLATE LIGHTS

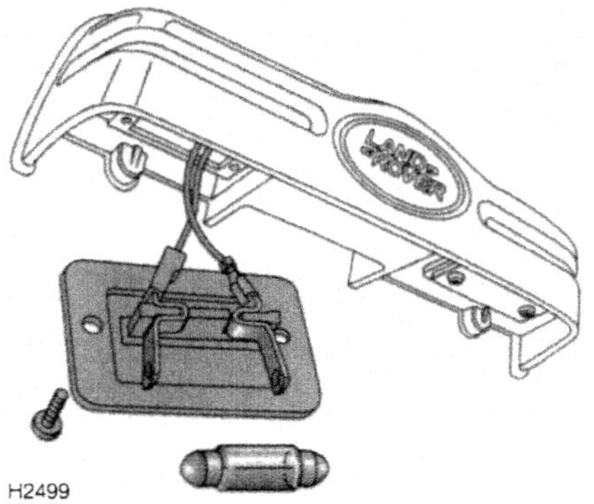

H2499

Remove both screws to release the light unit. Ease the light unit from its recess and pull the bulb to remove.

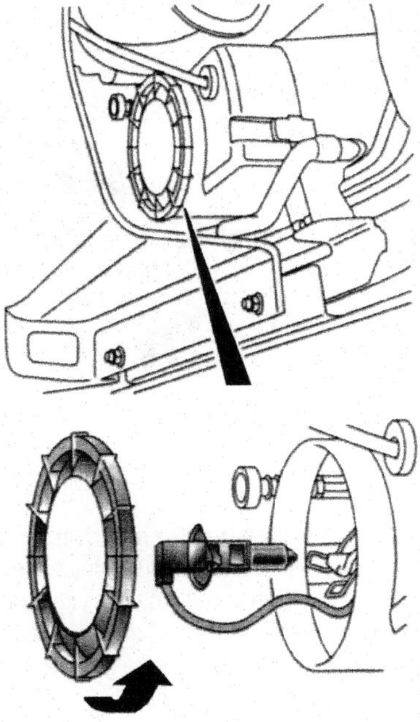
H3552

The front fog lights are mounted on the rear of the front bumpers and are shielded from behind by the lower wheelarch liners.

Access is severely restricted and will entail lying beneath the centre of the vehicle at the front and reaching between the wheelarch liner and the back of the fog light.

To access the bulb, remove the cover on the rear of the fog light by twisting it anti-clockwise.

Spring clips (similar to those in the headlights) hold the bulb in place. Unhook the clips to release the bulb from the light unit, then pull the bulb from the connector. Because access and vision are severely restricted (these operations must be carried out largely by 'feel'), it may be helpful to first examine the way in which similar spring clips in the headlight unit retain the headlight bulb.

Before fitting the replacement bulb, note the 'flat' on the otherwise circular shape of the bulb mounting flange. The flat acts as a key to enable correct positioning of the bulb in the light unit.

NOTE: *Do not touch the bulb glass with your fingers. If necessary, clean the bulb with methylated spirits.*

HIGH MOUNTED STOP LIGHT

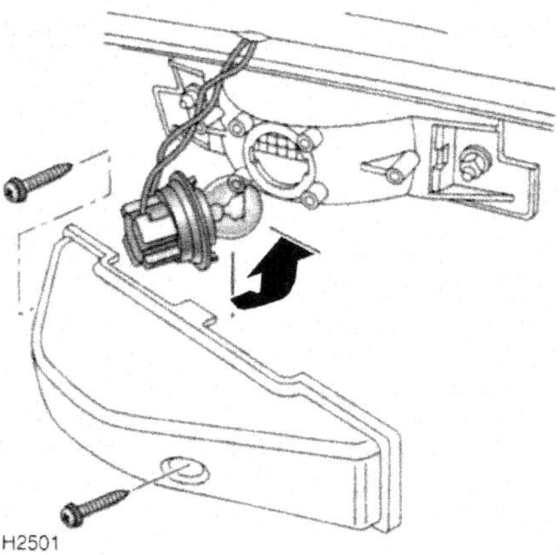

H2501

Remove both retaining screws and the cover from the rear of the light unit. Twist the bulb holder anti-clockwise to remove. Push and twist anti-clockwise to release the bulb.

GLOVEBOX LIGHT

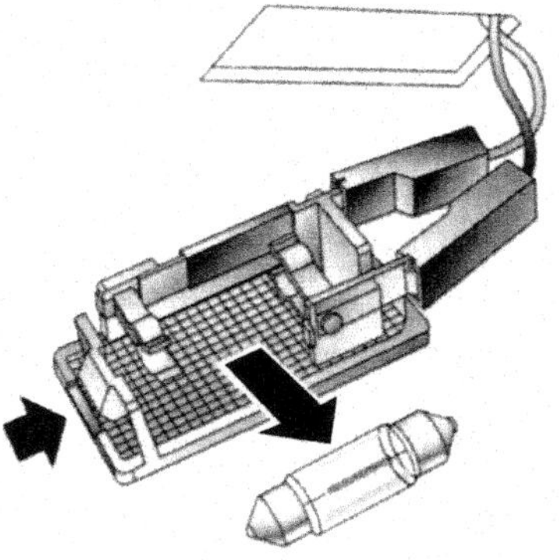

H2611

Insert a small flat-bladed screwdriver (preferably with a short handle, due to limited access) into the indent (arrowed in illustration) on the left hand side of the light unit, and carefully prise the unit from the glovebox panel. Remove the bulb from its clips.

INTERIOR COURTESY LIGHTS

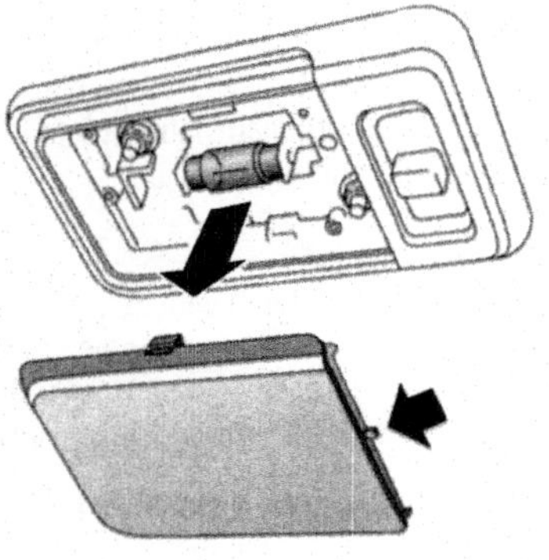

H2462

Insert a small flat-bladed screwdriver into the indent on the side of the lens and carefully prise the lens from the light unit, then pull the bulb to remove.

When replacing the lens, first locate the lug (arrowed in illustration), then push the lens into position.

INTERIOR LIGHT

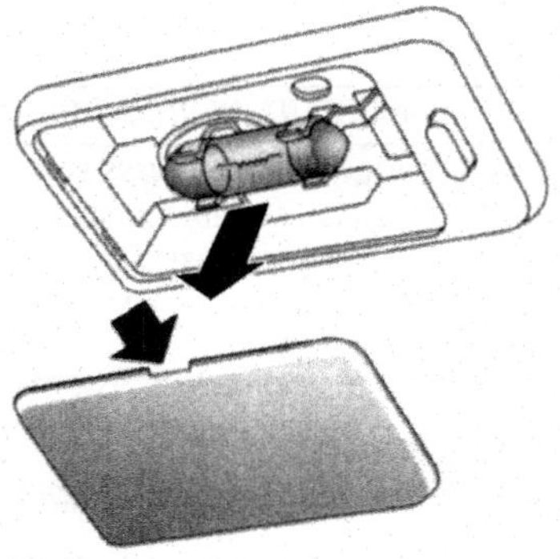

H2463

Insert a small flat-bladed screwdriver into the indent on the side of the lens (where arrowed) and prise the lens from the light unit, then pull the bulb out from the clips.

✱ Bulb Replacement

REPLACING BULBS

Check the operation of all exterior lights before you drive the vehicle.

IMPORTANT INFORMATION
Before replacing a bulb, always switch off the starter switch and appropriate lighting switch to prevent any possibility of a short circuit. Only replace bulbs with the same type and specification.

Replacement bulbs

NOTE: *All bulbs must be rated at 12 volts*

Bulb	Watts
Headlights dipped beam	55 (H7)
Headlights main beam	55 (H7)
Front side lights	5
Direction indicators	21
Front fog lights	55 (H7)
Side repeater lights	5
Reverse lights	6 (H6)
Rear fog guard lights	21
Tail lights	5
Number plate lights	5
Door/puddle lights	5
Interior lights	6
Luggage/footwell lights	5
Luggage/tailgate lights	6
Glovebox light	5
Vanity mirror light	1.2

NOTE: *In certain territories it is a legal requirement to carry spare bulbs, in case of bulb failure. A replacement bulb kit is available as an approved accessory from your Land Rover dealer.*

Halogen bulbs

Halogen bulbs are used for main beam, dipped beam, front fog and reverse lights. Take care NOT to touch this type of bulb with your fingers; always use a cloth to handle them. If necessary, clean the bulb with methylated spirits to remove fingerprints.

Xenon light units*

Some vehicles are fitted with Xenon dipped beam headlight units. Xenon lights provide significantly improved visibility, especially during adverse weather and driving conditions.

The operational life of a Xenon light is significantly longer than that of a conventional or Halogen bulb. However, the very high voltage required to ignite the gas and metal vapour used to power Xenon lights could cause very serious injury. Replacement or maintenance of Xenon lights should only be carried out by qualified personnel.

Used Xenon light units contain mercury, which is hazardous and can be injurious to health. Seek advice about the proper disposal of Xenon light units from a Land Rover dealer or your local authority.

Light emitting diodes (LEDs)

Controls, displays and some lights and other equipment items inside your vehicle have light emitting diodes (LEDs) behind a cover as their light source. These LEDs resemble conventional lasers and are classified by law as "Class 1 light emitting diodes". Replacement LEDs should be fitted only by qualified personnel.

WARNING

DO NOT remove the cover or expose the eyes directly to the unfiltered light source for several hours at a time, as this could cause irritation to the iris.

FRONT LIGHT UNIT

Light unit removal

To replace any of the bulbs, remove the light unit as follows:

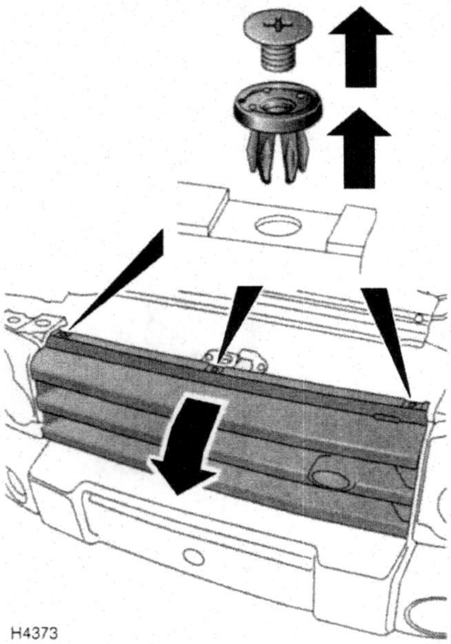

H4373

First unfasten the grille by unscrewing the 3 scrivets as indicated, then remove the grille by pulling forward.

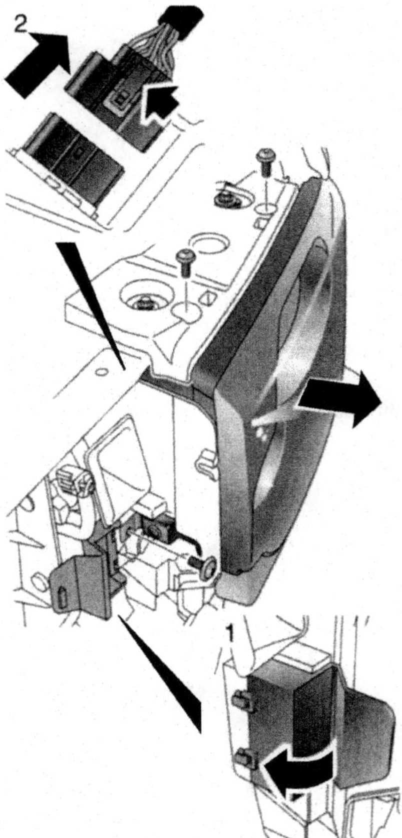

H4375

Open the cover flap (1) and remove the 3 screws as indicated. Pull the light unit forward and disconnect the electrical multi-plug (2) to release the unit.

✱ Bulb Replacement

Bulb location

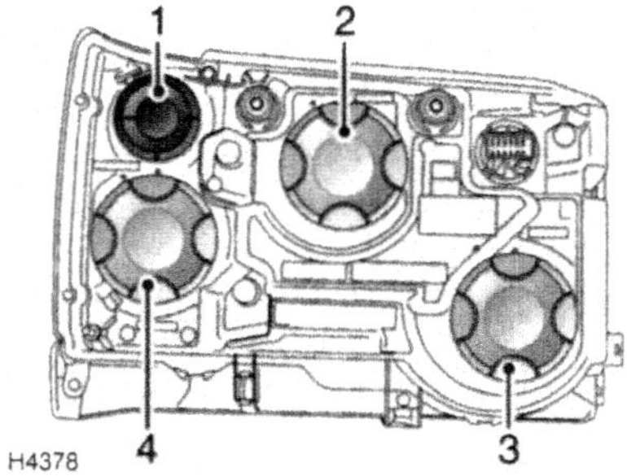

1. Indicator
2. Headlight (Dipped beam)
3. Headlight (Main beam)
4. Sidelight

Bulb covers

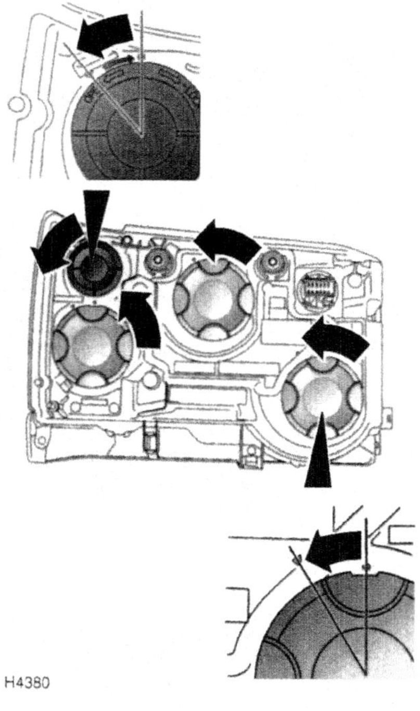

Headlight (Dipped beam) bulb replacement

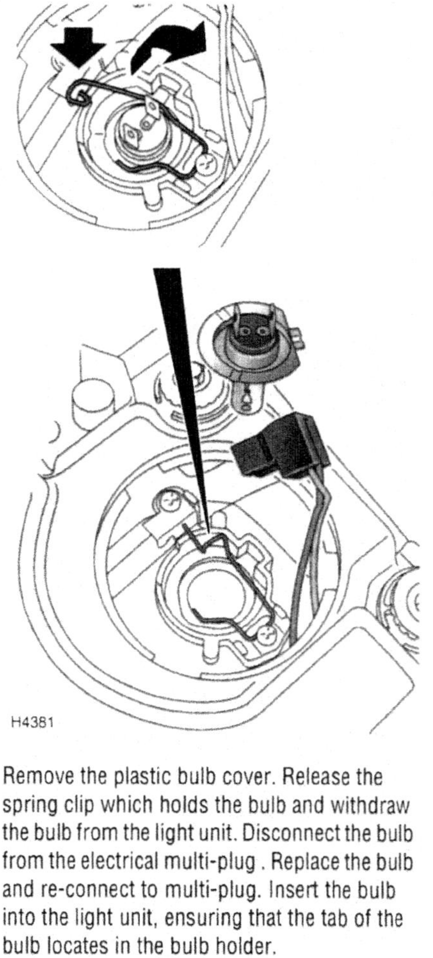

Remove the plastic bulb cover. Release the spring clip which holds the bulb and withdraw the bulb from the light unit. Disconnect the bulb from the electrical multi-plug . Replace the bulb and re-connect to multi-plug. Insert the bulb into the light unit, ensuring that the tab of the bulb locates in the bulb holder.
Replace the spring clip and plastic bulb cover.

NOTE: *Do not touch the bulb glass with your fingers. If necessary, clean the bulb with methylated spirits.*

Headlight (Main beam) bulb replacement

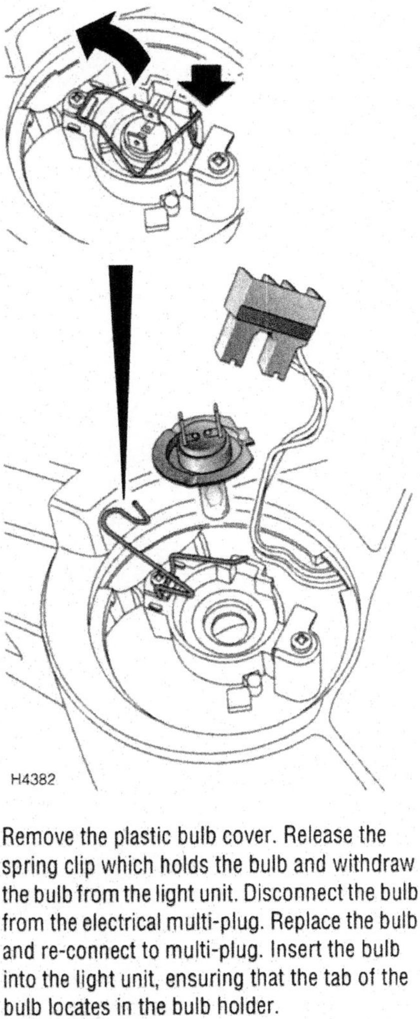

H4382

Remove the plastic bulb cover. Release the spring clip which holds the bulb and withdraw the bulb from the light unit. Disconnect the bulb from the electrical multi-plug. Replace the bulb and re-connect to multi-plug. Insert the bulb into the light unit, ensuring that the tab of the bulb locates in the bulb holder.
Replace the spring clip and plastic bulb cover.

NOTE: *Do not touch the bulb glass with your fingers. If necessary, clean the bulb with methylated spirits.*

Sidelight bulb replacement

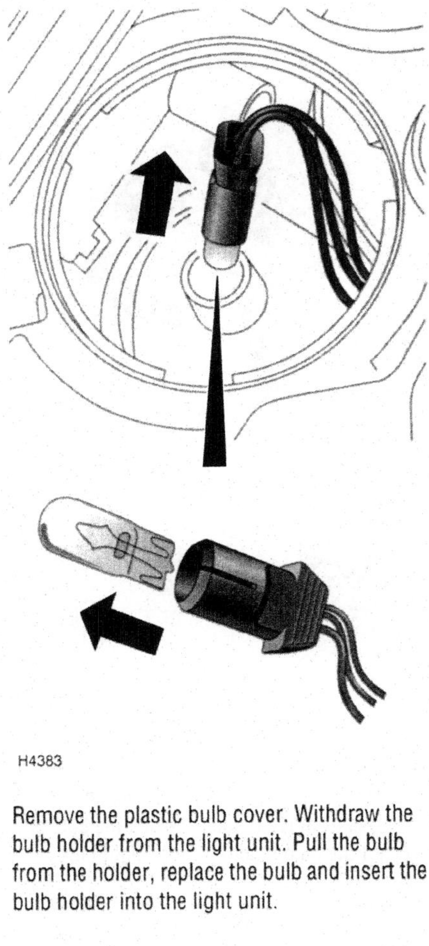

H4383

Remove the plastic bulb cover. Withdraw the bulb holder from the light unit. Pull the bulb from the holder, replace the bulb and insert the bulb holder into the light unit.

✱ Bulb Replacement

Front direction indicator bulb replacement

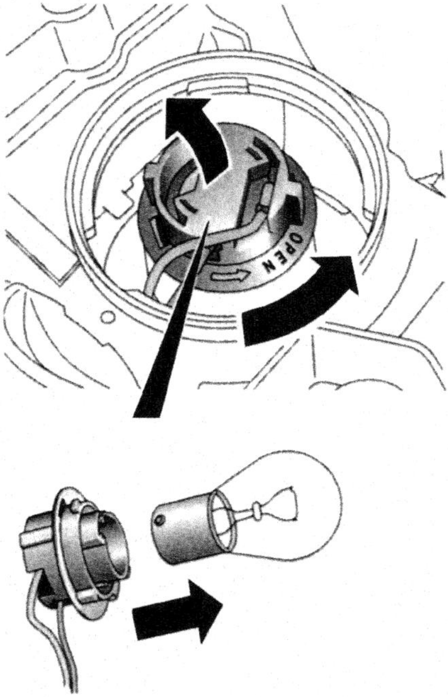

H4385

Remove the plastic bulb cover. Unscrew the bulb holder as indicated above and withdraw from the light unit. Push and twist the bulb to release from the holder, replace the bulb and insert the bulb holder into the light unit.

Re-fitting the front light unit

Re-fitting the unit is a reversal of the removal procedure.

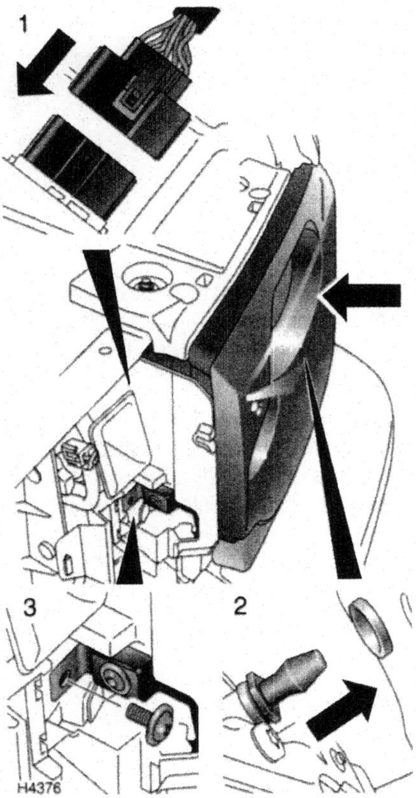

Re-connect the electrical multi-plug (1) and carefully push the unit back into place, ensuring that the pin (2) is engaged as illustrated. Replace the screw (3) and tighten.

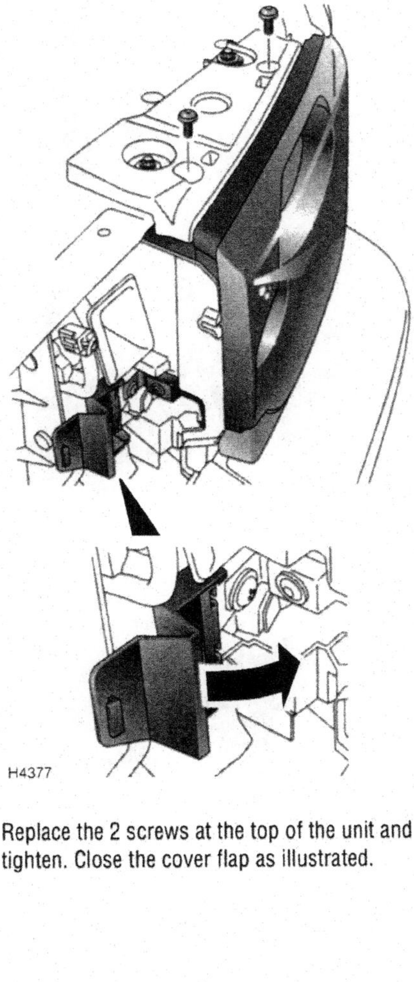

Replace the 2 screws at the top of the unit and tighten. Close the cover flap as illustrated.

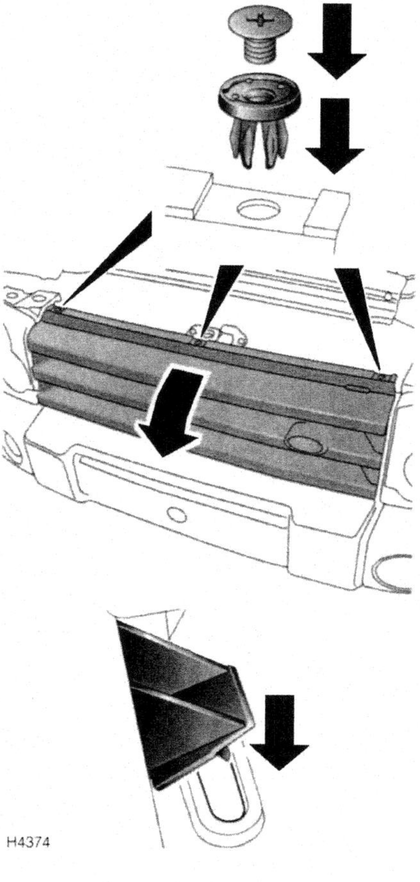

H4374

Re-fit the grille by first engaging the two lugs as illustrated, then insert the 3 scrivets to the top of the grille and tighten.

SIDE REPEATER LIGHT

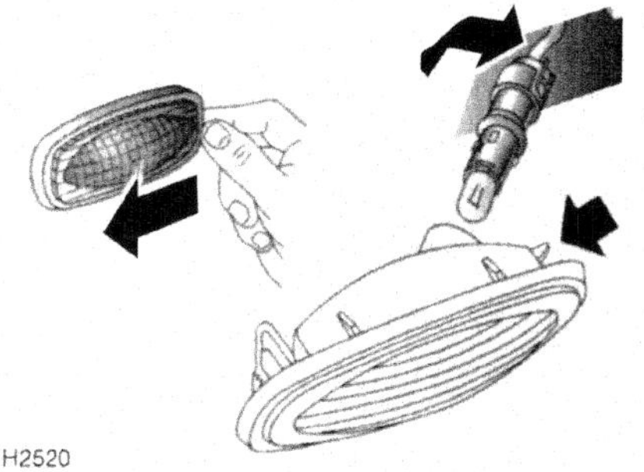

H2520

Push the lens firmly to the left and withdraw the light unit from the wing. Twist to release the bulb holder from the lens unit, then pull the bulb from its socket.

When refitting, ensure that the little tabs (arrowed in illustration) are pointed to the right and are inserted into the aperture before pushing the light unit into position in the wing.

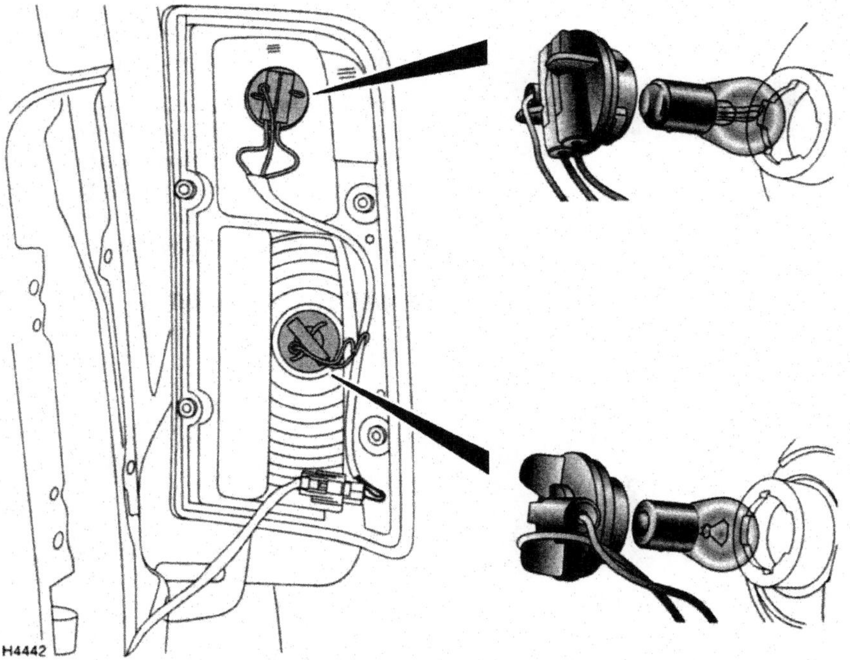

H4442

REAR LIGHT CLUSTER

(Tail, stop & direction indicator lights)

From outside the vehicle remove the four retaining screws to release the light unit from the vehicle (see right).

The Tail/Stop light bulb is located above the Indicator bulb.To replace either of the bulbs, unscrew the bulb holder from the light unit and then push and twist to release the required bulb from the holder. Replace the required bulb and re-fit the bulb holder into the light unit, then the light unit to the vehicle body.

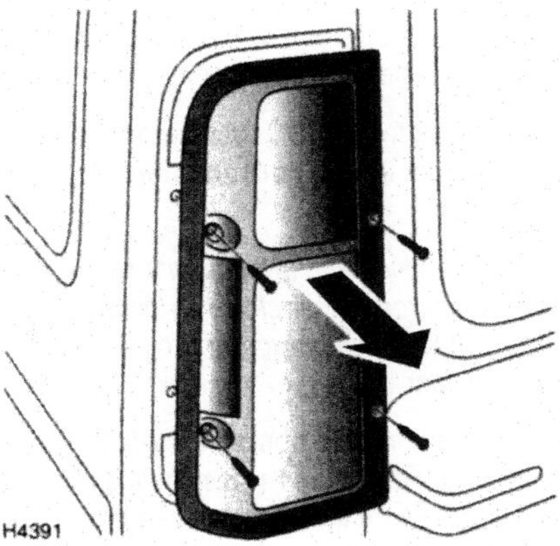

H4391

BUMPER MOUNTED LIGHTS
(Fog guard & reverse lights)

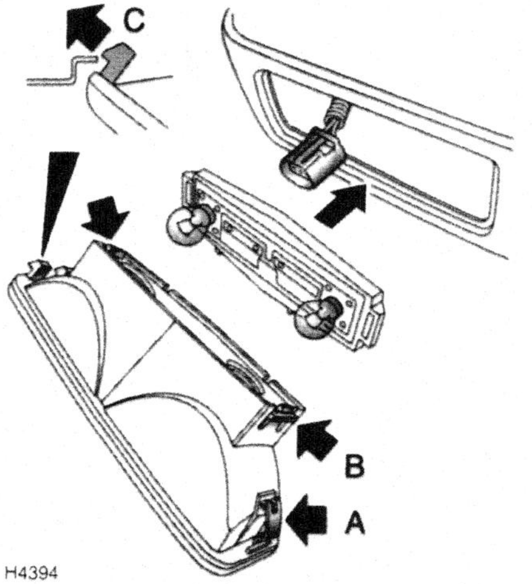

H4394

WARNING

If the engine is warm, the exhaust system may be hot - to prevent personal injury, avoid contact with a hot exhaust system when reaching behind the bumper.

Reach behind the bumper and press the spring clip 'A' to release the light unit.

Squeeze both levers 'B' to release the bulb holder from the lens. Push and twist to release the bulbs.

NOTE: *If necessary, the light unit can first be detached from the electrical harness by releasing the multi-plug from the rear of the bulb holder.*

Replace the required bulb and re-fit the holder to the light unit.Before reassembling the light unit, make sure the seal (between holder and lens) is in place.

To re-fit the light unit to the bumper, first locate the hooks 'C' in the bumper aperture and firmly push the other side of the light against spring pressure until it clicks into place.

NOTE: *The reverse bulbs in these units are Halogen bulbs and therefore as with all bulbs of this type, special care should be taken. Do not touch the bulb glass with your fingers. If necessary, clean the bulb with methylated spirits to remove any fingerprints.*

NUMBER PLATE LIGHTS

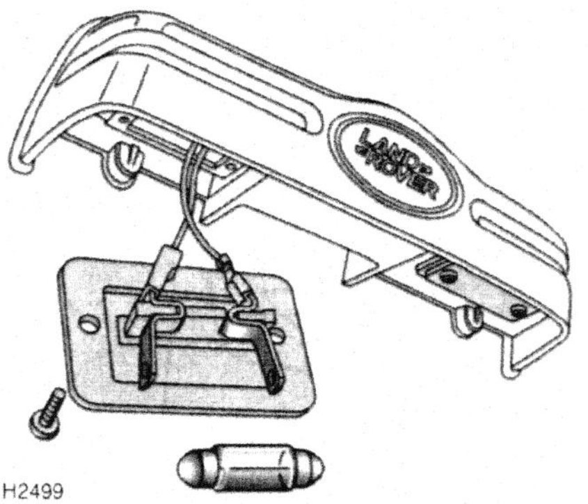

H2499

Remove both screws to release the light unit. Ease the light unit from its recess and pull the bulb to remove.

FRONT FOG LIGHTS

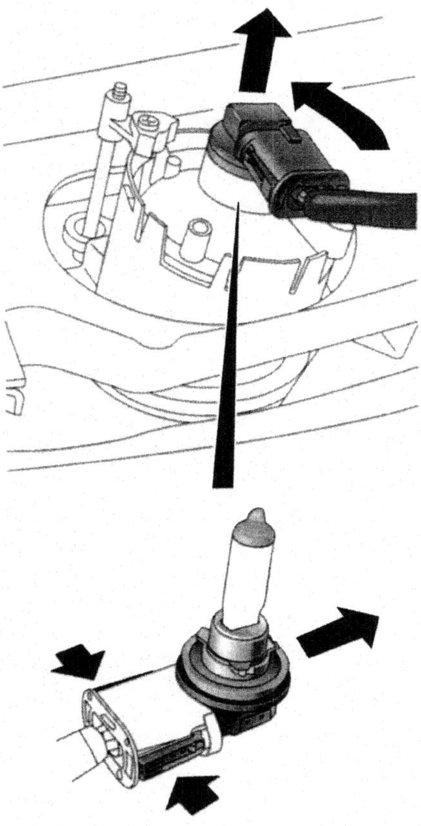

H4372

The front fog lights are accessible from the rear of the front bumpers and are shielded by the lower wheelarch liners.

Access is restricted and will entail lying beneath the centre of the vehicle at the front and reaching between the wheelarch liner and the back of the fog light.

To remove the bulb from the light unit, twist and pull, press in the two lock tabs on the electrical connector to release the bulb. Fit a new bulb to the connector and re-fit into the fog light unit.

NOTE: *Do not touch the bulb glass with your fingers. If necessary, clean the bulb with methylated spirits.*

HIGH MOUNTED STOP LIGHT

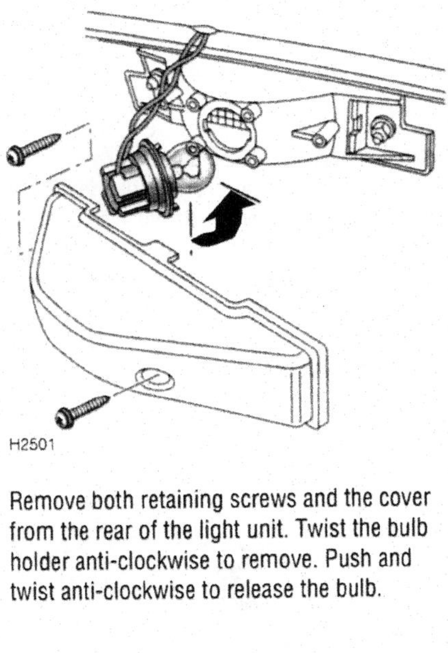

H2501

Remove both retaining screws and the cover from the rear of the light unit. Twist the bulb holder anti-clockwise to remove. Push and twist anti-clockwise to release the bulb.

GLOVEBOX LIGHT

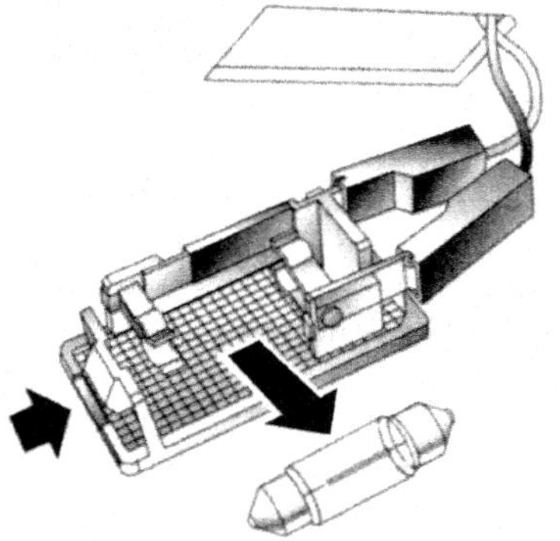

H2611

Insert a small flat-bladed screwdriver (preferably with a short handle, due to limited access) into the indent (arrowed in illustration) on the left hand side of the light unit, and carefully prise the unit from the glovebox panel. Remove the bulb from its clips.

INTERIOR LIGHT

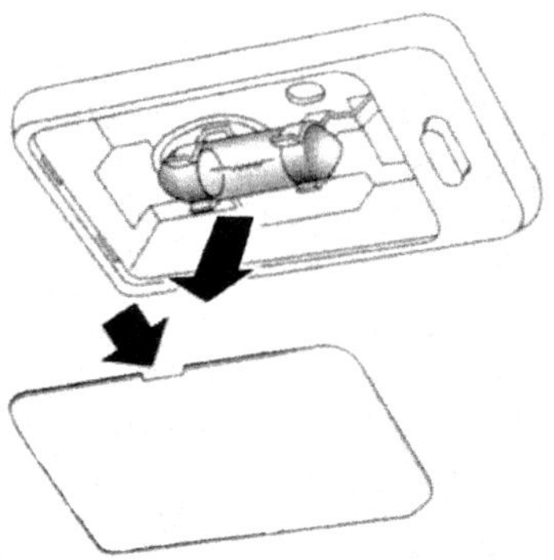

H2463

Insert a small flat-bladed screwdriver into the indent on the side of the lens (where arrowed) and prise the lens from the light unit, then pull the bulb out from the clips.

INTERIOR COURTESY LIGHTS

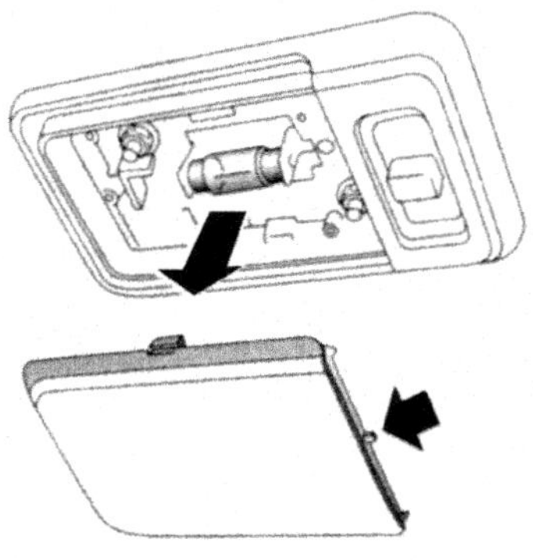

H2462

Insert a small flat-bladed screwdriver into the indent on the side of the lens and carefully prise the lens from the light unit, then pull the bulb to remove.

When replacing the lens, first locate the lug (arrowed in illustration), then push the lens into position.

Technical Data

LUBRICANTS AND FLUIDS

Recommendations for all climates and conditions.

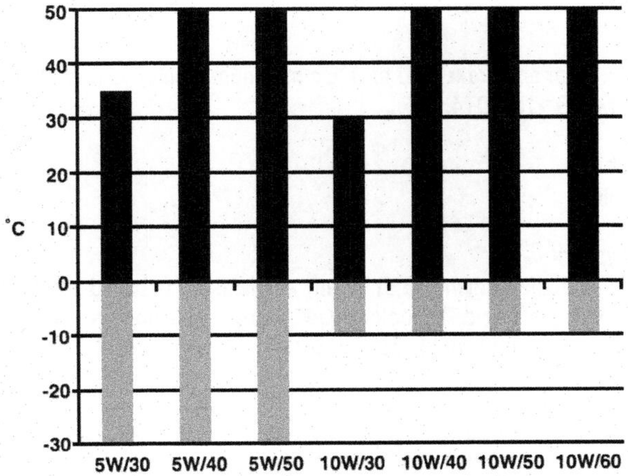

H3540

Engine oil - Petrol engines

Use a 5W/30, 5W/40, 5W/50, 10W/30, 10W/40, 10W/50 or 10W/60 oil meeting specification ACEA: A1 and having a viscosity band recommended for the temperature range of your locality.

NOTE: *ACEA A2 oils are also suitable.*

Engine oil - Diesel engines

Use a 5W/30, 5W/40, 5W/50 or 10W/40 oil meeting specification ACEA: A1 and B1, and having a viscosity band recommended for the temperature range of your locality.

NOTE: *ACEA B2 oils are also suitable.*

Manual gearbox

Use Texaco MTF 94 oil.

Automatic gearbox

Use ATF Dexron IID.

Transfer gearbox

Multigear Texaco 75W/90R or oil to meet API GL5.

Axles
Multigear Texaco 75W/90R or oil to meet API GL5.

Power steering and ACE
Texaco Cold Climate PAS fluid 14315.

Brake reservoir
Universal brake fluids or any brake fluid having a minimum boiling point of 260°C (500°F) and complying with FMVSS 116 DOT4.

Windscreen washers
Screen washer fluid.

Engine cooling system
Use Havoline Extended Life Coolant (XLC), or any ethylene glycol based anti-freeze (containing no methanol) with only Organic Acid Technology (OAT) corrosion inhibitors. Use one part anti-freeze to one part water for protection down to -36° C (-33° F).

Air conditioning compressor
Nippondenso ND-8 or Unipart ND-8.

Inertia reel seat belts
DO NOT LUBRICATE. These components are lubricated for life during manufacture.

CAPACITIES

The following capacities are approximate and provided as a guide only. All oil levels must be checked using the dipstick or level plugs as applicable.

Fuel tank	95 litre (21 gall)
Engine oil (from dry):	
- Diesel vehicles	8,20 litre (14.3 pt)
- Petrol vehicles - with oil cooler	6,60 litre (11.5 pt)
- Petrol vehicles - without oil cooler	6,15 litre (10.7 pt)
Engine oil refill and filter change:	
- Diesel vehicles	7,20 litre (12.6 pt)
- Petrol vehicles - with and without oil cooler	5,80 litre (10.1 pt)
Manual gearbox	2,70 litre (4.7 pt)
Automatic gearbox	9,70 litre (17.0 pt)
Transfer box	2,10 litre (3.7 pt)
Front differential	1,70 litre (2.9 pt)
Rear differential	1,70 litre (2.9 pt)
Washer reservoir	6,00 litre (10.5 pt)
Cooling system:	
- Diesel vehicles	13 litre (22.75 pt)
- Petrol vehicles	13 litre (22.75 pt)
Cooling system refill:	
- Diesel vehicles	7,5 litre (13.1 pt)
- Petrol vehicles	7,5 litre (13.1 pt)

ENGINES

Diesel

Fuel	Diesel or Automotive Gas Oil (AGO) to EN 590 specification
Capacity	2495 cm^3 (152.5 in^3)
Firing order	1-2-4-5-3
Bore	84,45 mm (3.3248 in)
Stroke	88,95 mm (3.5020 in)
Number of cylinders	5
Compression ratio	19.5:1

V8 Petrol - High compression

Fuel	UNLEADED 95 RON to EN 228 specification
Capacity	3950 cm^3 (241in^3)
Firing order	1-8-4-3-6-5-7-2
Idle speed	660 ± 50 rev/min
Bore	94,0 mm (3.700 in)
Stroke	71,04 mm (2.800 in)
Number of cylinders	8
Compression ratio	9.35:1
Spark plugs	Champion RC11PYPB4
Spark plug gap	0,95 - 1,05 mm

V8 Petrol - Low compression

Fuel: - Catalyst vehicles - Non-catalyst vehicles	 UNLEADED 91 RON to EN 228 specification UNLEADED 91 RON or 95 RON LEADED
Capacity	3950 cm^3 (241in^3)
Firing order	1-8-4-3-6-5-7-2
Idle speed	660 ± 50 rev/min
Bore	94,0 mm (3.700 in)
Stroke	71,04 mm (2.800 in)
Number of cylinders	8
Compression ratio	8.23:1
Spark plugs	Champion RC11PYPB4
Spark plug gap	0,95 - 1,05 mm

ELECTRICAL SYSTEM

Battery type:	
Petrol vehicles	Group 24, sealed for life
Diesel vehicles	Group 31, sealed for life
Battery rating:	
Petrol vehicles	72 amp/hr
Diesel vehicles	110 amp/hr
Voltage and polarity	12 V, negative (-) earth
Charging circuit	Alternator

STEERING

Steering wheel turns lock to lock	3.5
Turning circle between kerbs	11,9 metres (39.1 ft)
Camber angle	0°
Castor angle	3.6° to 3.8°
King pin inclination	13°
Front wheel toe-out included angle	0° 5' ± 2.5' (per side) 0° 10' ± 5' (total)

WHEELS & TYRES

Wheel size and type

Type	Size
Steel wheels	7J x 16
Alloy wheels	7J x 16 8J x 16 8J x 18
Road wheel nut torque	140 Nm (103 lbf/ft)

Tyre specification

Wheel size	Tyre
7J x 16 (steel wheel)	215/75 R16 Pirelli Scorpion S/T 107T 235/70 R16 Michelin XPC* 105H 235/70 R16 Goodyear Wrangler HP 105H
7J x 16 (alloy wheel)	235/70 R16 Goodyear Wrangler HP 105H 235/70 R16 Michelin XPC* 105H
8J x 16 (alloy wheel)	255/65 R16 Goodyear Wrangler HP 109H 255/65 R16 Michelin XPC* 109H
8J x 18 (alloy wheel)	255/55 R18 Goodyear Wrangler HP 109H

Tyre pressures

Loading condition		Pressure
Normal operating conditions	Front	1.9 bar (28 lbf/in^2)
	Rear	2.6 bar (38 lbf/in^2)
Vehicle loaded to maximum gross vehicle weight	Front	1.9 bar (28 lbf/in^2)
	Rear	3.2 bar (46 lbf/in^2)

NOTE: *When towing, the additional load imposed may cause the tyre maximum load rating to be exceeded. This is permissible provided the load rating is not exceeded by more than 15% and that road speeds are limited to 62 mph (100 km/h) and tyre pressures are increased by at least 0.2 bar (3 lbf/in^2).*

DIMENSIONS

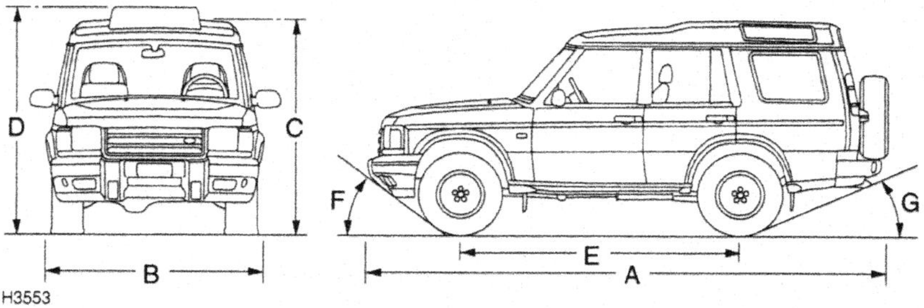

A	Overall length (including spare wheel)	4705 mm (185.2 in)
	Overall length (including tow hitch)	4715 mm (185.6 in)
B	Overall width (excluding mirrors)	1885 mm (74.2 in)
C	Overall height (no roof bars)	1940 mm (76.4 in)
D	Overall height (open sunroof)	2015 mm (79.3 in)
E	Wheelbase	2540 mm (100.0 in)
	Track:	
	- Front	1540 mm (61.6 in)
	- Rear	1560 mm (61.4 in)

Off road performance

	Maximum gradient (at EEC kerb weight)	45°
F	Approach angle (at EEC kerb weight)	
	- Vehicles with coil spring suspension	30.9°
	- Vehicles with self-levelling suspension	31.2°
G	Departure angle with tow hitch fitted (at EEC kerb weight)	
	- Vehicles with coil spring suspension	18.8°
	- Vehicles with self-levelling suspension	18.1°
	- Vehicles with self-levelling suspension (raised)	21.0°
G	Departure angle without tow hitch (at EEC kerb weight)	
	- Vehicles with coil spring suspension	21.1°
	- Vehicles with self-levelling suspension	21.4°
	Wading depth	500 mm (21.0 in)
	Minimum ground clearance (unladen)	253,5 mm (10.0 in)

VEHICLE WEIGHTS

Approximate EEC kerb weights (full fuel tank, excluding options)	
- Petrol engine vehicles	2095 - 2235 kg (4619 - 4928 lb)
- Diesel engine vehicles	2150 - 2280 kg (4740 - 5027 lb)
Maximum gross vehicle weight	
- All 5 seat vehicles (coil spring suspension)	2750 kg (6063 lb)
- 7 seat petrol engine vehicles (coil spring suspension)	2825 kg (6228 lb)
- 7 seat diesel engine vehicles (coil spring suspension)	2880 kg (6349 lb)
- Petrol engine vehicles (self-levelling suspension)	2825 kg (6228 lb)
- Diesel engine vehicles (self levelling suspension)	2880 kg (6349 lb)
Maximum front axle load	
- All vehicles	1200 kg (2646 lb)
Maximum rear axle load	
- 5 seat vehicles with coil spring suspension	1720 kg (3792 lb)
- 7 seat vehicles with coil spring suspension	1800 kg (3968 lb)
- Vehicles with self-levelling suspension	1800 kg (3968 lb)

NOTE: *The rear axle load for vehicles with self-levelling suspension can be increased to a maximum of 1928 kg when towing, provided road speed is limited to 62 mph (100 km/h).*

NOTE: *Axle weights are non additive. The individual maximum axle weights and gross vehicle weight must not be exceeded.*

TOW BAR DIMENSIONS

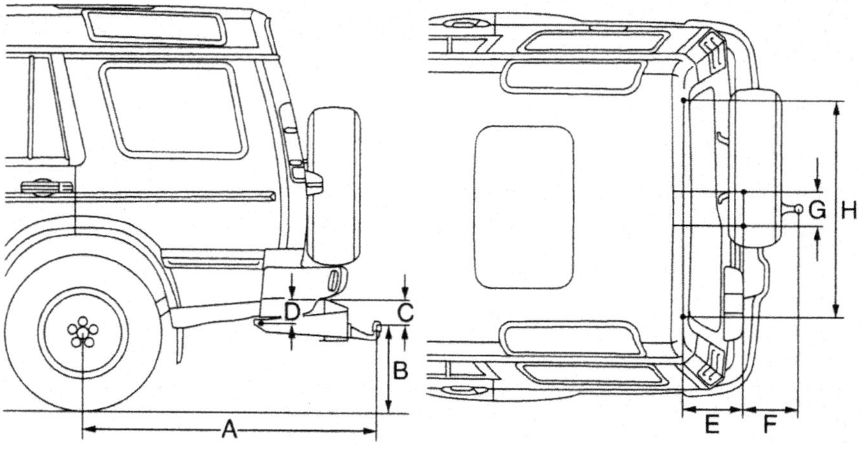

H3554

A	Wheel centre to centre of towball	1336 mm
B	Ground to centre of towball	518 mm
C	Centre of inner attachment points to centre of towball	91 mm
D	Centre inner attachments to centre outer attachments	136 mm
E	Centre inner attachments to centre outer attachments	260 mm
F	Centre inner attachments to centre of towball	324 mm
G	Distance between centres of inner attachments	140 mm
H	Distance between centres of outer attachments	628 mm
Dimensions refer to towing equipment officially released by Land Rover		

TOWING WEIGHTS

Maximum permissible towed weights	On-road	Off-road
Unbraked trailers	750 kg (1653 lb)	750 kg (1653 lb)
Trailers with overrun brakes	3500 kg (7716 lb)	1000 kg (2204 lb)
Roof rack load	50 kg (110 lb)	30 kg (66 lb)

NOTE: *The maximum roof rack load when using the approved roof bar and cross rail roof rack system allows for the weight of the cross rails. However, if an alternative roof rack system is to be used, the weight of the roof rack system must be included as part of the load weight.*

Vehicle, trailer and tow hitch loads

Maximum trailer weight	Maximum vehicle load	Maximum tow hitch load
2000 kg (2 tons)	All vehicles loaded to gross vehicle weight	150 kg (330 lb)

Maximum trailer weight (trailers with overrun brakes)	Vehicle loading limit when pulling max trailer weight	Maximum tow hitch load
Coil spring rear suspension vehicles 3500 kg (3.4 tons)	Driver, and one passenger (or equivalent load)	250 kg (551 lb)
Self-levelling rear suspension vehicles 3500 kg (3.4 tons)	Driver, plus four passengers (or equivalent load stowed forward of luggage comp.)	250 kg (551 lb)

FUEL CONSUMPTION

The fuel consumption figures shown below have been calculated using a standard testing procedure (the new EC test procedure from Directive 93/116/EC), and produced in accordance with The Passenger Car Fuel Consumption (Amendment) Order 1996. Under normal use, a vehicle's actual fuel consumption figures may differ from those achieved through the test procedure, depending on driving technique, road and traffic conditions, environmental factors, vehicle load and condition.

Fuel consumption figures

	URBAN		EXTRA-URBAN		COMBINED	
	mpg	l/100km	mpg	l/100km	mpg	l/100km
Petrol - manual	12.1	23,3	22.2	12,7	17.0	16,6
Petrol - automatic	11.6	24,4	21.8	12,9	16.5	17,1
Diesel - manual	24.6	11,5	34.4	8,2	30.0	9,4
Diesel - automatic	22.2	12,7	31.4	9,0	27.4	10,3

Urban cycle

The urban test cycle is carried out from a cold start and consists of a series of accelerations, decelerations and periods of steady speed driving and engine idling. The maximum speed attained during the test is 31 mph (50 km/h) with an average speed of 12 mph (19 km/h).

Extra-urban cycle

The extra urban test cycle is carried out immediately after the urban test. Approximately half of the test comprises steady-speed driving, while the remainder consists of a series of accelerations, decelerations and engine idling. The maximum test speed is 75 mph (120 km/h) and the average speed 39 mph (63 km/h). The test is carried out over a distance of 4.3 miles (7 km).

Combined

The combined figure is an average of the urban and extra-urban test cycle results, which has been weighted to take account of the different distances covered during the two tests.

NOTE: *These figures should not be compared with the figures produced using the ECE/EEC procedure previously required by The Passenger Car Fuel Consumption Order 1983. Because of the changes in test procedure, even the urban figures would differ if the same car were subjected to both tests.*

DECLARATIONS OF CONFORMITY

IMPORTANT INFORMATION

The Declarations of Conformity detailed on the following pages are from manufacturers of RF (Radio Frequency) equipment, whose components are used in the manufacture of your Land Rover Discovery.

These manufacturers state that their components comply with relevant rules of the R & TTE (Radio and Telecommunication Terminal Equipment) directive.

The directive requires the manufacturer of short range radio devices to self certify that RF parts fitted to Land Rover vehicles are fit for use and that the declarations are supplied with the vehicle documentation. If at a future date a technical inspection is required, the declarations will provide all necessary information.

NOTE: *The Declarations of Conformity are published in the native language of the RF equipment manufacturer, in compliance with the R & TTE Directive.*

DECLARATION OF CONFORMITY

CE 0682

This declaration is the responsibility of the manufacturer / authorised representative within the Community:

Supplier
Connaught Electronics Ltd.

Supplier Address
Dunmore Road,
Tuam
Co. Galway,
Ireland

This certifies that the following designated product

RECEIVER 433MHz PART No.1824

(Product identification)

complies with the essential protection requirements of R&TTE Directive 1999/5/ EC on the approximation of the laws of the Member States relating to ***Radio Spectrum Matters, EMC*** and ***Electrical Safety.***
This declaration applies to all specimens manufactured in accordance with the technical documentation described in the annex II. Connaught Electronics Ltd. keep this documentation at the proposal of the relevant national authorities of any Member State for inspection purpose.
Assessment of compliance of the product with the requirements relating to the essential requirements acc. to Article 3 R&TTE was based on Annex IV of the Directive 1999/5/ EC and the following standards:

Radio Spectrum:	EN 300 220-1 (Identification of regulations / standards)
EMC:	EN300 683 (Identification of regulations / standards)
Safety:	EN 60950 (Identification of regulations / standards)

(Place, date)

Tuam, Ireland

22/02/2001

(Signature)

Valeo
SÉCURITÉ HABITACLE

DIVISION SYSTÈMES D'ACCEÈS
42 rue le Corbusier
94042 Créteil Cedex - France
Tel : 01 56 71 53 00
Fax : 01 5671 53 71

DECLARATION OF CONFORMITY

We, **VALEO Sécurité Habitacle 42, Rue le Corbusier~94042 CRETEIL — France** hereby declare, At our sole responsibility, that the following product conforms to the Essential Requirements of the Radio and Telecommunications Terminal Equipment Directive 1999/5/EC in accordance with the tests conducted to the appropriate requirements of the relevant standards, as listed herewith.

Product	: **Remote Control Systems and Immobiliser systems**
Model/Type Number	: Valtx03 / Valrx03 and Valtkt03
Directive and Standards used	: **Radio** EN 300-220 and EN 300-330 **EMC** 95/54/EC, ISO 7637-1 : 1990 **Safety** EN 60065

Year of affixing CE marking: **2000**

CE marking:

CE 0165

Countries intended for use: All EU+EFTA Countries.

VALEO ELECTRONIQUE
Siege Social
2 avenue Fernand Pouillon
94042 Créteil Cedex France
S A au capital
de 10 479 765 Euros
606 020 071 RCS Creteil
APE 343 Z

Index

Index

Index

Index

Land Rover Discovery

Detailed engine data and work instructions for both petrol and diesel fuel systems. Covering 4.0 V8 petrol engines and Td5 diesel engines. A detailed guide to maintenance and repair covering of all parts of the car and engine.
A total of 824 fully illustrated pages.
VDR 100090. Soft Bound.
SKU: LRY2WH
ISBN: 9781855208681

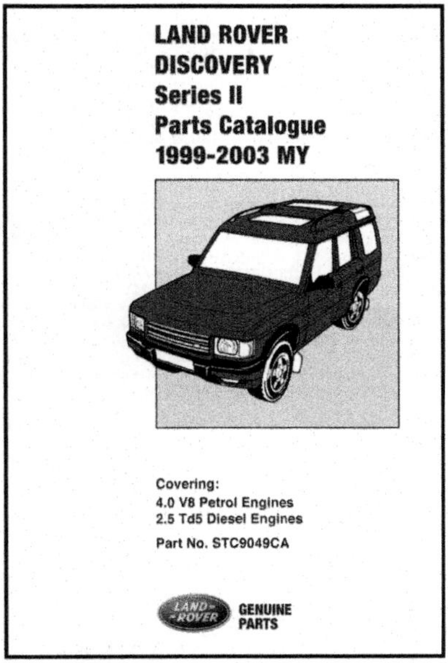

This catalogue covers all Land Rover Discovery vehicles from model year 1999 up to and including 2003, fitted with the 4.0 V8 petrol engines and the 2.5 Td5 diesel engines. There is a full listing of all the part numbers with exploding diagrams.
With 252 pages and well illustrated.
STC9049CA. Soft Bound.
SKU: LR99PH
ISBN: 9781855208858

www.brooklandsbooks.com

Available from Amazon and all good motoring bookshops.

Brooklands Books Ltd., PO Box 146, Cobham, Surrey, KT11 1LG, England

www.brooklands-books.com

LAND ROVER OFFICIAL FACTORY PUBLICATIONS

Land Rover Series 1 Workshop Manual	4291
Land Rover Series 1 1948-53 Parts Catalogue	4051
Land Rover Series 1 1954-58 Parts Catalogue	4107
Land Rover Series 1 Instruction Manual	4277
Land Rover Series 1 and II Diesel Instruction Manual	4343
Land Rover Series II and IIA Workshop Manual	AKM8159
Land Rover Series II and Early IIA Bonneted Control Parts Catalogue	605957
Land Rover Series IIA Bonneted Control Parts Catalogue	RTC9840CC
Land Rover Series IIA, III and 109 V8 Optional Equipment Parts Catalogue	RTC9842CE
Land Rover Series IIA/IIB Instruction Manual	LSM64IM
Land Rover Series 2A and 3 88 Parts Catalogue Supplement (USA Spec)	606494
Land Rover Series III Workshop Manual	AKM3648
Land Rover Series III Workshop Manual V8 Supplement (edn. 2)	AKM8022
Land Rover Series III 88, 109 and 109 V8 Parts Catalogue	RTC9841CE
Land Rover Series III Owners Manual 1971-1978	607324B
Land Rover Series III Owners Manual 1979-1985	AKM8155
Military Land Rover (Lightweight) Series III Parts Catalogue	61278
Military Land Rover Series III (L.W.B.) User Handbook	608179
Military Land Rover (Lightweight) Series III User Manual	608180
Land Rover 90/110 and Defender Workshop Manual 1983-1992	SLR621ENWM
Land Rover Defender Workshop Manual 1993-1995	LDAWMEN93
Land Rover Defender 300 Tdi and Supplements Workshop Manual 1996-1998	LRL0097ENGBB
Land Rover Defender Td5 Workshop Manual and Supplements 1999-2006	LRL0410BB
Land Rover Defender Electrical Manual Td5 1999-06 and 300Tdi 2002-2006	LRD5EHBB
Land Rover 110 Parts Catalogue 1983-1986	RTC9863CE
Land Rover Defender Parts Catalogue 1987-2006	STC9021CC
Land Rover 90 • 110 Handbook 1983-1990 MY	LSM0054
Land Rover Defender 90 • 110 • 130 Handbook 1991 MY - Feb. 1994	LHAHBEN93
Land Rover Defender 90 • 110 • 130 Handbook Mar. 1994 - 1998 MY	LRL0087ENG/2
Military Land Rover 90/110 All Variants (Excluding APV and SAS) User Manual	2320-D-122-201
Military Land Rover 90 and 110 2.5 Diesel Engine Versions User Handbook	SLR989WDHB
Military Land Rover Defender XD - Wolf Workshop Manual - 2320D128 -	302 522 523 524
Military Land Rover Defender XD - Wolf Parts Catalogue	2320D128711
Discovery Workshop Manual 1990-1994 (petrol 3.5, 3.9, Mpi and diesel 200 Tdi)	SJR900ENWM
Discovery Workshop Manual 1995-1998 (petrol 2.0 Mpi, 3.9, 4.0 V8 and diesel 300 Tdi)	LRL0079BB
Discovery Series II Workshop Manual 1999-2003 (petrol 4.0 V8 and diesel Td5 2.5)	VDR100090/6
Discovery Parts Catalogue 1989-1998 (2.0 Mpi, 3.5, 3.9 V8 and 200 Tdi and 300 Tdi)	RTC9947CF
Discovery Parts Catalogue 1999-2003 (petrol 4.0 V8 and diesel Td5 2.5)	STC9049CA
Discovery Owners Handbook 1990-1991 (petrol 3.5 V8 and diesel 200 Tdi)	SJR820ENHB90
Discovery Series II Handbook 1999-2004 MY (petrol 4.0 V8 and Td5 diesel)	LRL0459BB
Freelander Workshop Manual 1998-2000 (petrol 1.8 and diesel 2.0)	LRL0144
Freelander Workshop Manual 2001-2003 ON (petrol 1.8L, 2.5L and diesel Td4 2.0)	LRL0350ENG/4
Land Rover 101 1 Tonne Forward Control Workshop Manual	RTC9120
Land Rover 101 1 Tonne Forward Control Parts Catalogue	608294B
Land Rover 101 1 Tonne Forward Control User Manual	608239
Range Rover Workshop Manual 1970-1985 (petrol 3.5)	AKM3630
Range Rover Workshop Manual 1986-1989 (petrol 3.5 and diesel 2.4 Turbo VM)	SRR660ENWM & LSM180WS4/2
Range Rover Workshop Manual 1990-1994 (petrol 3.9, 4.2 and diesel 2.5 Turbo VM, 200 Tdi)	LHAWMENA02
Range Rover Workshop Manual 1995-2001 (petrol 4.0, 4.6 and BMW 2.5 diesel)	LRL0326ENGBB
Range Rover Workshop Manual 2002-2005 (BMW petrol 4.4 and BMW 3.0 diesel)	LRL0477
Range Rover Electrical Manual 2002-2005 UK version (petrol 4.4 and 3.0 diesel)	RR02KEMBB
Range Rover Electrical Manual 2002-2005 USA version (BMW petrol 4.4)	RR02AEMBB
Range Rover Parts Catalogue 1970-1985 (petrol 3.5)	RTC9846CH
Range Rover Parts Catalogue 1986-1991 (petrol 3.5, 3.9 and diesel 2.4 and 2.5 Turbo VM)	RTC9908CB
Range Rover Parts Catalogue 1992-1994 MY and 95 MY Classic (petrol 3.9, 4.2 and diesel 2.5 Turbo VM, 200 Tdi and 300 Tdi)	RTC9961CB
Range Rover Parts Catalogue 1995-2001 MY (petrol 4.0, 4.6 and BMW 2.5 diesel)	RTC9970CE
Range Rover Owners Handbook 1970-1980 (petrol 3.5)	606917
Range Rover Owners Handbook 1981-1982 (petrol 3.5)	AKM8139
Range Rover Owners Handbook 1983-1985 (petrol 3.5)	LSM0001HB
Range Rover Owners Handbook 1986-1987 (petrol 3.5 and diesel 2.4 Turbo VM)	LSM129HB

Engine Overhaul Manuals for Land Rover and Range Rover

300 Tdi Engine, R380 Manual Gearbox and LT230T Transfer Gearbox Overhaul Manuals	LRL003, 070 & 081
Petrol Engine V8 3.5, 3.9, 4.0, 4.2 and 4.6 Overhaul Manuals	LRL004 & 164
Land Rover/Range Rover Driving Techniques	LR369
Working in the Wild - Manual for Africa	SMR684MI
Winching in Safety - Complete guide to winching Land Rovers and Range Rovers	SMR699MI

Workshop Manual Owners Edition

Land Rover 2 / 2A / 3 Owners Workshop Manual 1959-1983
Land Rover 90, 110 and Defender Workshop Manual Owners Edition 1983-1995
Land Rover Discovery Workshop Manual Owners Edition 1990-1998

All titles available from Amazon or Land Rover specialists

Brooklands Books Ltd., P.O. Box 146, Cobham, Surrey, KT11 1LG, England, UK
Phone: +44 (0) 1932 865051 info@brooklands-books.com www.brooklands-books.com

www.brooklandsbooks.com

Printed by Printforce, United Kingdom